Fundamentals of Statistics

Fundamentals of Statistics

Krishnendu Mi
Nisha P R
Theja Jayan

2026

Agri Horti Press
New Delhi-110 084

ISBN: 978-93-49690-24-0 (Hardbound)

Published By
Agri Horti Press
New Delhi
E-mail: agrihortipress@gmail.com

Digitally Printed at : Replika Press Pvt. Ltd.

Preface

Fundamentals of Statistics is designed to provide a thorough and accessible introduction to the principles and methods of statistical analysis. Statistics plays a vital role across disciplines—be it the natural and social sciences, business, health, or engineering—by enabling researchers, professionals, and decision-makers to make informed judgments based on data. As we move further into the era of big data and evidence-based reasoning, a sound grasp of statistical fundamentals has become more essential than ever.

This book is intended for undergraduate students, beginners in data analysis, and professionals seeking a foundational understanding of statistics. It aims to present statistical concepts in a clear and logical manner, emphasizing both theoretical understanding and practical application. No prior knowledge of advanced mathematics is assumed, making this book suitable for a wide audience.

The content progresses from the basics of descriptive statistics—such as measures of central tendency and dispersion—to the core ideas of probability, probability distributions, sampling techniques, and inferential statistics. Topics like hypothesis testing, correlation and regression, analysis of variance (ANOVA), and non-parametric methods are also included to provide a comprehensive toolkit for data interpretation. Each chapter is enriched with real-world examples, step-by-step problem-solving approaches, and exercises to reinforce learning and facilitate self-assessment.

Particular attention is given to the use of statistics in the context of research design and decision-making, helping students understand not only how to perform analyses but also why certain methods are appropriate in specific situations. Where applicable, modern computational tools and software applications are introduced to demonstrate how technology can aid statistical analysis.

We hope that Fundamentals of Statistics will serve as a reliable foundation for those beginning their journey into statistical thinking and practice. By emphasizing clarity, relevance, and practical understanding, this book aspires to demystify statistics and inspire confidence in its application.

Krishnendu Mi
Nisha P R
Theja Jayan

Contents

Preface v

1. **Introduction** **1**
   - Definition and meaning of Statisitcs
   - Scope
   - Statistical methods
   - Statistics as a method of research
   - Types of Research Studies
   - Modern Statistics
   - Statistical Thinking and Modern Management
   - Relation of Statistics with other sciences
   - Statisitcs and its Functions
   - Distrust of Statistics
2. **Correlation** **29**
3. **Measures of Variability** **87**
   - Introduction
   - Concept of Variation
   - Properties of a good measure of variation
   - Types of Measures of Dispersion
   - Different Methods of Measuring Dispersion
   - Merits and Demerits of Range
   - Inter-Quatile Range
   - Percentile Range
   - Standard Deviation
   - Quartile Deviation
3. **Skewness, Moment & Kurtosis** **103**
   - Types of Frequency Distributions
   - Measures of Skewness
   - Kurtosis
4. **Data Collection** **113**
   - Observational Study
   - Sampling a Dichotomous Population
   - History of development
   - Experimental designs after Fisher
5. **Descriptive Statistics for Numerical Variables** **127**
   - Use in Statistical Analysis
   - Measures of statistical dispersion
6. **Probability** **133**
   - Classical Definition
   - Relation to Randomness
   - Sample Spaces and Probability

7. Probability Distributions **145**
- Introduction
- Cumulative density
- Specification
- Definition
- Alternative parametrizations
- Properties
- The central limit theorem

8. Sampling Distributions and Confidence Intervals **179**
- Sampling Distribution
- Standard error
- Conceptual basis
- Confidence band

9. Hypothesis Testing **195**
- Variations and sub-classes
- Statistical significance test
- Origins and early controversy
- A comparison between Fisherian, frequentist (Neyman-Pearson)
- Chi-squared test for variance in a normal population

10. Regression Analysis **217**
- History
- Regression models
- "Limited dependent" variables
- Interpolation and extrapolation

11. Quality and Six Sigma Management Application of Statistic **225**
- Doctrine
- Etymology of "six sigma process"
- Criticism
- Total quality management
- Notable definitions

12. Understanding Advanced Statistical Methods **237**
- DEFINITIONS
- Use of Statistical Methods
- Divisions of Statistics
- Development of Modern Statistics
- Distrust of Statistics
- Statistics and its Importance
- Importance of Basic Statistics
- Main Functions of Statistics
- Whether Statistics is a science or an Art
- Is statistics a science?

Bibliography **257**

Index **259**

1

Introduction

Statistics is the study of the collection, organization, analysis, interpretation and presentation of data. It deals with all aspects of data including the planning of data collection in terms of the design of surveys and experiments. When analyzing data, it is possible to use one or both of statistics methodologies: descriptive and inferential statistics in the analysis data.

Definition and meaning of Statisitcs

Statistics is the study of how to collect, organize, analyze, and interpret numerical information from data. Descriptive statistics involves methods of organizing, picturing and summarizing information from data. Inferential statistics involves methods of using information from a sample to draw conclusions about the population.

Definitions according to the first concept in which 'Statistics' has been taken in the sense of numerical data

(a) According to this concept, the most exhaustive definition has been given by Prof. Horace Secrist. He defines :

"By statistics we mean aggregate of facts affected to a marked extent by multiplicity of causes, numerically expressed, enumerated or estimated according to reasonable standards of accuracy, collected in a systematic manner for a pre-determined purpose and placed in relation to each other."

Meaning

The word statistics has three different meanings (sense) which are discussed below:

(1) Plural Sense (2) Singular Sense (3) Plural of the word "Statistic" :

(1) Plural Sense: In plural sense, the word statistics refer to numerical facts and figures collected in a systematic manner with a definite purpose in any field of study. In this sense, statistics are also aggregates of facts which are expressed in numerical form. For example, Statistics on industrial production, statistics or population growth of a country in different years etc.

(2) Singular Sense: In singular sense, it refers to the science comprising methods which are used in collection, analysis, interpretation and presentation of numerical data. These methods are used to draw conclusion about the population parameter.

For Example: If we want to have a study about the distribution of weights of students in a certain college.

First of all, we will collect the information on the weights which may be obtained from the records of the college or we may collect from the students directly. The large number of weight figures will confuse the mind. In this situation we may arrange the weights in groups such as: "50 Kg to 60 Kg" "60 Kg to 70 Kg" and so on and find the number of students fall in each group. This step is called a presentation of data. We may still go further and compute the averages and some other measures which may give us complete description of the original data.

(3) Plural of Word "Statistic":The word statistics is used as the plural of the word "Statistic" which refers to a numerical quantity like mean, median, variance etc..., calculated from sample value.

For Example: If we select 15 student from a class of 80 students, measure their heights and find the average height. This average would be a statistic.

In applying statistics to a scientific, industrial, or societal problem, it is necessary to begin with a population or process to be studied. Populations can be diverse topics such as "all persons living in a country" or "every atom composing a crystal". A population can also be composed of observations of a process at various times, with the data from each observation serving as a different member of the overall group. Data collected about this kind of "population" constitutes what is called a time series.

For practical reasons, a chosen subset of the population called a sample is studied — as opposed to compiling data about the entire group (an operation called census). Once a sample that is representative of the population is determined, data are collected for the sample members in an observational or experimental setting. This data can then be subjected to statistical analysis, serving two related purposes: description and inference.

- Descriptive statistics summarize the population data by describing what was observed in the sample numerically or graphically. Numerical descriptors include mean and standard deviation for continuous data types (like heights or weights), while frequency and percentage are more useful in terms of describing categorical data (like race).
- Inferential statistics uses patterns in the sample data to draw inferences about the population represented, accounting for randomness. These inferences may take the form of: answering yes/no questions about the data (hypothesis testing), estimating numerical characteristics of the data (estimation), describing associations within the data (correlation) and modeling relationships within the data (for example, using regression analysis). Inference can extend to forecasting, prediction and estimation of unobserved values either in or associated with the population being studied; it can include extrapolation and interpolation of time series or spatial data, and can also include data mining.

The concept of correlation is particularly noteworthy for the potential confusion it can cause. Statistical analysis of a data set often reveals that two variables (properties) of the population under consideration tend to vary together, as if they were connected. For example, a study of annual income that also looks at age of death might find that poor people tend to have shorter lives than affluent people. The two variables are said to be correlated; however, they may or may not be the cause of one another. The correlation phenomena could be caused by a third, previously unconsidered phenomenon, called a lurking variable or confounding variable. For this reason, there is no way to immediately infer the existence of a causal relationship between the two variables.

For a sample to be used as a guide to an entire population, it is important that it is truly a representative of that overall population. Representative sampling assures that the inferences and conclusions can be safely extended from the sample to the population as a whole. A major problem lies in determining the extent to which the sample chosen is actually representative. Statistics offers methods to estimate and correct for any random trending within the sample and data collection procedures. There are also methods of experimental design for experiments that can lessen these issues at the outset of a study, strengthening its capability to discern truths about the population.

Randomness is studied using the mathematical discipline of probability theory. Probability is used in "mathematical statistics" (alternatively, "statistical theory") to study the sampling distributions of sample statistics and, more generally, the properties of statistical procedures. The use of any statistical method is valid when the system or population under consideration satisfies the assumptions of the method.

Misuse of statistics can produce subtle, but serious errors in description and interpretation — subtle in the sense that even experienced professionals make such errors, and serious in the sense that they can lead to devastating decision errors. For instance, social policy, medical practice, and the reliability of structures like bridges all rely on the proper use of statistics. See below for further discussion.

Even when statistical techniques are correctly applied, the results can be difficult to interpret for those lacking expertise. The statistical significance of a trend in the data — which measures the extent to which a trend could be caused by random variation in the sample — may or may not agree with an intuitive sense of its significance. The set of basic statistical skills (and skepticism) that people need to deal with information in their everyday lives properly is referred to as statistical literacy.

Scope

Statistics is described as a mathematical body of science that pertains to the collection, analysis, interpretation or explanation, and presentation of data, or as a branch of mathematics concerned with collecting and interpreting data. Because of its empirical roots and its focus on applications, statistics is typically considered a distinct mathematical science rather than as a branch of mathematics. Some tasks a statistician may involve are less mathematical; for example, ensuring that data collection is undertaken in a way that produces valid conclusions, coding data, or reporting results in ways comprehensible to those who must use them.

Statisticians improve data quality by developing specific experiment designs and survey samples. Statistics itself also provides tools for prediction and forecasting the use of data through statistical models. Statistics is applicable to a wide variety of academic disciplines, including natural and social sciences, government, and business. Statistical consultants can help organizations and companies that don't have in-house expertise relevant to their particular questions.

Statistical methods can summarize or describe a collection of data. This is called *descriptive statistics*. This is particularly useful in communicating the results of experiments and research. In addition, data patterns may be modeled in a way that accounts for randomness and uncertainty in the observations.

These models can be used to draw inferences about the process or population under study—a practice called *inferential statistics*. Inference is a vital element of scientific advance, since it provides a way to draw conclusions from data that are subject to random variation. To prove the propositions being investigated further, the conclusions are tested as well, as part of the scientific method. Descriptive statistics and analysis of the new data tend to provide more information as to the truth of the proposition.

"Applied statistics" comprises descriptive statistics and the application of inferential statistics. *Theoretical statistics* concerns both the logical arguments underlying justification of approaches to statistical inference, as well encompassing *mathematical statistics*. Mathematical statistics includes not only the manipulation of probability distributions necessary for deriving results related to methods of estimation and inference, but also various aspects of computational statistics and the design of experiments.

Statistics is closely related to probability theory, with which it is often grouped. The difference is, roughly, that probability theory starts from the given parameters of a total population to deduce probabilities that pertain to samples. Statistical inference, however, moves in the opposite direction—inductively inferring from samples to the parameters of a larger or total population. Statistics has many ties to machine learning and data mining.

History

Statistical methods date back at least to the 5th century BC.

Some scholars pinpoint the origin of statistics to 1663, with the publication of *Natural and Political Observations upon the Bills of Mortality* by John Graunt. Early applications of statistical thinking revolved around the needs of states to base policy on demographic and economic data, hence its *stat-* etymology. The scope of the discipline of statistics broadened in the early 19th century to include the collection and analysis of data in general. Today, statistics is widely employed in government, business, and natural and social sciences.

Its mathematical foundations were laid in the 17th century with the development of the probability theory by Blaise Pascal and Pierre de Fermat. Mathematical probability theory arose from the study of games of chance, although the concept of probability was already examined in medieval law and by philosophers such as Juan Caramuel. The method of least squares was first described by Adrien-Marie Legendre in 1805.

The modern field of statistics emerged in the late 19th and early 20th century in three stages. The first wave, at the turn of the century, was led by the work of Sir Francis Galton and Karl Pearson, who transformed statistics into a rigorous mathematical discipline used for analysis, not just in science, but in industry and politics as well. Galton's contributions to the field included introducing the concepts of standard deviation, correlation, regression and the application of these methods to the study of the variety of human characteristics - height, weight, eyelash length among others. Pearson developed the Correlation coefficient, defined as a product-moment, the method of moments for the fitting of distributions to samples and the Pearson's system of continuous curves, among many other things. Galton and Pearson founded *Biometrika* as the first journal of mathematical statistics and biometry, and the latter founded the world's first university statistics department at University College London.

The second wave of the 1910s and 20s was initiated by William Gosset, and reached its culmination in the insights of Sir Ronald Fisher, who wrote the textbooks that were to define the academic discipline in universities around the world. Fisher's most important publications were his 1916 seminal paper *The Correlation between Relatives on the*

Supposition of Mendelian Inheritance and his classic 1925 work *Statistical Methods for Research Workers*. His paper was the first to use the statistical term, variance. He developed rigorous experimental models and also originated the concepts of sufficiency, ancillary statistics, Fisher's linear discriminator and Fisher information.

The final wave, which mainly saw the refinement and expansion of earlier developments, emerged from the collaborative work between Egon Pearson and Jerzy Neyman in the 1930s. They introduced the concepts of "Type II" error, power of a test and confidence intervals. Jerzy Neyman in 1934 showed that stratified random sampling was in general a better method of estimation than purposive (quota) sampling. Today, statistical methods are applied in all fields that involve decision making, for making accurate inferences from a collated body of data and for making decisions in the face of uncertainty based on statistical methodology. The use of modern computers has expedited large-scale statistical computations, and has also made possible new methods that are impractical to perform manually.

Overview

In applying statistics to a scientific, industrial, or societal problem, it is necessary to begin with a population or process to be studied. Populations can be diverse topics such as "all persons living in a country" or "every atom composing a crystal". A population can also be composed of observations of a process at various times, with the data from each observation serving as a different member of the overall group. Data collected about this kind of "population" constitutes what is called a time series.

For practical reasons, a chosen subset of the population called a sample is studied—as opposed to compiling data about the entire group (an operation called census). Once a sample that is representative of the population is determined, data is collected for the sample members in an observational or experimental setting. This data can then be subjected to statistical analysis, serving two related purposes: description and inference.

- Descriptive statistics summarize the population data by describing what was observed in the sample numerically or graphically. Numerical descriptors include mean and standard deviation for continuous data types (like heights or weights), while frequency and percentage are more useful in terms of describing categorical data (like race).
- Inferential statistics uses patterns in the sample data to draw inferences about the population represented, accounting for randomness. These inferences may take the form of: answering yes/no questions about the data (hypothesis testing), estimating numerical characteristics of the data (estimation), describing associations within the data (correlation) and modeling relationships within the data (for example, using regression analysis). Inference can extend to forecasting, prediction and estimation of unobserved values either in or associated with the population being studied; it can include extrapolation and interpolation of time series or spatial data, and can also include data mining.

The concept of correlation is particularly noteworthy for the potential confusion it can cause. Statistical analysis of a data set often reveals that two variables (properties) of the population under consideration tend to vary together, as if they were connected. For example, a study of annual income that also looks at age of death might find that poor people tend to have shorter lives than affluent people. The two variables are said to be correlated;

however, they may or may not be the cause of one another. The correlation phenomena could be caused by a third, previously unconsidered phenomenon, called a lurking variable or confounding variable. For this reason, there is no way to immediately infer the existence of a causal relationship between the two variables.

To use a sample as a guide to an entire population, it is important that it truly represent the overall population. Representative sampling assures that inferences and conclusions can safely extend from the sample to the population as a whole. A major problem lies in determining the extent that the sample chosen is actually representative. Statistics offers methods to estimate and correct for any random trending within the sample and data collection procedures. There are also methods of experimental design for experiments that can lessen these issues at the outset of a study, strengthening its capability to discern truths about the population.

Randomness is studied using the mathematical discipline of probability theory. Probability is used in "mathematical statistics" (alternatively, "statistical theory") to study the sampling distributions of sample statistics and, more generally, the properties of statistical procedures. The use of any statistical method is valid when the system or population under consideration satisfies the assumptions of the method.

Misuse of statistics can produce subtle, but serious errors in description and interpretation—subtle in the sense that even experienced professionals make such errors, and serious in the sense that they can lead to devastating decision errors. For instance, social policy, medical practice, and the reliability of structures like bridges all rely on the proper use of statistics. See below for further discussion.

Even when statistical techniques are correctly applied, the results can be difficult to interpret for those lacking expertise. The statistical significance of a trend in the data—which measures the extent to which a trend could be caused by random variation in the sample—may or may not agree with an intuitive sense of its significance. The set of basic statistical skills (and skepticism) that people need to deal with information in their everyday lives properly is referred to as statistical literacy.

Statistical methods

Experimental and observational studies

A common goal for a statistical research project is to investigate causality, and in particular to draw a conclusion on the effect of changes in the values of predictors or independent variables on dependent variables or response. There are two major types of causal statistical studies: experimental studies and observational studies. In both types of studies, the effect of differences of an independent variable (or variables) on the behavior of the dependent variable are observed. The difference between the two types lies in how the study is actually conducted. Each can be very effective. An experimental study involves taking measurements of the system under study, manipulating the system, and then taking additional measurements using the same procedure to determine if the manipulation has modified the values of the measurements. In contrast, an observational study does not involve experimental manipulation. Instead, data are gathered and correlations between predictors and response are investigated.

Experiments

The basic steps of a statistical experiment are:

1. Planning the research, including finding the number of replicates of the study, using the following information: preliminary estimates regarding the size of treatment effects, alternative hypotheses, and the estimated experimental variability. Consideration of the selection of experimental subjects and the ethics of research is necessary. Statisticians recommend that experiments compare (at least) one new treatment with a standard treatment or control, to allow an unbiased estimate of the difference in treatment effects.
2. Design of experiments, using blocking to reduce the influence of confounding variables, and randomized assignment of treatments to subjects to allow unbiased estimates of treatment effects and experimental error. At this stage, the experimenters and statisticians write the *experimental protocol* that shall guide the performance of the experiment and that specifies the *primary analysis* of the experimental data.
3. Performing the experiment following the experimental protocol and analyzing the data following the experimental protocol.
4. Further examining the data set in secondary analyses, to suggest new hypotheses for future study.
5. Documenting and presenting the results of the study.

Experiments on human behavior have special concerns. The famous Hawthorne study examined changes to the working environment at the Hawthorne plant of the Western Electric Company. The researchers were interested in determining whether increased illumination would increase the productivity of the assembly line workers. The researchers first measured the productivity in the plant, then modified the illumination in an area of the plant and checked if the changes in illumination affected productivity. It turned out that productivity indeed improved (under the experimental conditions). However, the study is heavily criticized today for errors in experimental procedures, specifically for the lack of a control group and blindness. The Hawthorne effect refers to finding that an outcome (in this case, worker productivity) changed due to observation itself. Those in the Hawthorne study became more productive not because the lighting was changed but because they were being observed.

Observational study

An example of an observational study is one that explores the correlation between smoking and lung cancer. This type of study typically uses a survey to collect observations about the area of interest and then performs statistical analysis. In this case, the researchers would collect observations of both smokers and non-smokers, perhaps through a case-control study, and then look for the number of cases of lung cancer in each group.

Levels of measurement

Various attempts have been made to produce a taxonomy of levels of measurement. The psychophysicist Stanley Smith Stevens defined nominal, ordinal, interval, and ratio scales. Nominal measurements do not have meaningful rank order among values, and permit any one-to-one transformation. Ordinal measurements have imprecise differences between consecutive values, but have a meaningful order to those values, and permit any order-preserving transformation. Interval measurements have meaningful distances between measurements defined, but the zero value is arbitrary (as in the case with longitude and temperature measurements in Celsius or Fahrenheit), and permit any linear transformation. Ratio measurements have both a meaningful zero value and the distances between different measurements defined, and permit any rescaling transformation.

Because variables conforming only to nominal or ordinal measurements cannot be reasonably measured numerically, sometimes they are grouped together as categorical variables, whereas ratio and interval measurements are grouped together as quantitative variables, which can be either discrete or continuous, due to their numerical nature.

Other categorizations have been proposed. For example, Mosteller and Tukey (1977) distinguished grades, ranks, counted fractions, counts, amounts, and balances. Nelder (1990) described continuous counts, continuous ratios, count ratios, and categorical modes of data. See also Chrisman (1998), van den Berg (1991).

The issue of whether or not it is appropriate to apply different kinds of statistical methods to data obtained from different kinds of measurement procedures is complicated by issues concerning the transformation of variables and the precise interpretation of research questions. "The relationship between the data and what they describe merely reflects the fact that certain kinds of statistical statements may have truth values which are not invariant under some transformations. Whether or not a transformation is sensible to contemplate depends on the question one is trying to answer" (Hand, 2004, p. 82).

Key terms used in statistics

Statistics, estimators and pivotal quantities

Consider n independent identically distributed (iid) random variables with a given probability distribution: standard statistical inference and estimation theory defines a random sample as the random vector given by the column vector of these iid variables. The population being examined is described by a probability distribution which may have unknown parameters.

A statistic is random variable which is a function of the random sample, but *not a function of unknown parameters*. The probability distribution of the statistics, though, may have unknown parameters.

Consider now a function of the unknown parameter: an estimator is a statistic used to estimate such function. Commonly used estimators include sample mean, unbiased sample variance and sample covariance.

A random variable which is a function of the random sample and of the unknown parameter, but whose probability distribution *does not depend on the unknown parameter* is called a pivotal quantity or pivot. Widely used pivots include the z-score, the chi square statistic and Student's t-value.

Between two estimators of a given parameter, the one with lower mean squared error is said to be more efficient. Furthermore an estimator is said to be unbiased if it's expected value is equal to the true value of the unknown parameter which is being estimated and asymptotically unbiased if its expected value converges at the limit to the true value of such parameter.

Other desirable properties for estimators include: UMVUE estimators which have the lowest variance for all possible values of the parameter to be estimated (this is usually an easier property to verify than efficiency) and consistent estimators which converges in probability to the true value of such parameter.

This still leaves the question of how to obtain estimators in a given situation and carry the computation, several methods have been proposed: the method of moments, the maximum likelihood method, the least squares method and the more recent method of estimating equations.

Null hypothesis and alternative hypothesis

Interpretation of statistical information can often involve the development of a null hypothesis in that the assumption is that whatever is proposed as a cause has no effect on the variable being measured.

The best illustration for a novice is the predicament encountered by a jury trial. The null hypothesis, H0, asserts that the defendant is innocent, whereas the alternative hypothesis, H1, asserts that the defendant is guilty. The indictment comes because of suspicion of the guilt. The H0 (status quo) stands in opposition to H1 and is maintained unless H1 is supported by evidence "beyond a reasonable doubt". However, "failure to reject H0" in this case does not imply innocence, but merely that the evidence was insufficient to convict. So the jury does not necessarily *accept* H0 but *fails to reject* H0. While one can not "prove" a null hypothesis, one can test how close it is to being true with a power test, which tests for type II errors.

What statisticians call a alternative hypothesis is simply an hypothesis which contradicts the null hypothesis.

Error

Working from a null hypothesis two basic forms of error are recognized:

- Type I errors where the null hypothesis is falsely rejected giving a "false positive".
- Type II errors where the null hypothesis fails to be rejected and an actual difference between populations is missed giving a "false negative".

Standard deviation refers to the extent to which individual observations in a sample differ from a central value, such as the sample or population mean, while Standard error refers to an estimate of difference between sample mean and population mean.

A statistical error is the amount by which an observation differs from its expected value, a residual is the amount an observation differs from the value the estimator of the expected value assumes on a given sample (also called prediction).

Mean squared error is used for obtaining efficient estimators, a widely used class of estimators. Root mean square error is simply the square root of mean squared error. Many statistical methods seek to minimize the residual sum of squares, and these are called "methods of least squares" in contrast to Least absolute deviations. The later gives equal weight to small and big errors, while the former gives more weight to large errors. Residual sum of squares is also differentiable, which provides a handy property for doing regression. Least squares applied to linear regression is called ordinary least squares method and least squares applied to nonlinear regression is called non-linear least squares. Also in a linear regression model the non deterministic part of the model is called error term, disturbance or more simply noise.

Measurement processes that generate statistical data are also subject to error. Many of these errors are classified as random (noise) or systematic (bias), but other important types of errors (e.g., blunder, such as when an analyst reports incorrect units) can also be important. The presence of missing data and/or censoring may result in biased estimates and specific techniques have been developed to adress these problems.

Interval estimation

Most studies only sample part of a population, so results don't fully represent the whole population. Any estimates obtained from the sample only approximate the population value. Confidence intervals allow statisticians to express how closely the sample estimate matches the true value in the whole population. Often they are expressed as 95% confidence intervals. Formally, a 95% confidence interval for a value is a range where, if the sampling and analysis were repeated under the same conditions (yielding a different dataset), the interval would include the true (population) value in 95% of all possible cases. This does *not* imply that the probability that the true value is in the confidence interval is 95%. From the frequentist perspective, such a claim does not even make sense, as the true value is not a random variable. Either the true value is or is not within the given interval. However, it is true that, before any data are sampled and given a plan for how to construct the confidence interval, the probability is 95% that the yet-to-be-calculated interval will cover the true value: at this point, the limits of the interval are yet-to-be-observed random variables. One approach that does yield an interval that can be interpreted as having a given probability of containing the true value is to use a credible interval from Bayesian statistics: this approach depends on a different way of interpreting what is meant by "probability", that is as a Bayesian probability.

In principle confidence intervals can be symmetrical or asymmetrical. An interval can be asymmetrical because it works as lower or upper bound for a parameter (left-sided interval or right sided interval), but it can also be asymmetrical because the two sided interval is built violating symmetry around the estimate. Sometimes the bounds for a confidence interval are reached asymptotically and these are used to approximate the true bounds.

Significance

Statistics rarely give a simple Yes/No type answer to the question asked of them. Interpretation often comes down to the level of statistical significance applied to the numbers and often refers to the probability of a value accurately rejecting the null hypothesis (sometimes referred to as the p-value).

Referring to statistical significance does not necessarily mean that the overall result is significant in real world terms. For example, in a large study of a drug it may be shown that the drug has a statistically significant but very small beneficial effect, such that the drug is unlikely to help the patient noticeably.

Criticisms arise because the hypothesis testing approach forces one hypothesis (the null hypothesis) to be "favored," and can also seem to exaggerate the importance of minor differences in large studies. A difference that is highly statistically significant can still be of no practical significance, but it is possible to properly formulate tests in account for this.

One response involves going beyond reporting only the significance level to include the *p*-value when reporting whether a hypothesis is rejected or accepted. The *p*-value, however, does not indicate the size of the effect. A better and increasingly common approach is to report confidence intervals. Although these are produced from the same calculations as those of hypothesis tests or *p*-values, they describe both the size of the effect and the uncertainty surrounding it.

Examples

Some well-known statistical tests and procedures are:

- Analysis of variance (ANOVA)
- Chi-squared test
- Correlation
- Factor analysis
- Mann–Whitney *U*
- Mean square weighted deviation (MSWD)
- Pearson product-moment correlation coefficient
- Regression analysis
- Spearman's rank correlation coefficient
- Student's *t*-test
- Time series analysis

Specialized disciplines

Statistical techniques are used in a wide range of types of scientific and social research, including: biostatistics, computational biology, computational sociology, network biology, social science, sociology and social research. Some fields of inquiry use applied statistics so extensively that they have specialized terminology. These disciplines include:

- Actuarial science (assesses risk in the insurance and finance industries)
- Applied information economics
- Biostatistics
- Business statistics
- Chemometrics (for analysis of data from chemistry)
- Data mining (applying statistics and pattern recognition to discover knowledge from data)
- Demography
- Econometrics
- Energy statistics
- Engineering statistics

- Epidemiology
- Geography and Geographic Information Systems, specifically in Spatial analysis
- Image processing
- Psychological statistics
- Reliability engineering
- Social statistics

In addition, there are particular types of statistical analysis that have also developed their own specialised terminology and methodology:

- Bootstrap & Jackknife Resampling
- Multivariate statistics
- Statistical classification
- Statistical surveys
- Structured data analysis (statistics)
- Structural equation modelling
- Survival analysis
- Statistics in various sports, particularly baseball and cricket

Statistics form a key basis tool in business and manufacturing as well. It is used to understand measurement systems variability, control processes (as in statistical process control or SPC), for summarizing data, and to make data-driven decisions. In these roles, it is a key tool, and perhaps the only reliable tool.

Statistical computing

The rapid and sustained increases in computing power starting from the second half of the 20th century have had a substantial impact on the practice of statistical science. Early statistical models were almost always from the class of linear models, but powerful computers, coupled with suitable numerical algorithms, caused an increased interest in nonlinear models (such as neural networks) as well as the creation of new types, such as generalized linear models and multilevel models.

Increased computing power has also led to the growing popularity of computationally intensive methods based on resampling, such as permutation tests and the bootstrap, while techniques such as Gibbs sampling have made use of Bayesian models more feasible. The computer revolution has implications for the future of statistics with new emphasis on "experimental" and "empirical" statistics. A large number of both general and special purpose statistical software are now available.

Misuse

There is a general perception that statistical knowledge is all-too-frequently intentionally misused by finding ways to interpret only the data that are favorable to the presenter. A mistrust and misunderstanding of statistics is associated with the quotation, "There are three kinds of lies: lies, damned lies, and statistics". Misuse of statistics can be both inadvertent and intentional, and the book *How to Lie with Statistics* outlines a range of considerations. In an attempt to shed light on the use and misuse of statistics, reviews of statistical techniques used in particular fields are conducted (e.g. Warne, Lazo, Ramos, and Ritter (2012)).

Ways to avoid misuse of statistics include using proper diagrams and avoiding bias. Misuse can occur when conclusions are overgeneralized and claimed to be representative of more than they really are, often by either deliberately or unconsciously overlooking sampling bias. Bar graphs are arguably the easiest diagrams to use and understand, and they can be made either by hand or with simple computer programs. Unfortunately, most people do not look for bias or errors, so they are not noticed. Thus, people may often believe that something is true even if it is not well represented. To make data gathered from statistics believable and accurate, the sample taken must be representative of the whole. According to Huff, "The dependability of a sample can be destroyed by... allow yourself some degree of skepticism."

To assist in the understanding of statistics Huff proposed a series of questions to be asked in each case:

- Who says so? (Does he/she have an axe to grind?)
- How does he/she know? (Does he/she have the resources to know the facts?)
- What's missing? (Does he/she give us a complete picture?)
- Did someone change the subject? (Does he/she offer us the right answer to the wrong problem?)
- Does it make sense? (Is his/her conclusion logical and consistent with what we already know?)

Statistics applied to mathematics or the arts

Traditionally, statistics was concerned with drawing inferences using a semi-standardized methodology that was "required learning" in most sciences. This has changed with use of statistics in non-inferential contexts. What was once considered a dry subject, taken in many fields as a degree-requirement, is now viewed enthusiastically. Initially derided by some mathematical purists, it is now considered essential methodology in certain areas.

- In number theory, scatter plots of data generated by a distribution function may be transformed with familiar tools used in statistics to reveal underlying patterns, which may then lead to hypotheses.
- Methods of statistics including predictive methods in forecasting are combined with chaos theory and fractal geometry to create video works that are considered to have great beauty.
- The process art of Jackson Pollock relied on artistic experiments whereby underlying distributions in nature were artistically revealed. With the advent of computers, statistical methods were applied to formalize such distribution-driven natural processes to make and analyze moving video art.
- Methods of statistics may be used predicatively in performance art, as in a card trick based on a Markov process that only works some of the time, the occasion of which can be predicted using statistical methodology.

- Statistics can be used to predicatively create art, as in the statistical or stochastic music invented by Iannis Xenakis, where the music is performance-specific. Though this type of artistry does not always come out as expected, it does behave in ways that are predictable and tunable using statistics.

Statistics as a method of research

Research Methods

To understand the use of statistics, one needs to know a little bit about experimental design or how a researcher conducts investigations. A little knowledge about methodology will provide us with a place to hang our statistics. In other words, statistics are not numbers that just appear out of nowhere. Rather, the numbers (data) are generated out of research. Statistics are merely a tool to help us answer research questions. As such, an understanding of methodology will facilitate our understanding of basic statistics.

Validity

A key concept relevant to a discussion of research methodology is that of validity. When an individual asks, "Is this study valid?", they are questioning the validity of at least one aspect of the study. There are four types of validity that can be discussed in relation to research and statistics. Thus, when discussing the validity of a study, one must be specific as to which type of validity is under discussion. Therefore, the answer to the question asked above might be that the study is valid in relation to one type of validity but invalid in relation to another type of validity.

Each of the four types of validity will be briefly defined and described below. Be aware that this represents a cursory discussion of the concept of validity. Each type of validity has many threats which can pose a problem in a research study. Examples, but not an exhaustive discussion, of threats to each validity will be provided. For a comprehensive discussion of the four types of validity, the threats associated with each type of validity, and additional validity issues see Cook and Campbell (1979).

Statistical Conclusion Validity: Unfortunately, without a background in basic statistics, this type of validity is difficult to understand. According to Cook and Campbell (1979), "statistical conclusion validity refers to inferences about whether it is reasonable to presume covariation given a specified alpha level and the obtained variances (p. 41)." Essentially, the question that is being asked is - "Are the variables under study related?" or "Is variable A correlated (does it covary) with Variable B?". If a study has good statistical conclusion validity, we should be relatively certain that the answer to these questions is "yes". Examples of issues or problems that would threaten statistical conclusion validity would be random heterogeneity of the research subjects (the subjects represent a diverse group - this increases statistical error) and small sample size (more difficult to find meaningful relationships with a small number of subjects).

Internal Validity: Once it has been determined that the two variables (A & B) are related, the next issue to be determined is one of causality. Does A cause B? If a study is lacking internal validity, one can not make cause and effect statements based on the research; the study would be descriptive but not causal. There are many potential threats to internal validity. For example, if a study has a pretest, an experimental treatment, and a follow-up posttest, history is a threat to internal validity. If a difference is found between the pretest and posttest, it might be due to the experimental treatment but it might also be due to any other event that subjects experienced between the two times of testing (for example, a historical event, a change in weather, etc.).

Construct Validity: One is examining the issue of construct validity when one is asking the questions "Am I really measuring the construct that I want to study?" or "Is my study confounded (Am I confusing constructs)?". For example, if I want to know a particular drug (Variable A) will be effective for treating depression (Variable B) , I will need at least one measure of depression. If that measure does not truly reflect depression levels but rather anxiety levels (Confounding Variable X), than my study will be lacking construct validity. Thus, good construct validity means the we will be relatively sure that Construct A is related to Construct B and that this is possibly a causal relationship. Examples of other threats to construct validity include subjects apprehension about being evaluated, hypothesis guessing on the part of subjects, and bias introduced in a study by expectencies on the part of the experimenter.

External Validity: External validity addresses the issue of being able to generalize the results of your study to other times, places, and persons. For example, if you conduct a study looking at heart disease in men, can these results be generalized to women? Therefore, one needs to ask the following questions to determine if a threat to the external validity exists: "Would I find these same results with a difference sample?", "Would I get these same results if I conducted my study in a different setting?", and "Would I get these same results if I had conducted this study in the past or if I redo this study in the future?" If I can not answer "yes" to each of these questions, then the external validity of my study is threatened.

Types of Research Studies

There are four major classifications of research designs. These include observational research, correlational research, true experiments, and quasi-experiments. Each of these will be discussed further below.

Observational research: There are many types of studies which could be defined as observational research including case studies, ethnographic studies, ethological studies, etc. The primary characteristic of each of these types of studies is that phenomena are being observed and recorded. Often times, the studies are qualitative in nature. For example, a psychological case study would entail extensive notes based on observations of and interviews with the client. A detailed report with analysis would be written and reported constituting the study of this individual case. These studies may also be qualitative in nature or include qualitative components in the research. For example, an ethological study of primate behavior in the wild may include measures of behavior durations ie. the amount of time an animal engaged in a specified behavior. This measure of time would be qualitative.

Surveys are often classified as a type of observational research.

Correlational research: In general, correlational research examines the covariation of two or more variables. For example, the early research on cigarette smoking examine the covariation of cigarette smoking and a variety of lung diseases. These two variable, smoking and lung disease were found to covary together.

Correlational research can be accomplished by a variety of techniques which include the collection of empirical data. Often times, correlational research is considered type of observational research as nothing is manipulated by the experimenter or individual conducting the research. For example, the early studies on cigarette smoking did not manipulate how many cigarettes were smoked. The researcher only collected the data on the two variables. Nothing was controlled by the researchers.

It is important to not that correlational research is not causal research. In other words, we can not make statements concerning cause and effect on the basis of this type of research. There are two major reasons why we can not make cause and effect statements. First, we donÂ¹t know the direction of the cause. Second, a third variable may be involved of which we are not aware. An example may help clarify these points.

In major clinical depressions, the neurotransmitters serotonin and/or norepinephrine have been found to be depleted (Coppen, 1967; Schildkraut & Kety, 1967). In other words, low levels of these two neurotransmitters have been found to be associated with increased levels of clinical depression. However, while we know that the two variables covary - a relationship exists - we do not know if a causal relationship exists. Thus, it is unclear whether a depletion in serotonin/norepinephrine cause depression or whether depression causes a depletion is neurotransmitter levels. This demonstrates the first problem with correlational research; we don't know the direction of the cause. Second, a third variable has been uncovered which may be affecting both of the variables under study. The number of receptors on the postsynaptic neuron has been found to be increased in depression (Segal, Kuczenski, & Mandell, 1974; Ventulani, Staqarz, Dingell, & Sulser, 1976). Thus, it is possible that the increased number of receptors on the postsynaptic neuron is actually responsible for the relationship between neurotransmitter levels and depression. As you can see from the discussion above, one can not make a simple cause and effect statement concerning neurotransmitter levels and depression based on correlational research. To reiterate, it is inappropriate in correlational research to make statements concerning cause and effect.

Correlational research is often conducted as exploratory or beginning research. Once variables have been identified and defined, experiments are conductable.

True Experiments: The true experiment is often thought of as a laboratory study. However, this is not always the case. A true experiment is defined as an experiment conducted where an effort is made to impose control over all other variables except the one under study. It is often easier to impose this sort of control in a laboratory setting. Thus, true experiments have often been erroneously identified as laboratory studies.

To understand the nature of the experiment, we must first define a few terms:

1. Experimental or treatment group - this is the group that receives the experimental treatment, manipulation, or is different from the control group on the variable under study.
2. Control group - this group is used to produce comparisons. The treatment of interest is deliberately withheld or manipulated to provide a baseline performance with which to compare the experimental or treatment group's performance.

3. Independent variable - this is the variable that the experimenter manipulates in a study. It can be any aspect of the environment that is empirically investigated for the purpose of examining its influence on the dependent variable.
4. Dependent variable - the variable that is measured in a study. The experimenter does not control this variable.
5. Random assignment - in a study, each subject has an equal probability of being selected for either the treatment or control group.
6. Double blind - neither the subject nor the experimenter knows whether the subject is in the treatment of the control condition.

Now that we have these terms defined, we can examine further the structure of the true experiment. First, every experiment must have at least two groups: an experimental and a control group. Each group will receive a level of the independent variable. The dependent variable will be measured to determine if the independent variable has an effect. As stated previously, the control group will provide us with a baseline for comparison. All subjects should be randomly assigned to groups, be tested a simultaneously as possible, and the experiment should be conducted double blind. Perhaps an example will help clarify these points.

Wolfer and Visintainer (1975) examined the effects of systematic preparation and support on children who were scheduled for inpatient minor surgery. The hypothesis was that such preparation would reduce the amount of psychological upset and increase the amount of cooperation among thee young patients. Eighty children were selected to participate in the study. Children were randomly assigned to either the treatment or the control condition. During their hospitalization the treatment group received the special program and the control group did not. Care was take such that kids in the treatment and the control groups were not roomed together. Measures that were taken included heart rates before and after blood tests, ease of fluid intake, and self-report anxiety measures. The study demonstrated that the systematic preparation and support reduced the difficulties of being in the hospital for these kids.

Let us examine now the features of the experiment described above. First, there was a treatment and control group. If we had had only the treatment group, we would have no way of knowing whether the reduced anxiety was due to the treatment or the weather, new hospital food, etc. The control group provides us with the basis to make comparisons The independent variable in this study was the presence or absence of the systematic preparation program. The dependent variable consisted of the heart rates, fluid intake, and anxiety measures. The scores on these measures were influenced by and depended on whether the child was in the treatment or control group. The children were randomly assigned to either group. If the "friendly" children had been placed in the treatment group we would have no way of knowing whether they were less anxious and more cooperative because of the treatment or because they were "friendly". In theory, the random assignment should balance the number of "friendly" children between the two groups. The two groups were also tested at about the same time. In other words, one group was not measured during the summer and the other during the winter. By testing the two groups as simultaneously as possible, we can rule out any bias due to time. Finally, the children were unaware that they were participants in an experiment (the parents had agreed to their children's participation in research and the program), thus making the study single blind. If the individuals who were responsible for the dependent measures were also unaware of whether the child was in the treatment or control group, then the experiment would have been double blind.

A special case of the true experiment is the clinical trial. A clinical trial is defined as a carefully designed experiment that seeks to determine the clinical efficacy of a new treatment or drug. The design of a clinical trial is very similar to that of a true experiment. Once again, there are two groups: a treatment group (the group that receives the therapeutic agent) and a control group (the group that receives the placebo). The control group is often called the placebo group. The independent variable in the clinical trial is the level of the therapeutic agent. Once again, subjects are randomly assigned to groups, they are tested simultaneously, and the experiment should be conducted double blind. In other words, neither the patient or the person administering the drug should know whether the patient is receiving the drug or the placebo.

Quasi-Experiments: Quasi-experiments are very similar to true experiments but use naturally formed or pre-existing groups. For example, if we wanted to compare young and old subjects on lung capacity, it is impossible to randomly assign subjects to either the young or old group (naturally formed groups). Therefore, this can not be a true experiment. When one has naturally formed groups, the variable under study is a subject variable (in this case - age) as opposed to an independent variable. As such, it also limits the conclusions we can draw from such an research study. If we were to conduct the quasi-experiment, we would find that the older group had less lung capacity as compared to the younger group. We might conclude that old age thus results in less lung capacity. But other variables might also account for this result. It might be that repeated exposure to pollutants as opposed to age has caused the difference in lung capacity. It could also be a generational factor. Perhaps more of the older group smoked in their early years as compared to the younger group due to increased awareness of the hazards of cigarettes. The point is that there are many differences between the groups that we can not control that could account for differences in our dependent measures. Thus, we must be careful concerning making statement of causality with quasi-experimental designs.

Quasi-experiments may result from studying the differences between naturally formed groups (ie. young & old; men & women). However, there are also instances when a researcher designs a study as a traditional experiment only to discover that random assignment to groups is restricted by outside factors. The researcher is forced to divide groups according to some pre-existing criteria. For example, if a corporation wanted to test the effectiveness of a new wellness program, they might decide to implement their program at one site and use a comporable site (no wellness program) as a control. As the employees are not shuffled and randomly assigned to work at each site, the study has pre-existing groups. After a few months of study, the researchers could then see if the wellness site had less absenteeism and lower health costs than the non-wellness site. The results are again restricted due to the quasi-correlational nature of the study. As the study has pre-existing groups, there may be other differences between those groups than just the presence or absence of a wellness program. For example, the wellness program may be in a significantly newer, more attractive building, or the manager from hell may work at the nonwellness program site. Either way, it a difference is found between the two sites it may or may not be due to the presence/absence of the wellness program.

Populations and Samples

When conducting research, one must often use a sample of the population as opposed to using the entire population. Before we go further into the reasons why, let us first discuss what differentiates between a population and a sample.

A population can be defined as any set of persons/subjects having a common observable characteristic. For example, all individuals who reside in the United States make up a population. Also, all pregnant women make up a population. The characteristics of a population are called a parameter. A statistic can be defined as any subset of the population. The characteristics of a sample are called a statistic.

Why Sample?

This brings us to the question of why sample. Why should we not use the population as the focus of study. There are at least four major reasons to sample.

First, it is usually too costly to test the entire population. The United States government spends millions of dollars to conduct the U.S. Census every ten years. While the U.S. government may have that kind of money, most researchers do not.

The second reason to sample is that it may be impossible to test the entire population. For example, let us say that we wanted to test the 5-HIAA (a serotonergic metabolite) levels in the cerebrospinal fluid (CSF) of depressed individuals. There are far too many individuals who do not make it into the mental health system to even be identified as depressed, let alone to test their CSF.

The third reason to sample is that testing the entire population often produces error. Thus, sampling may be more accurate. Perhaps an example will help clarify this point. Say researchers wanted to examine the effectiveness of a new drug on Alzheimer's disease. One dependent variable that could be used is an Activities of Daily Living Checklist. In other words, it is a measure of functioning o a day to day basis. In this experiment, it would make sense to have as few of people rating the patients as possible. If one individual rates the entire sample, there will be some measure of consistency from one patient to the next. If many raters are used, this introduces a source of error. These raters may all use a slightly different criteria for judging Activities of Daily Living. Thus, as in this example, it would be problematic to study an entire population.

The final reason to sample is that testing may be destructive. It makes no sense to lesion the lateral hypothalamus of all rats to determine if it has an effect on food intake. We can get that information from operating on a small sample of rats. Also, you probably would not want to buy a car that had the door slammed five hundred thousand time or had been crash tested. Rather, you probably would want to purchase the car that did not make it into either of those samples.

Nature of Statistics

The Graziano and Raulin textbook covered the basics of statistical procedures, but this section will review those critical concepts and expand on them.

Purpose of Statistics

Statistics serve two primary purposes. The first is to summarize and describe a set of data from a research study. The second is to provide an objective basis for drawing conclusions from the data collected in a research study.

Key Definitions

Listed here are definitions of critical terms for this section.

- descriptive statistics - statistics that are used to describe some aspect of the data, such as the typical score or the variability of scores.
- inferential statistics - statistical procedures that are used to draw conclusions about the populations under study based on the sample data from those populations.
- population - all people, objects, or events that are of interest. Populations are usually defined by one or more specific characteristics. For example, we might be studying the population of all college students, which is defined as all individuals currently attending college.
- sample - a subset of people, objects, or events drawn from the population. The word sample is also used as a verb to indicate the process of drawing the sample.
- population parameter - a descriptive statistic that is computed on the entire population.
- sample statistic - a descriptive statistic that is computed on a sample drawn from the population.
- sampling procedure - the method that is used to draw a samplc from the population.
- sample size - the number of individuals included in the sample that is drawn from the population. Traditionally, the uppercase letter N is used to denote this number.

Sampling Procedure

The object of sampling is to obtain a sample that is representative of the population from which the sample is drawn. A sample is representative of the population if it shows the same characteristics as the population. In other words, the sample statistics are very similar to the population parameters.

The best way of obtaining a representative sample is to sample randomly, which means sampling so that every individual in the population has an equal chance of being sampled and the selection of any one individual does not change the probability of sampling any other individual. As you will learn in the research methods textbook, random sampling is very difficult to actually carry out, and research rarely is based on true random samples from the population.

Subject matter of Statistics

Statistics has developed as a science in its own right, and its principles and methods form the foundation for statistical work in all fields. This is because, its principles and methods involve certain logical patterns which may exist in almost any problem area or in any subject-matter field. Statistical principles and methods are specially appropriate for handling data which are subject to variations that cannot be fully controlled by experimental methods."

Statistical methods are devices by the application of which quantitative data influenced by multiple causation are collected and so scientifically analysed and elucidated that they are brought within easy and clear grasp."

Croxton and Cowden write,"The methods of statistics are useful in ever widening range of human activities in any field of thought in which numerical data may be had ...Today, there is hardly a phase of endeavour which does not find statistical devices at least occasionally useful." Statistical principles and methods deal with the quantitative characteristics of objects. These are handmade of both physical and social sciences, but are of greater service to the latter.

Modern Statistics

A century ago H.G. Wells commented that "statistical thinking will one day be as necessary for efficient citizenship as the ability to read and write." Each day of our lives we are exposed to a wide assortment of numerical information pertaining to such phenomena as stock market activity, unemployment rates, medical research findings, opinion poll results, weather forecasts, and sports data. Frequently, such information has a profound impact on our lives.

"The subject of modern statistics encompasses the collection, presentation, and characterization of information to assist in both data analysis and the decision making process".

Growth and Development

Historically, the growth and development of modern statistics can be traced to two separate phenomena–the needs of government to collect information on its citizenry and the development of the mathematics of probability theory.

Data have been collected throughout recorded history. During the Egyptian, Greek, and Roman civilizations information was obtained primarily for the purposes of taxation and military conscription. In the Middle Ages, Church institutions often kept records concerning births, deaths, and marriages.

Descriptive Statistics

These and other needs for data on a nationwide basis were closely interwined with the development of descriptive statistics.

Descriptive statistics can be defined as those methods involving the collection, presentation, and characterization of a set of data in order to properly describe the various features of that set of data.

Although descriptive statistical methods are important for presenting and characterizing information, it has been the development of inferential statistical methods as an outgrowth of probability theory that has led to the wide application of statistics in all fields of research today.

Differential Statistics

The initial for formulation of the mathematics of probability theory came from the investigation of games of chance during the Renaissance. The foundations of the subject of probability can be traced back to the middle of the seventeenth century in the correspondence between the mathematician Pascal and the gambler Chevalier de Mere. These and other developments by such mathematicians as Bernoulli, DeMoivre, and Gauss were the forerunners of the subject of inferential statistics. However, it has only been since the turn of this century that statisticians such as Pearson, Fisher, Gosset, Neyman, Wald, and Tukey pioneered in the development of the methods of inferential statistics that are widely applied in to many fields today.

Inferential statistics can be defined as those methods that make possible the estimation of a characteristic of a population or the making of a decision concerning a population based only on sample results.

To clarify this, a few more definitions are necessary.

A population (or universe) is the totality of items or things under consideration.

A sample is the portion of the population that is selected for analysis.

A parameter is a summary measure that is computed to describe a characteristic of an entire population

A statistic is a summary measure that is computed to describe a characteristic from only a sample of the population

Thus, one major aspect of inferential statistics is the process of using sample statistics to draw conclusion about the true population parameters.

The need for interential statistical methods derives from the need for sampling. As a population becomes large, it is usually too costly, too time consuming, and too cumbersome to obtain our information from the entire population. Decisions pertaining to the population's characteristics have to be based on the information contained in a sample of that population. Probability theory provides the link by ascertaining the likelihood that the results from the sample reflect the results from the population.

These ideas can be clearly seen in the example of a political poll. If the pollster wishes to estimate the percentage of the votes a candidate will received in a particular election, he or she will not interview each of the thousands (or even millions) of voters. Instead, a sample of voters will be selected. Based on the outcome from the sample, conclusion will be drawn concerning the entire population of voters. Appended to these conclusion that the results from the sample reflect the true voting behavior in the population.

Statistical Thinking and Modern Management

Along with the major advances in information processing that have taken place in the past decade, there has occurred a reemergence of interest in the quality of products manufactured and services delivered. An integral part of this total quality management approach is the application of certain statistical methods and the use of a statistical thinking approach on the part of managers throughout a company. In this model, the strategic top of the triangle consists of management leadership, product quality and care of customers, people and teamwork, and constant improvement and innovation. The middle of the triangle, the quality management systems represents the link between the strategic and operational levels of activities. The bottom foundation of the triangle represents the operational of activities. The bottom foundation of the triangle represent the operational levels of activities, partially consisting of the use of statistical methods and tools. However, the use of statistical tools can only be valuable in the context of understanding their role in statistical thinking.

Statistical thinking can be defined as thought processes that focus on ways to manage (and thereby reduce variation.

It includes the recognition that data are inherently variable (no two things or people will be exactly alike in all ways) and that the identification, measurement control, and reduction of variation provide opportunities for quality improvement. Statistical methods can provide the vehicle for taking advantage of these opportunities. "Statistical workers have the task of organising and summarising the data, of observing the variations revealed, of analysing the relations, of preparing reports, explaining them and making recommendations." (Neiswanger). In performing these functions, a statistician is a practitioner of the art and science of statistics As such he must know the methods available to solve certain kinds of problems capable of numerical expression. In other words, he should understand the problem to be solved. He should also be able to discern what types of numerical information may throw light on the problem. For obtaining the necessary information, he must be well-versed with collection methods. He should be able to classify the information and communicate the results to others who will use the information to decide the issue at hand. However, "the statistician's job does not really end at this point, because he must keep in mind the necessity of adding new knowledge to the body of skills and methods which comprise the science of statistics." (C.H. Meyers)

A statistician can perform his functions efficiently only when he is master of statistical techniques and laws. Besides such knowledge, "good judgement, broad knowledge and experience and common sense are the most valued possessions of the statistician." His work is not merely of a routine nature. He has to work under various handicaps and he should be very cautious and vigilant.

Relation of Statistics with other sciences

Statistics is a way to formalize the operation of free will (unpredictable events).

All social sciences deal with operation of free will.

Using statistics in social science research provides a more organized way to present quantitative and qualitative findings. For instance, if you're reading a sociology or psychology report or scholarly paper, you would most likely find some sort of table of data, such as a frequency distribution or a graph for instance. These are both statistical methods to present data. Many researchers would agree that a social science research project would hardly be called legitimate without some sort quantitative (statistical) analysis included in it. To a certain degree, you could say that statistics provide real fact to social science theory because numbers are much more tangiblethan beliefs. Without statistics, the social sciences definitely would not be where they are today.

Relation of Statistics with Social Sciences. Statistical methods are extensively used in Social Sciences. Political Science, History, Geography, psychology, etc., all social sciences use statistical methods in investigation and research in their respective fields. Computation of

I.Q. (Intelligence Quotient) done in psychology is based on statistical methods. In many social sciences, data are firse collected to study special problems. Even non-quantitative facts are presented in numerical terms for statistical analysis. The political analysis of voters' behaviour are the new areas where statistical methods are being used. In the words of G. Kalton," In the social sciences much of the research undertaken involves, at some stage the collection of statistical information. For example, economists collect data on the proportion of a famil 's income that is spent on housing, sociologists on the housing conditions, of immigrants, social psychologists on the attitudes of nurses towards their patients and educational psychologists on the effectiveness of a teaching machine in the teaching of algebra to school children. To carry on such research project, a knowledge of statistics is required."2

The development of social sciences owes much to the use of statistical methods. The extensive use of statistical methods in social sciences has resulted in the development of new statistical methods and techniques. Statistical methods are indispensable to the analysis and research in the problems pertaining to the field of social sciences, In social sciences, the role of statistician is not only in the measurement of social conditions but also in testing hypotheses and making suitable changes in them. For this, he (1) examines theory and hypothesis on the criteria of empirical tests, (2) examines the existing principles to find out their validity in the existing circumstances, and (3) substitutes better principles in place of incomplete or false ones. It is the job of statistician to make the loose principles precise, by collecting relevant facts, The principles falsified by the collected facts are revised and those passing tests are continuously examine by further rigid tests.

Relation of Statistics with Physical Sciences. In physical sciences, like Biology, Physics, Chemistry, Astronomy, Medicine, etc., the use of statistical methods is constantly increasing .In these sciences, statistical data are collected from the results of experiments. Different experiments give different results. It is found out whether the difference in various results is statistically significant. With more and more facts, which are made available, the different estimates in the areas of physical sciences, like that of distance between different planets in the universe, become more and more accurate. Karl pearson's doctrine of evolution and heredity is based on statistical methods. The method of Least squares was propounded by an astronomer. In fact, "our actual knowledge of concrete thing is of an essentially statistical nature."

Ever since the work of Isaac Newton (right), mathematics has been the language and the basic tool of theoretical physics. Mathematics models the motion of the planets, the flow of heat, the propagation of electromagnetic waves, the quantum behaviour of electrons, the curvature of space and time, the flow of liquids and gasses, and much else besides.

The last few decades have seen a hugely fruitful interaction between pure mathematics and the more speculative end of theoretical physics. There are fascinating parallels with the situation in the last century, when Joseph Fourier made spectacular advances in the theory of heatflow using some rather strange manipulations with infinite series, which made no sense when interpreted literally. Nonetheless, it later proved possible to reinterpret Fourier's arguments rigorously, vindicating his confidence in the essential correctness of his arguments and leading the way to many generalisations and extensions of his theory. A similar story could be told about the "delta-function" introduced by the physicist Paul Dirac, which inspired and was made rigorous by Laurent Schwartz 's theory of distributions.

Today we have a similar situation on a much grander scale, where physicists (exemplified by Edward Witten, right) have used their intuition about possible models of quantum mechanics (with neither a solid mathematical basis nor a realistic possibility of experimental test) to suggest profound conjectures about higher-dimensional geometry. This has inspired a great deal of new mathematics designed to address these conjectures more rigorously; they have proved to be correct in a remarkable number of cases. A part of this story is surveyed at the Cambridge relativity home page. A more recent development is the use of mathematics in biology. One very early example was the use of statistics by John Snow in the mid 19th century to show that cholera was caused by contaminated water; this story (and much, much more) is told in Tom Körner's book "The Pleasures of Counting". The first half of the 20th century saw work of Fisher and Haldane using probability and statistics to study the spread of genes in an evolving population. There are also mathematical models of many biological processes: the conduction of signals along nerves, the flow of blood through the heart, the formation of scar tissue and so on. Some mathematical theory of the topology of knots has been used to study knotted strands of DNA. Some scientists have been inspired by this to construct strands of DNA knotted in bizarre and complicated shapes.

Statisitcs and its Functions

Statistics as a discipline is considered indispensable in almost all spheres of human knowledge. There is hardly any branch of study which does not use statistics. Scientific, social and economic studies use statistics in one form or another. These disciplines make-use of observations, facts and figures, enquiries and experiments etc. using statistics and statistical methods. Statistics studies almost all aspects in an enquiry. It mainly aims at simplifying the complexity of information collected in an enquiry. It presents data in a simplified form as to make them intelligible. It analyses data and facilitates drawal of conclusions. Now let us briefly discuss some of the important functions of statistics.

1. **Presents facts in. simple form:** Statistics presents facts and figures in a definite form. That makes the statement logical and convincing than mere description. It condenses the whole mass of figures into a single figure. This makes the problem intelligible.
2. **Reduces the Complexity of data:** Statistics simplifies the complexity of data. The raw data are unintelligible. We make them simple and intelligible by using different statistical measures. Some such commonly used measures are graphs, averages, dispersions, skewness, kurtosis, correlation and regression etc. These measures help in interpretation and drawing infcrcnccs. Thcrcforc, statistics cnablcs to cnlargc thc horizon of onc's knowledge.
3. **Facilitates comparison:** Comparison between different sets of observation is an important function of statistics. Comparison is necessary to draw conclusions as Professor Boddington rightly points out." the object of statistics is to enable comparison between past and present results to ascertain the reasons for changes, which have taken place and the effect of such changes in future. So to determine the efficiency of any measure comparison is necessary. Statistical devices like averages, ratios, coefficients etc. are used for the purpose of comparison.
4. **Testing hypothesis:** Formulating and testing of hypothesis is an important function of statistics. This helps in developing new theories. So statistics examines the truth and helps in innovating new ideas.

5. **Formulation of Policies:** Statistics helps in formulating plans and policies in different fields. Statistical analysis of data forms the beginning of policy formulations. Hence, statistics is essential for planners, economists, scientists and administrators to prepare different plans and programmes.
6. **Forecasting:** The future is uncertain. Statistics helps in forecasting the trend and tendencies. Statistical techniques are used for predicting the future values of a variable. For example a producer forecasts his future production on the basis of the present demand conditions and his past experiences. Similarly, the planners can forecast the future population etc. considering the present population trends.
7. **Derives valid inferences:** Statistical methods mainly aim at deriving inferences from an enquiry. Statistical techniques are often used by scholars planners and scientists to evaluate different projects. These techniques are also used to draw inferences regarding population parameters on the basis of sample information.

Distrust of Statistics

Statistical methodology has yielded (and is yielding) important results in many fields of knowledge. Statistics, as a quantitative method of analysis, eliminates haphazard guesses and the bias of individual opinion and hunches, and replaces them with highly useful measurements and conclusions. Science of statistics is very useful indeed, but its usefulness lies in the figures themselves, but in the correct interpretations of those figures. Due to ignorance and bias people misuse this delicate tool of knowledge, that has created distruse about the science of statistics among the common men.

The science of statistics is looked upon with a suspicious eye and consumed as a tissue of falsehood. Stephen Leacock wrote that," In earlier times they (people) had not statistics and so they had to fall back on lies. Hence the huge exaggerations of primitive literature- giants or miracles or wonders! They did it with lies and we do it with statistics, but it is all the same." He treats lies and statistics as sisters. Mark Twain once remarked that "There are three degrees of comparison in lying, lies, damned lies and statistics." He treats statistics as the superlative degree of lying. A famous writer has said that "History asserts without evidence, while Statistics asserts contrary to the evidence." According to La Gordia, Statistics are like alienists- they will testify for either side." It is also said that, "A statistician is a person who draws a mathematically precise line from an unwarranted assumption to a foregone conclusion." According to one statement,"Statistical analysis has often meant the manipulation of ambiguous data by means of dubious methods to solve a problem that has not been defined." People say that an ounce of truth will produce tons of statistics, or statistics are lies of the first order, It has been remarked that'there are black lies, white lies, multichromatic lies; Statistics is a rainbow of lies."

It is believed that statistics can prove any thing, which also means that you can prove almost nothing with statistics. Statistical facts are considered stranger than fiction. It is believed that," What statistics reveal is ordinary, but what they hide is vital." An or dinary citizen feels that he is being bluffed by statistics and he resents the clever statisticians who have made him feel inferior. He regards statisticians as naive and incautious. The statistician is offer regarded as something of a pseudo-magician.

These statements indicate the extent to which the science of statistics had come to disrepute. On the other hand it is also said that if figures say so it cannot be otherwise, or 'figures don't lie', or 'facts speak for themselves'.

The reason for this diversity of opinions lies in the innocence of figures. Figures by their nature are innocent and easily believed. It is human psychology that facts supported by statistics are easily believed. As data convey a sense of precision and accuracy, it is natural to have faith in them. Misuses unfortunately are probably as common as valid uses of statistics The ability to discriminate between a valid and an invalid use of statistics is more important for most people than knowing how themselves to make effective use of statistics. Figures supporting a fact may not be true. They may be incomplete, inaccurate and deliberately manipulated by prejudiced persons. Figures do not bear a trademark of their accuracy as stated by W.I. Knig," One of the shortcomings of statistics is that they do not always bear on their face the label of their quality. The crudest table founded on the most unreliable basis appears to the casual observer equally valuable with a table compiled after months of labour by a corps of skillful statisticians."

Statistical methods are delicate tools likely to be misused . Hence fault lies with the user and not with the science of statistics. Just as a knife may be used in cutting one's throat instead of cutting a sweet red apply, similarly, statistics may be wrongly used. These innocent things can be used in any way we like. Thus it is desirable that only experts and trained persons should use these delicate tools. Bowely says," Statistics only furnish a tool necessary, though imperfect, which is dangerous in the hands of those who do not know its uses and deficiencies." A statistician should not give up his common sense and professional integrity. Neither statistics are lies nor the science of statistics is a science of liars. Hence, it is not necessary that, the scientific investigator must seek the truth above all. It is not enough to avoid outright falsehood; the investigator must be on the alert to detect possible distortion of truth. Therefore, Yule and kendall have said, " Statistics is one of those sciences whose adepts must exercise the self-restraint of an artist." Prof. Mill writes, " as a tool, statistical method requires intelligent usage and that the results secured through statistical analysis require intelligent usage and that the results secured through statistical analysis require intelligent interpretation." According to wallis and Roberts, "Eternal vigilance is the price of freedom from serious statistical blunders."

Prof. W. I. King has made it clear that," It is true that one can prove anything by statistics but he can do so by unscientific handling of his data or deliberate manipulation of the figures with the purpose of showing the desired result. It is also a fact that some set of figures are hard to analyse and their meaning is often doubtful and debatable, but in a large percentage of cases a clear and undisputable result may be arrived at, if the analysis is conducted in a scientific and unbiased manner. The science of statistics is the most useful servant but only of a great value to those who understand its proper use." Tippett has observed," the statistical method, like scientific method in general, is based on certain fundamental principles, it is not entirely automatic in its operation, and progress in knowledge depends to a considerable degree on the personal qualities of the investigator."

Whether correct or not, the misconception about statistics in the past helped to build up a mass of antipathy which is even now considerable, despite the rapid advances and the contribution.

which statistical method has been able to make in the organisation of our affairs and resources. The persons either due to their ignorance or design of dishonesty give a tarnished image of statistics. But it should be remembered that because some people habitually misuse grammar, it does not mean that grammar itself is bad. The distrust is, however, slowly decreasing, because of the increasing interest evinced in the study of statistics and in the recognition of its limitations as well as improvement in statistical methods. Now on one, whether he is as administrator or a scientist or a responsible citizen can afford to be misled by bad statistics and everybody needs knowledge that can be gained only through the effective use of statistics. It is necessary to examine the reliability of data, before believing in them. To disbelieve or believe statistics blindly is not desirable. Hence it can be said, "He who accepts statistics indiscriminately will often be duped unnecessarily. But he who distrusts statistics indiscriminately will often be ignorant unnccessarily. Reliable statistics are lamps that light our path on the road of knowledge." The statistical methods are to be considered as tools which, in proper hands, and applied to the situation for which they are designed, can produce useful results, but which, by themselves, have no power to work miracles."

2

Correlation

Statistics is a branch of mathematics working with data collection, organization, analysis, interpretation and presentation. In applying statistics to a scientific, industrial, or social problem, it is conventional to begin with a statistical population or a statistical model to be studied. Populations can be diverse groups of people or objects such as "all people living in a country" or "every atom composing a crystal". Statistics deals with every aspect of data, including the planning of data collection in terms of the design of surveys and experiments. See glossary of probability and statistics. When census data cannot be collected, statisticians collect data by developing specific experiment designs and survey samples. Representative sampling assures that inferences and conclusions can reasonably extend from the sample to the population as a whole. An experimental study involves taking measurements of the system under study, manipulating the system, and then taking additional measurements using the same procedure to determine if the manipulation has modified the values of the measurements. In contrast, an observational study does not involve experimental manipulation.

Two main statistical methods are used in data analysis: descriptive statistics, which summarize data from a sample using indexes such as the mean or standard deviation, and inferential statistics, which draw conclusions from data that are subject to random variation (e.g., observational errors, sampling variation). Descriptive statistics are most often concerned with two sets of properties of a distribution (sample or population): central tendency (or location) seeks to characterize the distribution's central or typical value, while dispersion (or variability) characterizes the extent to which members of the distribution depart from its center and each other. Inferences on mathematical statistics are made under the framework of probability theory, which deals with the analysis of random phenomena. A standard statistical procedure involves the test of the relationship between two statistical data sets, or a data set and synthetic data drawn from an idealized model. A hypothesis is proposed for the statistical relationship between the two data sets, and this is compared as an alternative to an idealized null hypothesis of no relationship between two data sets. Rejecting or disproving the null hypothesis is done using statistical tests that quantify the sense in which the null can be proven false, given the data that are used in the test. Working from a null hypothesis, two basic forms of error are recognized: Type I errors (null hypothesis is falsely rejected giving a "false positive") and Type II errors (null hypothesis fails to be rejected and an actual difference between populations is missed giving a "false negative"). Multiple problems have come to be associated with this framework: ranging from obtaining a sufficient sample size to specifying an adequate null hypothesis.

In statistics, dependence or association is any statistical relationship, whether causal or not, between two random variables or bivariate data. In the broadest sense correlation is any statistical association, though it commonly refers to the degree to which a pair of variables arelinearly related. Familiar examples of dependent phenomena include the correlation between the physical statures of parents and their offspring, and the correlation between the demand for a limited supply product and its price.

Correlations are useful because they can indicate a predictive relationship that can be exploited in practice. For example, an electrical utility may produce less power on a mild day based on the correlation between electricity demand and weather. In this example, there is a causal relationship, because extreme weather causes people to use more electricity for heating or cooling. However, in general, the presence of a correlation is not sufficient to infer the presence of a causal relationship (i.e., correlation does not imply causation). Formally, random variables are dependent if they do not satisfy a mathematical property of probabilistic independence. In informal parlance, correlation is synonymous with dependence. However, when used in a technical sense, correlation refers to any of several specific types of relationship between mean values. There are several correlation coefficients, often denoted ñ or r, measuring the degree of correlation. The most common of these is the Pearson correlation coefficient, which is sensitive only to a linear relationship between two variables (which may be present even when one variable is a nonlinear function of the other). Other correlation coefficients have been developed to be more robust than the Pearson correlation – that is, more sensitive to nonlinear relationships. Mutual information can also be applied to measure dependence between two variables.

In a bivariate distribution, the correlation may be

1. Positive, Negative and Zero Correlation; and
2. Linear or Curvilinear (Non-linear).

1. Positive, Negative or Zero Correlation

When the increase in one variable (X) is followed by a corresponding increase in the other variable (Y); the correlation is said to be positive correlation. The positive correlations range from 0 to +1; the upper limit i.e.+1 is the perfect positive coefficient of correlation. The perfect positive correlation specifies that, for every unit increase in one variable, there is proportional increase in the other. For example "Heat" and "Temperature" have a perfect positive correlation. If, on the other hand, the increase in one variable (X) results in a corresponding decrease in the other variable (Y), the correlation is said to be negative correlation. The negative correlation ranges from 0 to – 1; the lower limit giving the perfect negative correlation. The perfect negative correlation indicates that for every unit increase in one variable, there is proportional unit decrease in the other. Zero correlation means no relationship between the two variables X and Y; i.e. the change in one variable (X) is not associated with the change in the other variable (Y). For example, body weight and intelligence, shoe size and monthly salary; etc. The zero correlation is the mid-point of the range – 1 to + 1.

2. Linear or Curvilinear Correlation

Linear correlation is the ratio of change between the two variables either in the same direction or opposite direction and the graphical representation of the one variable with respect to other variable is straight line. Consider another situation. First, with increase of one variable, the second variable increases proportionately upto some point; after that with an increase in the first variable the second variable starts decreasing.

Methods of Studying Correlation

Following are the methods for studying correlation:

1. Scatter Diagram Method
2. Graphic Method
3. Karl Pearson's Coefficient of Correlation
4. Method of Least Squares

Types of correlation coefficient

Several types of correlation coefficient exist, each with their own definition and own range of usability and characteristics. They all assume values in the range from "1 to +1, where ±1 indicates the strongest possible agreement and 0 the strongest possible disagreement. As tools of analysis, correlation coefficients present certain problems, including the propensity of some types to be distorted by outliers and the possibility of incorrectly being used to infer a causal relationship between the variables.

1. Pearson correlation coefficient
2. Intraclass correlation (ICC)
3. Rank correlation

Pearson Correlation Coefficient

The Pearson product-moment correlation coefficient, also known as r, R, or Pearson's r, is a measure of the strength and direction of the linear relationship between two variables that is defined as the covariance of the variables divided by the product of their standard deviations. This is the best known and most commonly used type of correlation coefficient; when the term "correlation coefficient" is used without further qualification, it usually refers to the Pearson product-moment correlation coefficient.

For a population

Pearson's correlation coefficient when applied to a population is commonly represented by the Greek letter ñ (rho) and may be referred to as the population correlation coefficient or the population Pearson correlation coefficient. Given a pair of random variables (X, Y), the formula for ñ is:

$$\rho_{X,Y} = \frac{\text{cov}(X,Y)}{\sigma_X \sigma_Y} \qquad \text{(Eq.1)}$$

where:

- cov is the covariance
- óXis the standard deviation of X
- óYis the standard deviation of Y

The formula for ñcan be expressed in terms of mean and expectation. Since

$$\text{cov}(X,Y) = \text{E}[(X-\mu_X)(Y-\mu_Y)],$$

the formula for ñcan also be written as

$$\rho_{X,Y} = \frac{\mathrm{E}[(X-\mu_X)(Y-\mu_Y)]}{\sigma_X \sigma_Y} \qquad \text{(Eq.2)}$$

where:

- óY and óX are defined as above
- ìX is the mean of X
- ìY is the mean of Y
- E is the expectation.

The formula for ñcan be expressed in terms of uncentered moments. Since

- $\mu_X = \mathrm{E}[X]$
- $\mu_Y = \mathrm{E}[Y]$
- $\sigma_X^2 = \mathrm{E}[(X-\mathrm{E}[X])^2] = \mathrm{E}[X^2] - [\mathrm{E}[X]]^2$]
- $\sigma_Y^2 = \mathrm{E}[(Y-\mathrm{E}[Y])^2] = \mathrm{E}[Y^2] - [\mathrm{E}[Y]]^2$
- $\mathrm{E}[(X-\mu_X)(Y-\mu_Y)] = \mathrm{E}[(X-\mathrm{E}[X])(Y-\mathrm{E}[Y])] = \mathrm{E}[XY] - \mathrm{E}[X]\mathrm{E}[Y],$

$$\rho_{X,Y} = \frac{\mathrm{E}[XY] - \mathrm{E}[X]\mathrm{E}[Y]}{\sqrt{\mathrm{E}[X^2] - [\mathrm{E}[X]]^2}\sqrt{\mathrm{E}[Y^2] - [\mathrm{E}[Y]]^2}}.$$

the formula for ñcan also be written as

$$r_{xy} = \frac{\sum_{i=1}^{n}(x_i - \bar{x})(y_i - \bar{y})}{\sqrt{\sum_{i=1}^{n}(x_i - \bar{x})^2}\sqrt{\sum_{i=1}^{n}(y_i - \bar{y})^2}}$$

For a sample

Pearson's correlation coefficient when applied to a sample is commonly represented by rxyand may be referred to as the sample correlation coefficient or the sample Pearson correlation coefficient. We can obtain a formula for rxyby substituting estimates of the covariances and variances based on a sample into the formula above. Given paired data { (x1, y1) , … , (xn , yn) }consisting of npairs, rxyis defined as:

$$\bar{x} = \frac{1}{n}\sum_{i=1}^{n} x_i \qquad \text{(Eq.3)}$$

where:

- nis sample size
- xi, yiare the individual sample points indexed with i
- $\bar{y}$ (t h e s a m p l e m e a n) ; a n d a n a l o g o u s l y f o r

$$r_{xy} = \frac{n\sum x_i y_i - \sum x_i \sum y_i}{\sqrt{n\sum x_i^2 - (\sum x_i)^2}\sqrt{n\sum y_i^2 - (\sum y_i)^2}}.$$

Rearranging gives us this formula for rxy:

$$r_{xy} = \frac{\sum x_i y_i - n\bar{x}\bar{y}}{\sqrt{(\sum x_i^2 - n\bar{x}^2)}\sqrt{(\sum y_i^2 - n\bar{y}^2)}}.$$

where:

- n, xi , yiare defined as above

This formula suggests a convenient single-pass algorithm for calculating sample correlations, but, depending on the numbers involved, it can sometimes be numerically unstable

Rearranging again gives us this formula for rxy:

$$n, x_i, y_i, \bar{x}, \bar{y}$$

where:

- $r_{xy} = \frac{1}{n-1}\sum_{i=1}^{n}\left(\frac{x_i - \bar{x}}{s_x}\right)\left(\frac{y_i - \bar{y}}{s_y}\right)$ are defined as above

An equivalent expression gives the formula for rxyas the mean of the products of the standard scores as follows:

$$n, x_i, y_i, \bar{x}, \bar{y}$$

where:

- $\left(\frac{x_i - \bar{x}}{s_x}\right)$ are defined as above, and sx, syare defined below
- $r_{xy} = \frac{\sum x_i y_i - n\bar{x}\bar{y}}{(n-1)s_x s_y}$ is the standard score (and analogously for the standard score of y)

Alternative formulae for rxyare also available. One can use the following formula for rxy:

$$n, x_i, y_i, \bar{x}, \bar{y}$$

where:

- $s_x = \sqrt{\frac{1}{n-1}\sum_{i=1}^{n}(x_i - \bar{x})^2}$ are defined as above and:

- $X_i - \overline{X}$ (the sample standard

deviation); and analogously for sy

Practical issues

Under heavy noise conditions, extracting the correlation coefficient between two sets of stochastic variables is nontrivial, in particular where Canonical Correlation Analysis reports degraded correlation values due to the heavy noise contributions. A generalization of the approach is given elsewhere.

Mathematical properties

The absolute values of both the sample and population Pearson correlation coefficients are less than or equal to 1. Correlations equal to 1 or "1 correspond to data points lying exactly on a line (in the case of the sample correlation), or to a bivariate distribution entirely supported on a line (in the case of the population correlation). The Pearson correlation coefficient is symmetric: corr(X,Y) = corr(Y,X). A key mathematical property of the Pearson correlation coefficient is that it is invariant under separate changes in location and scale in the two variables. That is, we may transform X to a + bX and transform Y to c + dY, where a, b, c, and d are constants with b, d> 0, without changing the correlation coefficient. (This holds for both the population and sample Pearson correlation coefficients.).

Interpretation

The correlation coefficient ranges from "1 to 1. A value of 1 implies that a linear equation describes the relationship between X and Y perfectly, with all data points lying on a line for which Y increases as X increases. A value of"1 implies that all data points lie on a line for which Y decreases as X increases. A value of 0 implies that there is no linear correlation between the

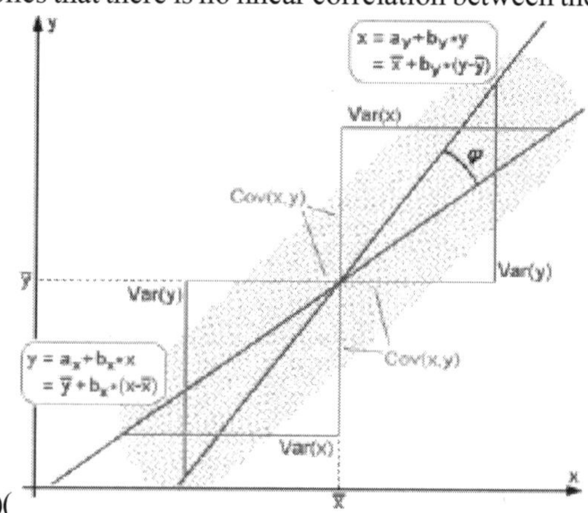

variables. More generally, note that ($Y_i - \overline{Y}$)( ) is positive if and only if Xi and Yi lie on the same side of their respective means. Thus the correlation coefficient is positive if Xi and Yi tend to be simultaneously greater than, or simultaneously less than, their respective means. The correlation coefficient is negative (anti-correlation) if Xi and Yi tend to lie on opposite sides of their respective means. Moreover, the stronger is either tendency, the larger is the absolute value of the correlation coefficient.

Rogers and Nicewander cataloged thirteen ways of interpreting correlation:

- Function of raw scores and means.
- Standardized covariance.
- Standardized slope of the regression line
- Geometric mean of the two regression slopes.
- Square root of the ratio of two variances.
- Mean cross-product of standardized variables.
- Function of the angle between two standardized regression lines.
- Function of the angle between two variable vectors.
- Rescaled variance of the difference between standardized scores.
- Estimated from the balloon rule.
- Related to the bivariate ellipses of isoconcentration.
- Function of test statistics from designed experiments.
- Ratio of two means.

Geometric interpretation

For uncentered data, there is a relation between the correlation coefficient and the angle ö between the two regression lines, y = gx(x) and x = gy(y), obtained by regressing y on x and x on y respectively. (Here ö is measured counterclockwise within the first quadrant formed around the lines' intersection point if r> 0, or counterclockwise from the fourth to the second quadrant if r< 0.) One can show] that if the standard deviations are equal, then r = sec ö " tan ö, where sec and tan are trigonometric functions.

$$\cos\theta = \frac{\mathbf{x}\cdot\mathbf{y}}{\|\mathbf{x}\|\|\mathbf{y}\|} = \frac{2.93}{\sqrt{103}\sqrt{0.0983}} = 0.920814711.$$

Regression lines for y = gx(x) [red] and x = gy(y) [blue] For centered data (i.e., data which have been shifted by the sample means of their respective variables so as to have an average of zero for each variable), the correlation coefficient can also be viewed as the cosine of the angleè between the two observed vectors in N-dimensional space (for N observations of each variable) (as illustrated for a special case in the next paragraph). Both the uncentered (non-Pearson-compliant) and centered correlation coefficients can be determined for a dataset. As an example, suppose five countries are found to have gross national products of 1, 2, 3, 5, and 8 billion dollars, respectively. Suppose these same five countries (in the same order) are found to have 11%, 12%, 13%, 15%, and 18% poverty. Then let x and y be ordered 5-element vectors containing the above data: x = (1, 2, 3, 5, 8) and y = (0.11, 0.12, 0.13, 0.15, 0.18).

By the usual procedure for finding the angle è between two vectors (see dot product), the uncentered correlation coefficient is:

$$\cos\theta = \frac{\mathbf{x}\cdot\mathbf{y}}{\|\mathbf{x}\|\|\mathbf{y}\|} = \frac{0.308}{\sqrt{30.8}\sqrt{0.00308}} = 1 = \rho_{xy},$$

This uncentred correlation coefficient is identical with the cosine similarity. Note that the above data were deliberately chosen to be perfectly correlated: y = 0.10 + 0.01 x. The Pearson correlation coefficient must therefore be exactly one. Centering the data (shifting x by E(x) = 3.8 and y by E(y) = 0.138) yields x = (“2.8, “1.8, “0.8, 1.2, 4.2) and y = (“0.028, “0.018, “0.008, 0.012, 0.042), from which as expected.

$$E[r] = \rho - \frac{\rho(1-\rho^2)}{2n} + \cdots,$$

Interpretation of the size of a correlation Several authors have offered guidelines for the interpretation of a correlation coefficient. However, all such criteria are in some ways arbitrary. The interpretation of a correlation coefficient depends on the context and purposes. A correlation of 0.8 may be very low if one is verifying a physical law using high-quality instruments, but may be regarded as very high in the social sciences where there may be a greater contribution from complicating factors.

Sensitivity to the data distribution

Existence

The population Pearson correlation coefficient is defined in terms of moments, and therefore exists for any bivariate probability distribution for which the populationcovariance is defined and the marginalpopulation variances are defined and are non-zero. Some probability distributions such as the Cauchy distribution have undefined variance and hence ñ is not defined if X or Y follows such a distribution. In some practical applications, such as those involving data suspected to follow a heavy-tailed distribution, this is an important consideration. However, the existence of the correlation coefficient is usually not a concern; for instance, if the range of the distribution is bounded, ñ is always defined.

Sample size

- If the sample size is moderate or large and the population is normal, then, in the case of the bivariate normal distribution, the sample correlation coefficient is the maximum likelihood estimate of the population correlation coefficient, and is asymptoticallyunbiased and efficient, which roughly means that it is impossible to construct a more accurate estimate than the sample correlation coefficient.
- If the sample size is large and the population is not normal, then the sample correlation coefficient remains approximately unbiased, but may not be efficient.
- If the sample size is large, then the sample correlation coefficient is a consistent estimator of the population correlation coefficient as long as the sample means, variances, and covariance are consistent (which is guaranteed when the law of large numbers can be applied).
- If the sample size is small, then the sample correlation coefficient r is not an unbiased estimate of ñ. The adjusted correlation coefficient must be used instead: see elsewhere in this article for the definition.
- Correlations can be different for imbalanced dichotomous data when there is variance error in sample.

Robustness

Like many commonly used statistics, the sample statistic r is not robust, so its value can be misleading if outliers are present. Specifically, the PMCC is neither distributionally robust, nor outlier resistant. Inspection of the scatterplot between X and Y will typically reveal a situation where lack of robustness might be an issue, and in such cases it may be advisable to use a robust measure of association. Note however that while most robust estimators of association measure statistical dependence in some way, they are generally not interpretable on the same scale as the Pearson correlation coefficient.

Statistical inference for Pearson's correlation coefficient is sensitive to the data distribution. Exact tests, and asymptotic tests based on the Fisher transformation can be applied if the data are approximately normally distributed, but may be misleading otherwise. In some situations, the bootstrap can be applied to construct confidence intervals, and permutation tests can be applied to carry out hypothesis tests. These non-parametric approaches may give more meaningful results in some situations where bivariate normality does not hold.

However the standard versions of these approaches rely on exchangeability of the data, meaning that there is no ordering or grouping of the data pairs being analyzed that might affect the behavior of the correlation estimate. A stratified analysis is one way to either accommodate a lack of bivariate normality, or to isolate the correlation resulting from one factor while controlling for another. If W represents cluster membership or another factor that it is desirable to control, we can stratify the data based on the value of W, then calculate a correlation coefficient within each stratum. The stratum-level estimates can then be combined to estimate the overall correlation while controlling for W.

Variants

Variations of the correlation coefficient can be calculated for different purposes. Here are some examples.

Adjusted correlation coefficient

The sample correlation coefficient r is not an unbiased estimate of ñ. For data that follows a bivariate normal distribution, the expectation E(r) for the sample correlation coefficient r of a normal bivariate is

(1) $$r_{\text{adj}} = \boldsymbol{r}\,{}_2\mathbf{F}_1\left(\frac{1}{2},\frac{1}{2};\frac{n-1}{2};1-r^2\right),$$ thereforer is a biased estimator of ñ.

The unique minimum variance unbiased estimator radj is given by

(2) $$r = \mathrm{E}[r] = r_{\text{adj}} - \frac{r_{\text{adj}}(1-r_{\text{adj}}^2)}{2n}.$$

where:

- r, nare defined as above,
- 2 F1 (a, b; c; z) is the Gaussian hypergeometric function.

An approximately unbiased estimator radj can be obtained by truncating E[r] and solving this truncated equation:

(3) $$r_{adj} = r\left[1+\frac{1-r^2}{2n}\right],$$

An approximate solution to equation (2) is:

$$r_{\text{adj}} = \sqrt{1-\frac{(1-r^2)(n-1)}{(n-2)}}.$$

where in (3):

- r, nare defined as above,
- radj is a suboptimal estimator,
- radj can also be obtained by maximizing log(f(r)),
- radj has minimum variance for large values of n,
- radj has a bias of order 1/(n " 1).

Another proposed adjusted correlation coefficient is:

$$\mathrm{m}(x;w) = \frac{\sum_i w_i x_i}{\sum_i w_i}.$$

Note that radj H" r for large values of n.

Weighted correlation coefficient

Suppose observations to be correlated have differing degrees of importance that can be expressed with a weight vector w. To calculate the correlation between vectors x and y with the weight vector w (all of length n),

- Weighted mean

$$\mathrm{cov}(x,y;w) = \frac{\sum_i w_i(x_i - \mathrm{m}(x;w))(y_i - \mathrm{m}(y;w))}{\sum_i w_i}.$$

- Weighted covariance

$$\mathrm{corr}(x,y;w) = \frac{\mathrm{cov}(x,y,w)}{\sqrt{\mathrm{cov}(x,x;w)\,\mathrm{cov}(y,y;w)}}.$$

- Weighted correlation

$$\mathrm{Corr}_r(X,Y) = \frac{E[XY]}{\sqrt{EX^2 \cdot EY^2}}.$$

Reflective correlation coefficient

The reflective correlation is a variant of Pearson's correlation in which the data are not centered around their mean values. The population reflective correlation is

$$\mathrm{Corr}_r(X,Y) = \mathrm{Corr}_r(Y,X) = \mathrm{Corr}_r(X,bY) \neq \mathrm{Corr}_r(X,a+bY), \quad a \neq 0, b > 0.$$

The reflective correlation is symmetric, but it is not invariant under translation:

$$rr_{xy} = \frac{\sum x_i y_i}{\sqrt{(\sum x_i^2)(\sum y_i^2)}}.$$

The sample reflective correlation is equivalent to cosine similarity:

$$rr_{xy,w} = \frac{\sum w_i x_i y_i}{\sqrt{(\sum w_i x_i^2)(\sum w_i y_i^2)}}.$$

The weighted version of the sample reflective correlation is

$$K = \text{round}\left(\frac{T}{s}\right).$$

Scaled correlation coefficient

Scaled correlation is a variant of Pearson's correlation in which the range of the data is restricted intentionally and in a controlled manner to reveal correlations between fast components in time series. Scaled correlation is defined as average correlation across short segments of data. Let Kbe the number of segments that can fit into the total length of the signal Tfor a given scale s:

$\bar{r}_s$

The scaled correlation across the entire signals $\bar{r}_s = \frac{1}{K}\sum_{k=1}^{K} r_k$, is then computed as

$$d_{X,Y} = 1 - \rho_{X,Y}.$$

whererk is Pearson's coefficient of correlation for segment k.

By choosing the parameter s, the range of values is reduced and the correlations on long time scale are filtered out, only the correlations on short time scales being revealed. Thus, the contributions of slow components are removed and those of fast components are retained.

Pearson's distance

A distance metric for two variables X and Y known as Pearson's distance can be defined from their correlation coefficient as

$$r_{\text{circular}} = \frac{\sum_{i=1}^{n} \sin(x_i - \bar{x}) \sin(y_i - \bar{y})}{\sqrt{\sum_{i=1}^{n} \sin(x_i - \bar{x})^2} \sqrt{\sum_{i=1}^{n} \sin(y_i - \bar{y})^2}}$$

Considering that the Pearson correlation coefficient falls between ["1, 1], the Pearson distance lies in [0, 2]. The Pearson distance has been used in cluster analysis and data detection for communications and storage with unknown gain and offset.

Circular correlation coefficient

For variables X = {x1,...,xn} and Y = {y1,...,yn} that are defined on the unit circle [0, 2ð), it is possible to define a circular analog of Pearson's coefficient. This is done by transforming data points in X and Y with a sinefunction such that the correlation coefficient is given as:

$$\overline{x}$$

where $\overline{y}$ and $Z_{m,m}$ are the circular means of X and Y. This measure can be useful in fields like meteorology where the angular direction of data is important.

Partial correlation

If a population or data-set is characterized by more than two variables, a partial correlation coefficient measures the strength of dependence between a pair of variables that is not accounted for by the way in which they both change in response to variations in a selected subset of the other variables.

Decorrelation of n random variables

It is always possible to remove the correlations between all pairs of an arbitrary number of random variables by using a data transformation, even if the relationship between the variables is nonlinear. A presentation of this result for population distributions is given by Cox & Hinkley. A corresponding result exists for reducing the sample correlations to zero. Suppose a vector of n random variables is observed m times. Let X be a matrix where Xi, jis the jth variable of observation i. Let $D = X - \frac{1}{m} Z_{m,m} X$ be an m by m square matrix with every element 1. Then D is the data transformed so every random variable has zero mean, and T is the data transformed so all variables have zero mean and zero correlation with all other variables – the sample correlation matrix of T will be the identity matrix. This has to be further divided by the standard deviation to get unit variance. The transformed variables will be uncorrelated, even though they may not be independent.

$$T = D(D^{\mathsf{T}} D)^{-\frac{1}{2}},$$

$$d = x - \frac{1}{m} Z_{1,m} X,$$

where an exponent of "1/2 represents the matrix square root of the inverse of a matrix. The correlation matrix of T will be the identity matrix. If a new data observation x is a row vector of n elements, then the same transform can be applied to x to get the transformed vectors d and t:

$$t = d(D^{\mathsf{T}} D)^{-\frac{1}{2}}.$$

$$t = r\sqrt{\frac{n-2}{1-r^2}}$$

This decorrelation is related to principal components analysis for multivariate data.

Inference

Statistical inference based on Pearson's correlation coefficient often focuses on one of the following two aims:

- One aim is to test the null hypothesis that the true correlation coefficient ñ is equal to 0, based on the value of the sample correlation coefficient r.
- The other aim is to derive a confidence interval that, on repeated sampling, has a given probability of containing ñ.

We discuss methods of achieving one or both of these aims below.

Using a permutation test

Permutation tests provide a direct approach to performing hypothesis tests and constructing confidence intervals. A permutation test for Pearson's correlation coefficient involves the following two steps:

1. Using the original paired data (xi, yi), randomly redefine the pairs to create a new data set (xi, yi2), where the i2 are a permutation of the set {1,...,n}. The permutation i2 is selected randomly, with equal probabilities placed on all n! possible permutations. This is equivalent to drawing the i2 randomly without replacement from the set {1, ...,n}. In bootstrapping, a closely related approach, the i and the i2 are separately drawn with replacement from {1, ..., n};
2. Construct a correlation coefficient r from the randomized data.

To perform the permutation test, repeat steps (1) and (2) a large number of times. The p-value for the permutation test is the proportion of the r values generated in step (2) that are larger than the Pearson correlation coefficient that was calculated from the original data. Here "larger" can mean either that the value is larger in magnitude, or larger in signed value, depending on whether a two-sided or one-sided test is desired.

Using a bootstrap

The bootstrap can be used to construct confidence intervals for Pearson's correlation coefficient. In the "non-parametric" bootstrap, n pairs (xi, yi) are resampled "with replacement" from the observed set of npairs, and the correlation coefficient r is calculated based on the resampled data. This process is repeated a large number of times, and the empirical distribution of the resampled r values are used to approximate the sampling distribution of the statistic. A 95% confidence interval for ñ can be defined as the interval spanning from the 2.5th to the 97.5th percentile of the resampled r values.

Testing using Student's t-distribution

For pairs from an uncorrelated bivariate normal distribution, the sampling distribution of a certain function of Pearson's correlation coefficient follows Student's t-distribution with degrees of freedom n " 2. Specifically, if the underlying variables have a bivariate normal distribution, the variable

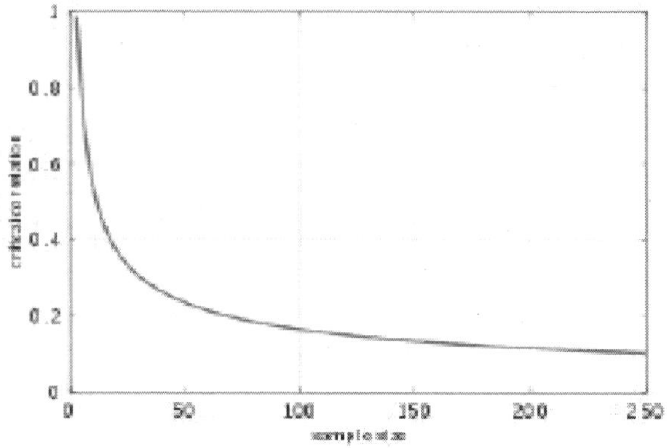

$$r = \frac{t}{\sqrt{n-2+t^2}}.$$

Critical values of Pearson's correlation coefficient that must be exceeded to be considered significantly nonzero at the 0.05 level. has a Student's t-distribution in the null case (zero correlation). This holds approximately in case of non-normal observed values if sample sizes are large enough. For determining the critical values for r the inverse function is needed:

$$f(r) = \frac{(n-2)\tilde{A}(n-1)(1-\rho^2)^{\frac{n-1}{2}}(1-r^2)^{\frac{n-4}{2}}}{\sqrt{2\pi}\tilde{A}\left(n-\frac{1}{2}\right)(1-\rho r)^{n-\frac{3}{2}}} {}_2\mathrm{F}_1\left(\frac{1}{2},\frac{1}{2};\frac{2n-1}{2};\frac{\rho r+1}{2}\right)$$

Alternatively, large sample, asymptotic approaches can be used. Another early paper provides graphs and tables for general values of ñ, for small sample sizes, and discusses computational approaches.

Using the exact distribution

For data that follows a bivariate normal distribution, the exact density function f(r) for the sample correlation coefficient r of a normal bivariate is

$(a,b;c;z)$

$$f(r) = \frac{(1-r^2)^{\frac{n-4}{2}}}{\mathbf{B}\left(\frac{1}{2},\frac{n-2}{2}\right)},$$

whereÃis the gamma function and 2 F 1 is the Gaussian hypergeometric function.

In the special case when ñ = 0, the exact density function f(r) can be written as:

Furness data set on metabolic rates of northern fulmars			
Sex	**Metabolic rate**	**Sex**	**Metabolic rate**
Male	525.8	Female	727.7
Male	605.7	Female	1086.5
Male	843.3	Female	1091.0
Male	1195.5	Female	1361.3
Male	1945.6	Female	1490.5
Male	2135.6	Female	1956.1
Male	2308.7		
Male	2950.0		

whereBis the beta function, which is one way of writing the density of a Student's t-distribution, as above.

Standard deviation

In statistics, the standard deviation (SD, also represented by the lower case Greek letter sigma ó for the population standard deviation or the Latin letter s for the sample standard deviation) is a measure that is used to quantify the amount of variation or dispersion of a set of data values. A low standard deviation indicates that the data points tend to be close to the mean (also called the expected value) of the set, while a high standard deviation indicates that the data points are spread out over a wider range of values. The standard deviation of a random variable, statistical population, data set, or probability distribution is the square root of its variance. It is algebraically simpler, though in practice less robust, than the average absolute deviation. A useful property of the standard deviation is that, unlike the variance, it is expressed in the same units as the data.

In addition to expressing the variability of a population, the standard deviation is commonly used to measure confidence in statistical conclusions. For example, the margin of error in polling data is determined by calculating the expected standard deviation in the results if the same poll were to be conducted multiple times. This derivation of a standard deviation is often called the "standard error" of the estimate or "standard error of the mean" when referring to a mean. It is computed as the standard deviation of all the means that would be computed from that population if an infinite number of samples were drawn and a mean for each sample were computed.

It is very important to note that the standard deviation of a population and the standard error of a statistic derived from that population (such as the mean) are quite different but related (related by the inverse of the square root of the number of observations). The reported margin of error of a poll is computed from the standard error of the mean (or alternatively from the product of the standard deviation of the population and the inverse of the square root of the sample size, which is the same thing) and is typically about twice the standard deviation—the half-width of a 95 percent confidence interval.

In science, many researchers report the standard deviation of experimental data, and only effects that fall much farther than two standard deviations away from what would have been expected are considered statistically significant—normal random error or variation in the measurements is in this way distinguished from likely genuine effects or associations. The standard deviation is also important in finance, where the standard deviation on the rate of return on an investment is a measure of the volatility of the investment. When only a sample of data from a population is available, the term standard deviation of the sample or sample standard deviation can refer to either the above-mentioned quantity as applied to those data or to a modified quantity that is an unbiased estimate of the population standard deviation (the standard deviation of the entire population).

Basic examples

Sample standard deviation of metabolic rate of northern fulmars Logan gives the following example. Furness and Bryant measured the resting metabolic rate for 8 male and 6 female breeding northern fulmars. The table shows the Furness data set.

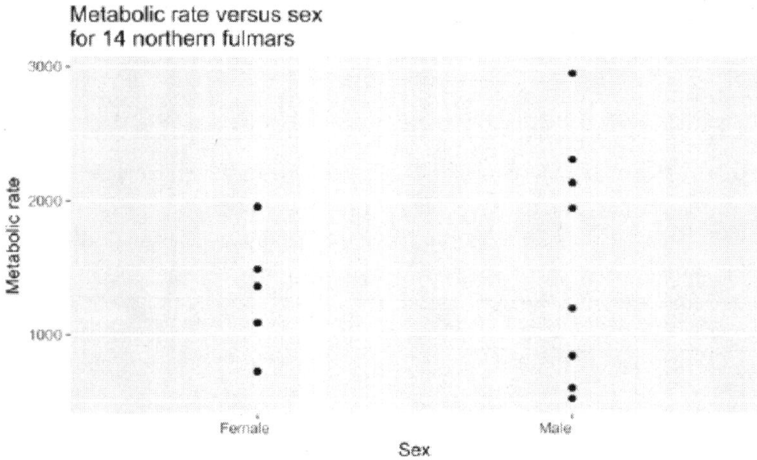

The graph shows the metabolic rate for males and females. By visual inspection, it appears that the variability of the metabolic rate is greater for males than for females.

$$s = \sqrt{\frac{1}{N-1}\sum_{i=1}^{N}(x_i - \overline{x})^2},$$

The sample standard deviation of the metabolic rate for the female fulmars is calculated as follows. The formula for the sample standard deviation is

$$\{x_1, x_2, \ldots, x_N\}$$

where $\overline{x}$ are the observed values of the sample items,

Sum of squares calculation for female fulmars					
Animal	**Sex**	**Metabolic rate**	**Mean**	**Difference from mean**	**Squared difference from mean**
1	Female	727.7	1285.5	-557.8	311140.84
2	Female	1086.5	1285.5	-199.0	39601.00
3	Female	1091.0	1285.5	-194.5	37830.25
4	Female	1361.3	1285.5	75.8	5745.64
5	Female	1490.5	1285.5	205.0	42025.00
6	Female	1956.1	1285.5	670.6	449704.36
Mean of metabolic rates			1285.5	*Sum of squared differences*	886047.09

is the mean value of these observations, and N is the number of observations in the sample. In the sample standard deviation formula, for this example, the numerator is the sum of the squared deviation of each individual animal's metabolic rate from the mean metabolic rate. The table below shows the calculation of this sum of squared deviations for the female fulmars. For females, the sum of squared deviations is 886047.09, as shown in the table.

$$s = \sqrt{\frac{\sum_{i=1}^{N}(x_i - \overline{x})^2}{N-1}} = \sqrt{\frac{886047.09}{5}} = 420.96.$$

The denominator in the sample standard deviation formula is N – 1, where N is the number of animals. In this example, there are N = 6 females, so the denominator is 6 – 1 = 5. The sample standard deviation for the female fulmars is therefore

$$2, 4, 4, 4, 5, 5, 7, 9.$$

For the male fulmars, a similar calculation gives a sample standard deviation of 894.37, approximately twice as large as the standard deviation for the females. The graph shows the metabolic rate data, the means (red dots), and the standard deviations (red lines) for females and males.

Population standard deviation of grades of eight students. Suppose that the entire population of interest was eight students in a particular class. For a finite set of numbers, the population standard deviation is found by taking the square root of the average of the squared deviations of the values subtracted from their average value. The marks of a class of eight students (that is, a statistical population) are the following eight values:

$$\mu = \frac{2+4+4+4+5+5+7+9}{8} = 5.$$

These eight data points have the mean (average) of 5:

$$\begin{array}{ll} (2-5)^2 = (-3)^2 = 9 & (5-5)^2 = 0^2 = 0 \\ (4-5)^2 = (-1)^2 = 1 & (5-5)^2 = 0^2 = 0 \\ (4-5)^2 = (-1)^2 = 1 & (7-5)^2 = 2^2 = 4 \\ (4-5)^2 = (-1)^2 = 1 & (9-5)^2 = 4^2 = 16. \end{array}$$

First, calculate the deviations of each data point from the mean, and square the result of each:

$$\sigma^2 = \frac{9+1+1+1+0+0+4+16}{8} = 4.$$

The variance is the mean of these values:

$$\sigma = \sqrt{4} = 2.$$

and the population standard deviation is equal to the square root of the variance:

$$\mathrm{E}[X] = \mu.$$

This formula is valid only if the eight values with which we began form the complete population. If the values instead were a random sample drawn from some large parent population (for example, they were 8 marks randomly and independently chosen from a class of 2 million), then one often divides by 7 (which is n " 1) instead of 8 (which is n) in the denominator of the last formula. In that case the result of the original formula would be called the sample standard deviation. Dividing by n " 1 rather than by n gives an unbiased estimate of the variance of the larger parent population. This is known as Bessel's correction.

Standard deviation of average height for adult men

If the population of interest is approximately normally distributed, the standard deviation provides information on the proportion of observations above or below certain values. For example, the average height for adult men in the United States is about 70 inches (177.8 cm), with a standard deviation of around 3 inches (7.62 cm). This means that most men (about 68%, assuming a normal distribution) have a height within 3 inches (7.62 cm) of the mean (67–73 inches (170.18–185.42 cm)) – one standard deviation – and almost all men (about 95%) have a height within 6 inches (15.24 cm) of the mean (64–76 inches (162.56–193.04 cm)) – two standard deviations. If the standard deviation were zero, then all men would be exactly 70 inches (177.8 cm) tall. If the standard deviation were 20 inches (50.8 cm), then men would have much more variable heights, with a typical range of about 50–90 inches (127–228.6 cm). Three standard deviations account for 99.7% of the sample population being studied, assuming the distribution is normal (bell-shaped). (See the 68-95-99.7 rule, or the empirical rule, for more information.)

Deviation of population values

Let Xbe a random variable with mean value ì:

$$\sigma = \sqrt{E[(X-\mu)^2]} = \sqrt{E[X^2] + E[-2\mu X] + E[\mu^2]} = \sqrt{E[X^2] - 2\mu\, E[X] + \mu^2}$$
$$= \sqrt{E[X^2] - 2\mu^2 + \mu^2} = \sqrt{E[X^2] - \mu^2} = \sqrt{E[X^2] - (E[X])^2}$$

Here the operator E denotes the average or expected value of X. Then the standard deviation of X is the quantity

$$\sigma = \sqrt{\frac{1}{N}\left[(x_1-\mu)^2 + (x_2-\mu)^2 + \cdots + (x_N-\mu)^2\right]}, \text{ where } \mu = \frac{1}{N}(x_1 + \cdots + x_N),$$

(derived using the properties of expected value).

In other words, the standard deviation ó (sigma) is the square root of the variance of X; i.e., it is the square root of the average value of (X " ì)2. The standard deviation of a (univariate) probability distribution is the same as that of a random variable having that distribution. Not all random variables have a standard deviation, since these expected values need not exist. For example, the standard deviation of a random variable that follows a Cauchy distribution is undefined because its expected value ì is undefined.

Discrete random variable

In the case where X takes random values from a finite data set x1, x2, ...,xN, with each value having the same probability, the standard deviation is

$$\sigma = \sqrt{\frac{1}{N}\sum_{i=1}^{N}(x_i - \mu)^2}, \text{ where } \mu = \frac{1}{N}\sum_{i=1}^{N} x_i.$$

or, using summation notation,

$$\sigma = \sqrt{\sum_{i=1}^{N} p_i (x_i - \mu)^2}, \text{ where } \mu = \sum_{i=1}^{N} p_i x_i.$$

If, instead of having equal probabilities, the values have different probabilities, let x1 have probability p1, x2 have probability p2, ...,xN have probability pN. In this case, the standard deviation will be

$$\sigma = \sqrt{\int_{\mathbf{X}} (x - \mu)^2 \, p(x) \mathrm{d}x}, \text{ where } \mu = \int_{\mathbf{X}} x \, p(x) \mathrm{d}x,$$

Continuous random variable

The standard deviation of a continuous real-valued random variableX with probability density functionp(x) is

$$\sqrt{(e^{\sigma^2} - 1)e^{2\mu + \sigma^2}}.$$

and where the integrals are definite integrals taken for x ranging over the set of possible values of the random variable X.

In the case of a parametric family of distributions, the standard deviation can be expressed in terms of the parameters. For example, in the case of the log-normal distribution with parameters ì and ó2, the standard deviation is

$$M = (\overline{x}, \overline{x}, \overline{x})$$

Interpretation and application

A large standard deviation indicates that the data points can spread far from the mean and a small standard deviation indicates that they are clustered closely around the mean. For example, each of the three populations {0, 0, 14, 14}, {0, 6, 8, 14} and {6, 6, 8, 8} has a mean of 7. Their standard deviations are 7, 5, and 1, respectively. The third population has a much smaller standard deviation than the other two because its values are all close to 7. It will have the same units as the data points themselves. If, for instance, the data set {0, 6, 8, 14} represents the ages of a population of four siblings in years, the standard deviation is 5 years.

As another example, the population {1000, 1006, 1008, 1014} may represent the distances traveled by four athletes, measured in meters. It has a mean of 1007 meters, and a standard deviation of 5 meters. Standard deviation may serve as a measure of uncertainty. In physical science, for example, the reported standard deviation of a group of repeated measurements gives the precision of those measurements. When deciding whether measurements agree with a theoretical prediction, the standard deviation of those measurements is of crucial importance: if the mean of the measurements is too far away from the prediction (with the distance measured in standard deviations), then the theory being tested probably needs to be revised. This makes sense since they fall outside the range of values that could reasonably be expected to occur, if the prediction were correct and the standard deviation appropriately quantified. See prediction interval. While the standard deviation does measure how far typical values tend to be from the mean, other measures are available. An example is the mean absolute deviation, which might be considered a more direct measure of average distance, compared to the root mean square distance inherent in the standard deviation.

Application examples

The practical value of understanding the standard deviation of a set of values is in appreciating how much variation there is from the average (mean).

Experiment, industrial and hypothesis testing

Standard deviation is often used to compare real-world data against a model to test the model. For example, in industrial applications the weight of products coming off a production line may need to comply with a legally required value. By weighing some fraction of the products an average weight can be found, which will always be slightly different to the long-term average. By using standard deviations, a minimum and maximum value can be calculated that the averaged weight will be within some very high percentage of the time (99.9% or more). If it falls outside the range then the production process may need to be corrected. Statistical tests such as these are particularly important when the testing is relatively expensive. For example, if the product needs to be opened and drained and weighed, or if the product was otherwise used up by the test.

In experimental science, a theoretical model of reality is used. Particle physics conventionally uses a standard of "5 sigma" for the declaration of a discovery. A five-sigma level translates to one chance in 3.5 million that a random fluctuation would yield the result. This level of certainty was required in order to assert that a particle consistent with the Higgs boson had been discovered in two independent experiments at CERN,] and this was also the significance level leading to the declaration of the first detection of gravitational waves.

Weather

As a simple example, consider the average daily maximum temperatures for two cities, one inland and one on the coast. It is helpful to understand that the range of daily maximum temperatures for cities near the coast is smaller than for cities inland. Thus, while these two cities may each have the same average maximum temperature, the standard deviation of the daily maximum temperature for the coastal city will be less than that of the inland city as, on any particular day, the actual maximum temperature is more likely to be farther from the average maximum temperature for the inland city than for the coastal one.

Finance

In finance, standard deviation is often used as a measure of the risk associated with price-fluctuations of a given asset (stocks, bonds, property, etc.), or the risk of a portfolio of assets (actively managed mutual funds, index mutual funds, or ETFs). Risk is an important factor in determining how to efficiently manage a portfolio of investments because it determines the variation in returns on the asset and/or portfolio and gives investors a mathematical basis for investment decisions (known as mean-variance optimization). The fundamental concept of risk is that as it increases, the expected return on an investment should increase as well, an increase known as the risk premium. In other words, investors should expect a higher return on an investment when that investment carries a higher level of risk or uncertainty. When evaluating investments, investors should estimate both the expected return and the uncertainty of future returns. Standard deviation provides a quantified estimate of the uncertainty of future returns.

For example, assume an investor had to choose between two stocks. Stock A over the past 20 years had an average return of 10 percent, with a standard deviation of 20 percentage points (pp) and Stock B, over the same period, had average returns of 12 percent but a higher standard deviation of 30 pp. On the basis of risk and return, an investor may decide that Stock A is the safer choice, because Stock B's additional two percentage points of return is not worth the additional 10 pp standard deviation (greater risk or uncertainty of the expected return). Stock B is likely to fall short of the initial investment (but also to exceed the initial investment) more often than Stock A under the same circumstances, and is estimated to return only two percent more on average. In this example, Stock A is expected to earn about 10 percent, plus or minus 20 pp (a range of 30 percent to "10 percent), about two-thirds of the future year returns. When considering more extreme possible returns or outcomes in future, an investor should expect results of as much as 10 percent plus or minus 60 pp, or a range from 70 percent to "50 percent, which includes outcomes for three standard deviations from the average return (about 99.7 percent of probable returns).

Calculating the average (or arithmetic mean) of the return of a security over a given period will generate the expected return of the asset. For each period, subtracting the expected return from the actual return results in the difference from the mean. Squaring the difference in each period and taking the average gives the overall variance of the return of the asset. The larger the variance, the greater risk the security carries. Finding the square root of this variance will give the standard deviation of the investment tool in question.

Population standard deviation is used to set the width of Bollinger Bands, a widely adopted technical analysis tool. For example, the upper Bollinger Band is given as x + nóx. The most commonly used value for n is 2; there is about a five percent chance of going outside, assuming a normal distribution of returns. Financial time series are known to be non-stationary series, whereas the statistical calculations above, such as standard deviation, apply only to stationary series. To apply the above statistical tools to non-stationary series, the series first must be transformed to a stationary series, enabling use of statistical tools that now have a valid basis from which to work.

Geometric interpretation

To gain some geometric insights and clarification, we will start with a population of three values, x1, x2, x3. This defines a point P = (x1, x2, x3) in R3. Consider the line L = {(r, r, r) :r"R}. This is the "main diagonal" going through the origin. If our three given values were all equal, then the standard deviation would be zero and P would lie on L. So it is not unreasonable to assume that the standard deviation is related to the distance of P to L. That is indeed the case. To move orthogonally from L to the point P, one begins at the point:

$$\sigma(r) = \sqrt{\frac{1}{N-1}\sum_{i=1}^{N}(x_i - r)^2}.$$

whose coordinates are the mean of the values we started out with.

Relationship between standard deviation and mean

The mean and the standard deviation of a set of data are descriptive statistics usually reported together. In a certain sense, the standard deviation is a "natural" measure of statistical dispersion if the center of the data is measured about the mean. This is because the standard deviation from the mean is smaller than from any other point. The precise statement is the following: suppose x1, ...,xn are real numbers and define the function:

$$r = \overline{x}.$$

Using calculus or by completing the square, it is possible to show that ó(r) has a unique minimum at the mean:

$$\sigma_{\text{mean}} = \frac{1}{\sqrt{N}}\sigma$$

Variability can also be measured by the coefficient of variation, which is the ratio of the standard deviation to the mean. It is a dimensionless number. Standard deviation of the mean Often, we want some information about the precision of the mean we obtained. We can obtain this by determining the standard deviation of the sampled mean. Assuming statistical independence of the values in the sample, the standard deviation of the mean is related to the standard deviation of the distribution by:

$$\operatorname{var}(X) \equiv \sigma_X^2$$
$$\operatorname{var}(X_1 + X_2) \equiv \operatorname{var}(X_1) + \operatorname{var}(X_2)$$

where N is the number of observations in the sample used to estimate the mean. This can easily be proven with (see basic properties of the variance):

$$\operatorname{var}(cX_1) \equiv c^2 \operatorname{var}(X_1)$$

(Statistical Independence is assumed.)

$$\operatorname{var}(\text{mean}) = \operatorname{var}\left(\frac{1}{N}\sum_{i=1}^{N} X_i\right) = \frac{1}{N^2}\operatorname{var}\left(\sum_{i=1}^{N} X_i\right) =$$

$$\frac{1}{N^2}\sum_{i=1}^{N}\operatorname{var}(X_i) = \frac{N}{N^2}\operatorname{var}(X) = \frac{1}{N}\operatorname{var}(X).$$

hence

$$\sigma_{\text{mean}} = \frac{\sigma}{\sqrt{N}}.$$

Resulting in:

$$s_j = \sum_{k=1}^{N} x_k^j.$$

It should be emphasized that in order to estimate the standard deviation of the mean ómeanit is necessary to know the standard deviation of the entire population óbeforehand. However, in most applications this parameter is unknown. For example, if a series of 10 measurements of a previously unknown quantity is performed in a laboratory, it is possible to calculate the resulting sample mean and sample standard deviation, but it is impossible to calculate the standard deviation of the mean.

Rapid calculation methods

The following two formulas can represent a running (repeatedly updated) standard deviation. A set of two power sums s1 and s2 are computed over a set of N values of x, denoted as x1, ...,xN:

$$\sigma = \frac{\sqrt{Ns_2 - s_1^2}}{N}$$

Given the results of these running summations, the values N, s1, s2 can be used at any time to compute the current value of the running standard deviation:

$$s = \sqrt{\frac{Ns_2 - s_1^2}{N(N-1)}}.$$

Where N, as mentioned above, is the size of the set of values (or can also be regarded as s0).

Similarly for sample standard deviation,

$$A_0 = 0$$

In a computer implementation, as the three sj sums become large, we need to consider round-off error, arithmetic overflow, and arithmetic underflow. The method below calculates the running sums method with reduced rounding errors. This is a "one pass" algorithm for calculating variance of n samples without the need to store prior data during the calculation. Applying this method to a time series will result in successive values of standard deviation corresponding to n data points as n grows larger with each new sample, rather than a constant-width sliding window calculation.

For k = 1, ...,n:

$$A_k = A_{k-1} + \frac{x_k - A_{k-1}}{k}$$

$$Q_0 = 0$$

$$Q_k = Q_{k-1} + \frac{k-1}{k}(x_k - A_{k-1})^2 = Q_{k-1} + (x_k - A_{k-1})(x_k - A_k)$$

where A is the mean value.

$$s_n^2 = \frac{Q_n}{n-1}$$

Note: Q1 = 0 since k " 1 = 0 or x1 = A1

Sample variance:

$$\sigma_n^2 = \frac{Q_n}{n}$$

Population variance:

$$s_j = \sum_{k=1}^{N} w_k x_k^j .$$

Weighted calculation When the values xi are weighted with unequal weights wi, the power sums s0, s1, s2 are each computed as:

$$W_0 = 0$$

$$W_k = W_{k-1} + w_k$$

And the standard deviation equations remain unchanged. Note that s0 is now the sum of the weights and not the number of samples N. The incremental method with reduced rounding errors can also be applied, with some additional complexity. A running sum of weights must be computed for each k from 1 to n:

$$A_0 = 0$$

$$A_k = A_{k-1} + \frac{w_k}{W_k}(x_k - A_{k-1})$$

$$Q_0 = 0$$

$$Q_k = Q_{k-1} + \frac{w_k W_{k-1}}{W_k}(x_k - A_{k-1})^2 = Q_{k-1} + w_k(x_k - A_{k-1})(x_k - A_k)$$

and places where 1/n is used above must be replaced by wi/Wn:

$$\sigma_n^2 = \frac{Q_n}{W_n}$$

In the final division,

$$s_n^2 = \frac{Q_n}{W_n - 1},$$

and

$$s_n^2 = \frac{n'}{n'-1}\sigma_n^2,$$

or

$$r = \frac{1}{Ns^2} \sum_{n=1}^{N} (x_{n,1} - \bar{x})(x_{n,2} - \bar{x}),$$

wheren is the total number of elements, and n' is the number of elements with non-zero weights. The above formulas become equal to the simpler formulas given above if weights are taken as equal to one.

Intraclass correlation

Intraclass correlation (ICC) is a descriptive statistic that can be used when quantitative measurements are made on units that are organized into groups; it describes how strongly units in the same group resemble each other.

Rank Correlation

Rank correlation is a measure of the relationship between the rankings of two variables or two rankings of the same variable:

- Spearman's rank correlation coefficient is a measure of how well the relationship between two variables can be described by a monotonic function.
- The Kendall tau rank correlation coefficient is a measure of the portion of ranks that match between two data sets.
- Goodman and Kruskal's gamma is a measure of the strength of association of the cross tabulated data when both variables are measured at the ordinal level.

In statistics, the intraclass correlation, or the intraclass correlation coefficient (ICC), is a descriptive statistic that can be used when quantitative measurements are made on units that are organized into groups. It describes how strongly units in the same group resemble each other. While it is viewed as a type of correlation, unlike most other correlation measures it operates on data structured as groups, rather than data structured as paired observations. The intraclass correlation is commonly used to quantify the degree to which individuals with a fixed degree of relatedness (e.g. full siblings) resemble each other in terms of a quantitative trait (see heritability). Another prominent application is the assessment of consistency or reproducibility of quantitative measurements made by different observers measuring the same quantity. Early ICC definition: unbiased but complex formula The earliest work on intraclass correlations focused on the case of paired measurements, and the first intraclass correlation (ICC) statistics to be proposed were modifications of the interclass correlation (Pearson correlation).

Consider a data set consisting of N paired data values (xn,1, xn,2), for n = 1, ..., N. The intraclass correlation r originally proposed by Ronald Fisher is

$$\bar{x} = \frac{1}{2N} \sum_{n=1}^{N} (x_{n,1} + x_{n,2}),$$

where

$$s^2 = \frac{1}{2N} \left\{ \sum_{n=1}^{N} (x_{n,1} - \bar{x})^2 + \sum_{n=1}^{N} (x_{n,2} - \bar{x})^2 \right\}.$$

$$r = \frac{1}{3Ns^2}\sum_{n=1}^{N}\left\{(x_{n,1}-\bar{x})(x_{n,2}-\bar{x})+(x_{n,1}-\bar{x})(x_{n,3}-\bar{x})+(x_{n,2}-\bar{x})(x_{n,3}-\bar{x})\right\}$$

Later versions of this statistic used the degrees of freedom 2N d1 in the denominator for calculating s2 and N d1 in the denominator for calculating r, so that s2 becomes unbiased, and r becomes unbiased if s is known. The key difference between this ICC and the interclass (Pearson) correlation is that the data are pooled to estimate the mean and variance.

The reason for this is that in the setting where an intraclass correlation is desired, the pairs are considered to be unordered. For example, if we are studying the resemblance of twins, there is usually no meaningful way to order the values for the two individuals within a twin pair. Like the interclass correlation, the intraclass correlation for paired data will be confined to the interval ["1, +1]. The intraclass correlation is also defined for data sets with groups having more than 2 values. For groups consisting of three values, it is defined as

$$\bar{x} = \frac{1}{3N}\sum_{n=1}^{N}(x_{n,1}+x_{n,2}+x_{n,3}),$$

where

$$s^2 = \frac{1}{3N}\left\{\sum_{n=1}^{N}(x_{n,1}-\bar{x})^2+\sum_{n=1}^{N}(x_{n,2}-\bar{x})^2+\sum_{n=1}^{N}(x_{n,3}-\bar{x})^2\right\}.$$

$$r - \frac{K}{K-1}\cdot\frac{N^{-1}\sum_{n=1}^{N}(\bar{x}_n-\bar{x})^2}{s^2} - \frac{1}{K-1},$$

As the number of values per group grows, the number of cross-product terms in this expression grows rapidly. The equivalent form

$$\bar{x}_n$$

$$r \geq \frac{-1}{K-1}.$$

whereK is the number of data values per group, and is the sample mean of the nth group, is simpler to calculate. This form is usually attributed to Harris. The left term is non-negative; consequently the intraclass correlation must satisfy

$$\frac{N^{-1}\sum_{n=1}^{N}(\bar{x}_n-\bar{x})^2}{s^2},$$

For Large K, this ICC is nearly equal to

$$Y_{ij} = \mu + \alpha_j + \varepsilon_{ij},$$

which can be interpreted as the fraction of the total variance that is due to variation between groups. Ronald Fisher devotes an entire chapter to intraclass correlation in his classic book Statistical Methods for Research Workers. For data from a population that is completely noise, Fisher's formula produces ICC values that are distributed about 0, i.e. sometimes being negative. This is because Fisher designed the formula to be unbiased, and therefore its estimates are sometimes overestimates and sometimes underestimates. For small or 0 underlying values in the population, the ICC calculated from a sample may be negative.

Modern ICC definitions: simpler formula but positive bias Beginning with Ronald Fisher, the intraclass correlation has been regarded within the framework of analysis of variance (ANOVA), and more recently in the framework of random effects models. A number of ICC estimators have been proposed. Most of the estimators can be defined in terms of the random effects model

$$\frac{\sigma_\alpha^2}{\sigma_\alpha^2+\sigma_\varepsilon^2}.$$

whereYij is the ith observation in the jth group, ì is an unobserved overall mean, áj is an unobserved random effect shared by all values in group j, and åij is an unobserved noise term. For the model to be identified, the áj and åij are assumed to have expected value zero and to be uncorrelated with each other. Also, the áj are assumed to be identically distributed, and the åij are assumed to be identically distributed. The variance of áj is denoted ó2á and the variance of åij is denoted ó2å.

The population ICC in this framework is

Rank	Degree of agreement	Number
1	Strongly agree	20
2	Agree somewhat	30
3	Not sure	20
4	Disagree somewhat	15
5	Strongly disagree	15

An advantage of this ANOVA framework is that different groups can have different numbers of data values, which is difficult to handle using the earlier ICC statistics. Note also that this ICC is always non-negative, allowing it to be interpreted as the proportion of total variance that is "between groups." This ICC can be generalized to allow for covariate effects, in which case the ICC is interpreted as capturing the within-class similarity of the covariate-adjusted data values. This expression can never be negative (unlike Fisher's original formula) and therefore, in samples from a population which has an ICC of 0, the ICCs in the samples will be higher than the ICC of the population. A number of different ICC statistics have been proposed, not all of which estimate the same population parameter. There has been considerable debate about which ICC statistics are appropriate for a given use, since they may produce markedly different results for the same data.

Relationship to Pearson's correlation coefficient

In terms of its algebraic form, Fisher's original ICC is the ICC that most resembles the Pearson correlation coefficient. One key difference between the two statistics is that in the ICC, the data are centered and scaled using a pooled mean and standard deviation, whereas in the Pearson correlation, each variable is centered and scaled by its own mean and standard deviation. This pooled scaling for the ICC makes sense because all measurements are of the same quantity (albeit on units in different groups). For example, in a paired data set where each "pair" is a single measurement made for each of two units (e.g., weighing each twin in a pair of identical twins) rather than two different measurements for a single unit (e.g., measuring height and weight for each individual), the ICC is a more natural measure of association than Pearson's correlation.

An important property of the Pearson correlation is that it is invariant to application of separate linear transformations to the two variables being compared. Thus, if we are correlating X and Y, where, say, Y = 2X + 1, the Pearson correlation between X and Y is 1 — a perfect correlation. This property does not make sense for the ICC, since there is no basis for deciding which transformation is applied to each value in a group. However, if all the data in all groups are subjected to the same linear transformation, the ICC does not change.

Use in assessing conformity among observers

The ICC is used to assess the consistency, or conformity, of measurements made by multiple observers measuring the same quantity. For example, if several physicians are asked to score the results of a CT scan for signs of cancer progression, we can ask how consistent the scores are to each other. If the truth is known (for example, if the CT scans were on patients who subsequently underwent exploratory surgery), then the focus would generally be on how well the physicians' scores matched the truth. If the truth is not known, we can only consider the similarity among the scores. An important aspect of this problem is that there is both inter-observer and intra-observer variability. Inter-observer variability refers to systematic differences among the observers — for example, one physician may consistently score patients at a higher risk level than other physicians. Intra-observer variability refers to deviations of a particular observer's score on a particular patient that are not part of a systematic difference. The ICC is constructed to be applied to exchangeable measurements — that is, grouped data in which there is no meaningful way to order the measurements within a group. In assessing conformity among observers, if the same observers rate each element being studied, then systematic differences among observers are likely to exist, which conflicts with the notion of exchangeability. If the ICC is used in a situation where systematic differences exist, the result is a composite measure of intra-observer and inter-observer variability. One situation where exchangeability might reasonably be presumed to hold would be where a specimen to be scored, say a blood specimen, is divided into multiple aliquots, and the aliquots are measured separately on the same instrument. In this case, exchangeability would hold as long as no effect due to the sequence of running the samples was present.

Since the intraclass correlation coefficient gives a composite of intra-observer and inter-observer variability, its results are sometimes considered difficult to interpret when the observers are not exchangeable. Alternative measures such as Cohen's kappa statistic, the Fleiss kappa, and the concordance correlation coefficient have been proposed as more suitable measures of agreement among non-exchangeable observers.

Karl pearson's coefficient of correlation in bivariate frequency table

In statistics, the Pearson correlation coefficient (PCC), also referred to as Pearson's r, the Pearson product-moment correlation coefficient (PPMCC) or the bivariate correlation, is a measure of the linear correlation between two variables X and Y. According to the Cauchy–Schwarz inequality it has a value between +1 and "1, where 1 is total positive linear correlation, 0 is no linear correlation, and "1 is total negative linear correlation. It is widely used in the sciences. It was developed by Karl Pearson from a related idea introduced by Francis Galton in the 1880s and for which the mathematical formula was derived and published by Auguste Bravais in 1844. The naming of the coefficient is thus an example of Stigler's Law.

Pearson's correlation coefficient is the covariance of the two variables divided by the product of their standard deviations. The form of the definition involves a "product moment", that is, the mean (the first moment about the origin) of the product of the mean-adjusted random variables; hence the modifier product-moment in the name. Frequency distribution In statistics, a frequency distribution is a list, table or graph that displays the frequency of various outcomes in a sample. Each entry in the table contains the frequency or count of the occurrences of values within a particular group or interval, and in this way, the table summarizes the distribution of values in the sample.

Example

Here is an example of a univariate (single variable) frequency table. The frequency of each response to a survey question is depicted.

Height range	Number of students	Cumulative number
less than 5.0 feet	25	25
5.0–5.5 feet	35	60
5.5–6.0 feet	20	80
6.0–6.5 feet	20	100

A different tabulation scheme aggregates values into bins such that each bin encompasses a range of values. For example, the heights of the students in a class could be organized into the following frequency table.

$$\text{number of classes} = C = 1 + 3.3 \log n$$

A frequency distribution shows us a summarized grouping of data divided into mutually exclusive classes and the number of occurrences in a class. It is a way of showing unorganized data notably to show results of an election, income of people for a certain region, sales of a product within a certain period, student loan amounts of graduates, etc. Some of the graphs that can be used with frequency distributions are histograms, line charts, bar charts and pie charts. Frequency distributions are used for both qualitative and quantitative data.

Construction

1. Decide about the number of classes. Too many classes or too few classes might not reveal the basic shape of the data set, also it will be difficult to interpret such frequency distribution. The maximum number of classes may be determined by Formula: $C = \sqrt{n}$ (approximately) or $h = \dfrac{\text{rangc}}{\text{number of classes}}$ where n is the total number of observations in the data.
2. Calculate the range of the data (Range = Max – Min) by finding minimum and maximum data value. Range will be used to determine the class interval or class width.
3. Decide about width of the class denote by h and obtained

Two-way contingency table with marginal frequencies				
	Dance	Sports	TV	Total
Men	2	10	8	20
Women	16	6	8	30
Total	18	16	16	50

by .

Generally the class interval or class width is the same for all classes. The classes all taken together must cover at least the distance from the lowest value (minimum) in the data set up to the highest (maximum) value. Also note that equal class intervals are preferred in frequency distribution, while unequal class interval may be necessary in certain situations to avoid a large number of empty, or almost empty classes.

1. Decide the individual class limits and select a suitable starting point of the first class which is arbitrary, it may be less than or equal to the minimum value. Usually it is started before the minimum value in such a way that the midpoint (the average of lower and upper class limits of the first class) is properly placed.
2. Take an observation and mark a vertical bar (|) for a class it belongs. A running tally is kept till the last observation.
3. Find the frequencies, relative frequency, cumulative frequency etc. as required.

Joint frequency distributions

Bivariate joint frequency distributions are often presented as (two-way) contingency tables:

$$\phi(x) = ce^{-h^2x^2},$$

The total row and total column report the marginal frequencies or marginal distribution, while the body of the table reports the joint frequencies.

Applications

Managing and Operating on frequency tabulated data is much simpler than operation on raw data. There are simple algorithms to calculate median, mean, standard deviation etc. from these tables. Statistical hypothesis testing is founded on the assessment of differences and similarities between frequency distributions. This assessment involves measures of central tendency or averages, such as the mean and median, and measures of variability or statistical dispersion, such as the standard deviation or variance. A frequency distribution is said to be skewed when its mean and median are different, or more generally when it is asymmetric, depending on the textbook. The kurtosis of a frequency distribution measures the rare, extreme values, which appear as outliers in a histogram. If the distribution is more outlier-prone than the normal distribution it is said to be leptokurtic; if less outlier-prone it is said to be platykurtic. Letter frequency distributions are also used in frequency analysis to crack ciphers, and are used to compare the relative frequency of letters in different languages.

Bivariate analysis

Bivariate analysis is one of the simplest forms of quantitative (statistical) analysis. It involves the analysis of two variables (often denoted as X, Y), for the purpose of determining the empirical relationship between them. Bivariate analysis can be helpful in testing simple hypotheses of association. Bivariate analysis can help determine to what extent it becomes easier to know and predict a value for one variable (possibly a dependent variable) if we know the value of the other variable (possibly the independent variable). Bivariate analysis can be contrasted with univariate analysis in which only one variable is analysed. Like univariate analysis, bivariate analysis can be descriptive or inferential. It is the analysis of the relationship between the two variables. Bivariate analysis is a simple (two variable) special case of multivariate analysis (where multiple relations between multiple variables are examined simultaneously).

When there is a dependent variable

If the dependent variable—the one whose value is determined to some extent by the other, independent variable— is a categorical variable, such as the preferred brand of cereal, then probit or logit regression (or multinomial probit or multinomial logit) can be used. If both variables are ordinal, meaning they are ranked in a sequence as first, second, etc., then a rank correlation coefficient can be computed. If just the dependent variable is ordinal, ordered probit or ordered logit can be used. If the dependent variable is continuous—either interval level or ratio level, such as a temperature scale or an income scale—then simple regression can be used. If both variables are time series, a particular type of causality known as Granger causality can be tested for, and vector autoregression can be performed to examine the intertemporal linkages between the variables.

When there is not a dependent variable

When neither variable can be regarded as dependent on the other, regression is not appropriate but some form of correlation analysis may be.

Graphical methods

Graphs that are appropriate for bivariate analysis depend on the type of variable. For two continuous variables, a scatterplot is a common graph. When one variable is categorical and the other continuous, a box plot is common and when both are categorical a mosaic plot is common. These graphs are part of descriptive statistics.

Probability

Probability is a measure quantifying the likelihood that events will occur. See glossary of probability and statistics. Probability quantifies as a number between 0 and 1, where, loosely speaking,[note 1] 0 indicates impossibility and 1 indicates certainty. The higher the probability of an event, the more likely it is that the event will occur. A simple example is the tossing of a fair (unbiased) coin. Since the coin is fair, the two outcomes ("heads" and "tails") are both equally probable; the probability of "heads" equals the probability of "tails"; and since no other outcomes are possible, the probability of either "heads" or "tails" is 1/2 (which could also be written as 0.5 or 50%). These concepts have been given an axiomatic mathematical formalization in probability theory, which is used widely in such areas of study as mathematics, statistics, finance, gambling, science(in particular physics), artificial intelligence/machine learning, computer science, game theory, and philosophy to, for example, draw inferences about the expected frequency of events. Probability theory is also used to describe the underlying mechanics and regularities of complex systems.

Interpretations

When dealing with experiments that are random and well-defined in a purely theoretical setting (like tossing a fair coin), probabilities can be numerically described by the number of desired outcomes divided by the total number of all outcomes. For example, tossing a fair coin twice will yield "head-head", "head-tail", "tail-head", and "tail-tail" outcomes. The probability of getting an outcome of "head-head" is 1 out of 4 outcomes, or, in numerical terms, 1/4, 0.25 or 25%. However, when it comes to practical application, there are two major competing categories of probability interpretations, whose adherents possess different views about the fundamental nature of probability:

1. Objectivists assign numbers to describe some objective or physical state of affairs. The most popular version of objective probability is frequentist probability, which claims that the probability of a random event denotes the relative frequency of occurrence of an experiment's outcome, when repeating the experiment. This interpretation considers probability to be the relative frequency "in the long run" of outcomes. A modification of this is propensity probability, which interprets probability as the tendency of some experiment to yield a certain outcome, even if it is performed only once.
2. Subjectivists assign numbers per subjective probability, i.e., as a degree of belief. The degree of belief has been interpreted as, "the price at which you would buy or sell a bet that pays 1 unit of utility if E, 0 if not E." The most popular version of subjective probability is Bayesian probability, which includes expert knowledge as well as experimental data to produce probabilities. The expert knowledge is represented by some (subjective) prior probability distribution. These data are incorporated in a likelihood function. The product of the prior and the likelihood, normalized, results in a posterior probability distribution that incorporates all the information known to date. By Aumann's agreement theorem, Bayesian agents whose prior beliefs are similar will end up with similar posterior beliefs. However, sufficiently different priors can lead to different conclusions regardless of how much information the agents share.

The scientific study of probability is a modern development of mathematics. Gambling shows that there has been an interest in quantifying the ideas of probability for millennia, but exact mathematical descriptions arose much later. There are reasons for the slow development of the mathematics of probability. Whereas games of chance provided the impetus for the mathematical study of probability, fundamental issues[clarification needed] are still obscured by the superstitions of gamblers.

According to Richard Jeffrey, "Before the middle of the seventeenth century, the term 'probable' (Latin probabilis) meant approvable, and was applied in that sense, unequivocally, to opinion and to action. A probable action or opinion was one such as sensible people would undertake or hold, in the circumstances." However, in legal contexts especially, 'probable' could also apply to propositions for which there was good evidence.

The first two laws of error that were proposed both originated with Pierre-Simon Laplace. The first law was published in 1774 and stated that the frequency of an error could be expressed as an exponential function of the numerical magnitude of the error, disregarding sign. The second law of error was proposed in 1778 by Laplace and stated that the frequency of the error is an exponential function of the square of the error. The second law of error is called the normal distribution or the Gauss law. "It is difficult historically to attribute that law to Gauss, who in spite of his well-known precocity had probably not made this discovery before he was two years old." Daniel Bernoulli (1778) introduced the principle of the maximum product of the probabilities of a system of concurrent errors. Adrien-Marie Legendre (1805) developed the method of least squares, and introduced it in his Nouvelles méthodes pour la détermination des orbites des comètes (New Methods for Determining the Orbits of Comets). In ignorance of Legendre's contribution, an Irish-American writer, Robert Adrain, editor of "The Analyst" (1808), first deduced the law of facility of error,

$$P(A)$$

wherehis a constant depending on precision of observation, and cis a scale factor ensuring that the area under the curve equals 1. He gave two proofs, the second being essentially the same as John Herschel's (1850). Gauss gave the first proof that seems to have been known in Europe (the third after Adrain's) in 1809. Further proofs were given by Laplace (1810, 1812), Gauss (1823), James Ivory (1825, 1826), Hagen (1837), Friedrich Bessel (1838), W.F. Donkin (1844, 1856), and Morgan Crofton (1870). Other contributors were Ellis (1844), De Morgan (1864), Glaisher (1872), and Giovanni Schiaparelli (1875). Peters's (1856) formula[clarification needed] for r, the probable error of a single observation, is well known.

In the nineteenth century authors on the general theory included Laplace, Sylvestre Lacroix (1816), Littrow (1833), Adolphe Quetelet (1853), Richard Dedekind (1860), Helmert (1872), Hermann Laurent (1873), Liagre, Didion, and Karl Pearson. Augustus De Morgan and George Boole improved the exposition of the theory. Andrey Markovintroduced the notion of Markov chains (1906), which played an important role in stochastic processes theory and its applications. The modern theory of probability based on the measure theory was developed by Andrey Kolmogorov (1931). On the geometric side (see integral geometry) contributors to The Educational Times were influential (Miller, Crofton, McColl, Wolstenholme, Watson, and Artemas Martin).

Theory of Probability

Like other theories, the theory of probability is a representation of its concepts in formal terms—that is, in terms that can be considered separately from their meaning. These formal terms are manipulated by the rules of mathematics and logic, and any results are interpreted or translated back into the problem domain.

There have been at least two successful attempts to formalize probability, namely the Kolmogorov formulation and the Cox formulation. In Kolmogorov's formulation (see probability space), sets are interpreted as events and probability itself as a measure on a class of sets. In Cox's theorem, probability is taken as a primitive (that is, not further analyzed) and the emphasis is on constructing a consistent assignment of probability values to propositions. In both cases, the laws of probability are the same, except for technical details. There are other methods for quantifying uncertainty, such as the Dempster–Shafer theory or possibility theory, but those are essentially different and not compatible with the laws of probability as usually understood.

Applications

Probability theory is applied in everyday life in risk assessment and modeling. The insurance industry and markets use actuarial science to determine pricing and make trading decisions. Governments apply probabilistic methods in environmental regulation, entitlement analysis (Reliability theory of aging and longevity), and financial regulation. A good example of the use of probability theory in equity trading is the effect of the perceived probability of any widespread Middle East conflict on oil prices, which have ripple effects in the economy as a whole. An assessment by a commodity trader that a war is more likely can send that commodity's prices up or down, and signals other traders of that opinion. Accordingly, the probabilities are neither assessed independently nor necessarily very rationally. The theory of behavioral finance emerged to describe the effect of such groupthink on pricing, on policy, and on peace and conflict.

In addition to financial assessment, probability can be used to analyze trends in biology (e.g. disease spread) as well as ecology (e.g. biological Punnett squares). As with finance, risk assessment can be used as a statistical tool to calculate the likelihood of undesirable events occurring and can assist with implementing protocols to avoid encountering such circumstances. Probability is used to design games of chance so that casinos can make a guaranteed profit, yet provide payouts to players that are frequent enough to encourage continued play. The discovery of rigorous methods to assess and combine probability assessments has changed society.

Another significant application of probability theory in everyday life is reliability. Many consumer products, such as automobiles and consumer electronics, use reliability theory in product design to reduce the probability of failure. Failure probability may influence a manufacturer's decisions on a product's warranty. The cache language model and other statistical language models that are used in natural language processing are also examples of applications of probability theory.

Mathematical treatment

Consider an experiment that can produce a number of results. The collection of all possible results is called the sample space of the experiment. The power set of the sample space is formed by considering all different collections of possible results. For example, rolling a dice can produce six possible results. One collection of possible results gives an odd number on the dice. Thus, the subset $\{1,3,5\}$ is an element of the power set of the sample space of dice rolls. These collections are called "events". In this case, $\{1,3,5\}$ is the event that the dice falls on some odd number. If the results that actually occur fall in a given event, the event is said to have occurred.

A probability is a way of assigning every event a value between zero and one, with the requirement that the event made up of all possible results (in our example, the event $\{1,2,3,4,5,6\}$) is assigned a value of one. To qualify as a probability, the assignment of values must satisfy the requirement that if you look at a collection of mutually exclusive events (events with no common results, e.g., the events $\{1,6\}$, $\{3\}$, and $\{2,4\}$ are all mutually exclusive), the probability that at least one of the events will occur is given by the sum of the probabilities of all the individual events.

$$\text{P.E.} = 0.6745\left[\frac{1-r^2}{\sqrt{n}}\right]$$

The probability of an eventA is written as , p (A), or Pr (A). This mathematical definition of probability can extend to infinite sample spaces, and even uncountable sample spaces, using the concept of a measure. If two events A and B occur on a single performance of an experiment, this is called the intersection or joint probability of A and B, denoted as P (A)" B).

Probable error

In statistics, probable error defines the half-range of an interval about a central point for the distribution, such that half of the values from the distribution will lie within the interval and half outside. Thus for a symmetric distribution it is equivalent to half the interquartile range, or the median absolute deviation. One such use of the term probable error in this sense is as the name for the scale parameter of the Cauchy distribution, which does not have a standard deviation. The probable error can also be expressed as a multiple of the standard deviation ó, , which requires that at least the second statistical moment of the distribution should exist, whereas the other definition does not. For a normal distribution this is ã = 0.6745 × ó. It is used to help in the determination of the Karl Pearson's coefficient of correlation ' r '. Due to this ' r ' is corrected to a great extent but note that ' r ' depends on the random sampling and its conditions. it is given by

$$\tilde{X} = \text{median}(X)$$

i. If the value of r is less than P. E., then there is no evidence of correlation i.e. r is not significant.

ii. If r is more than 6 times the P. E. ' r ' is practically certain .i.e. significant.

iii. By adding or subtracting P. E. to ' r ', we get the upper and Lower limits within which ' r ' of the population can be expected to lie.

Symbolically e = r ± P. E.

P = Correlation (coefficient) of the population.

Median absolute deviation

In statistics, the median absolute deviation (MAD) is a robust measure of the variability of a univariate sample of quantitative data. It can also refer to the populationparameter that is estimated by the MAD calculated from a sample. For a univariate data set X1, X2, ..., Xn, the MAD is defined as the median of the absolute deviations from the data's median $\text{MAD} = \text{median}(|X_i - \tilde{X}|)$.

$$\hat{\sigma} = k \cdot \text{MAD},$$

that is, starting with the residuals (deviations) from the data's median, the MAD is the median of their absolute values.

Example

Consider the data (1, 1, 2, 2, 4, 6, 9). It has a median value of 2. The absolute deviations about 2 are (1, 1, 0, 0, 2, 4, 7) which in turn have a median value of 1 (because the sorted absolute deviations are (0, 0, 1, 1, 2, 4, 7)). So the median absolute deviation for this data is 1.

Uses

The median absolute deviation is a measure of statistical dispersion. Moreover, the MAD is a robust statistic, being more resilient to outliers in a data set than the standard deviation. In the standard deviation, the distances from the mean are squared, so large deviations are weighted more heavily, and thus outliers can heavily influence it. In the MAD, the deviations of a small number of outliers are irrelevant. Because the MAD is a more robust estimator of scale than the sample variance or standard deviation, it works better with distributions without a mean or variance, such as the Cauchy distribution.

Relation to standard deviation

The MAD may be used similarly to how one would use the deviation for the average. In order to use the MAD as a consistent estimator for the estimation of the standard deviationó, one takes

$$k = 1/\left(\Phi^{-1}(3/4)\right) \approx 1.4826$$

wherekis a constant scale factor, which depends on the distribution.

For normally distributed data kis taken to be:

$$\Phi^{-1}$$

i.e., the reciprocal of the quantile function $Z = (X - \mu)/\sigma$ (also known as the inverse of the cumulative distribution function) for the standard normal distribution $\frac{1}{2} = P(|X - \mu| \leq \text{MAD}) = P\left(\left|\frac{X-\mu}{\sigma}\right| \leq \frac{\text{MAD}}{\sigma}\right) = P\left(|Z| \leq \frac{\text{MAD}}{\sigma}\right)$. The argument 3/4 is such that ± MAD covers 50% (between 1/4 and 3/4) of the standard normal cumulative distribution function, i.e.:

$$\Phi(\text{MAD}/\sigma) - \Phi(-\text{MAD}/\sigma) = 1/2$$

Therefore, we must have that:

$$\Phi(-\text{MAD}/\sigma) = 1 - \Phi(\text{MAD}/\sigma)$$

Noticing that:

$$\text{MAD}/\sigma = \Phi^{-1}(3/4) = 0.67449$$

we have that $k = 1/\Phi^{-1}(3/4) = 1.4826$ from which we obtain the scale factor

$$\text{MAD} = \sigma\sqrt{2}\,\text{erf}^{-1}(1/2) \approx 0.67449\sigma$$

Another way of establishing the relationship is noting that MAD equals the half-normal distribution median:

$$(\tilde{X}, \tilde{Y})$$

This form is used in, e.g., the probable error.

The population MAD

The population MAD is defined analogously to the sample MAD, but is based on the complete distribution rather than on a sample. For a symmetric distribution with zero mean, the population MAD is the 75th percentile of the distribution. Unlike the variance, which may be infinite or undefined, the population MAD is always a finite number. For example, the standard Cauchy distribution has undefined variance, but its MAD is 1. The earliest known mention of the concept of the MAD occurred in 1816, in a paper by Carl Friedrich Gauss on the determination of the accuracy of numerical observations.

Geometric median absolute deviation

Similarly to how the median generalizes to the geometric median in multivariate data, a geometric MAD can be constructed that generalizes the MAD. Given a 2 dimensional paired set of data (X1,Y1), (X2,Y2),..., (Xn,Yn) and a suitably calculated geometric median $\mathrm{MAD} = \left(\mathrm{median}(|X_i - \tilde{X}|)^2 + \mathrm{median}(|Y_i - \tilde{Y}|)^2\right)^{1/2}$ the geometric median absolute deviation is given by:

$$f(x_0 - \delta) = f(x_0 + \delta)$$

This gives the identical result as the univariate MAD in 1 dimension and extends easily to higher dimensions. In the case of complex values (X+iY), the relation of MAD to the standard deviation is unchanged for normally distributed data.

Symmetric probability distribution

In statistics, a symmetric probability distribution is a probability distribution—an assignment of probabilities to possible occurrences—which is unchanged when its probability density function or probability mass function is reflected around a vertical line at some value of the random variable represented by the distribution. This vertical line is the line of symmetry of the distribution. Thus the probability of being any given distance on one side of the value about which symmetry occurs is the same as the probability of being the same distance on the other side of that value.

Formal definition

A probability distribution is said to be symmetric if and only if there exists a value x0such that

$\mathcal{F}$ for all real numbers ä,

wheref is the probability density function if the distribution is continuous or the probability mass function if the distribution is discrete. For continuous symmetric spherical,

Mir M. Ali gave the following definition. Let $f(x_1, x_2, \ldots, x_n) = g(x_1^2 + x_1^2 + \ldots + x_n^2)$ denote the class of spherically symmetric distributions of the absolutely continuous type in the n-dimensional Euclidean space having joint density of the form $(x - x_0)^{2k}$ inside a sphere with center at the origin with a prescribed radius which may be finite or infinite and zero elsewhere.

Properties

- The median and the mean (if it exists) of a symmetric distribution both occur at the point x0about which the symmetry occurs.
- If a symmetric distribution is unimodal, the mode coincides with the median and mean.
- All odd central moments of a symmetric distribution equal zero (if they exist), because in the calculation of such moments the negative terms arising from negative deviations from x0exactly balance the positive terms arising from equal positive deviations from x0.
- Every measure of skewness equals zero for a symmetric distribution.

Probability density function

Typically a symmetric continuous distribution's probability density function contains the index value xonly in the context of a term $x = x_0 - \delta$ where kis some positive integer (usually 1). This quadratic or other even-powered term takes on the same value for $x = x_0 + \delta$ as for $|x - x_0|$, giving symmetry about x0. Sometimes the density function contains the term $f(x \mid \mu, \sigma^2) = \frac{1}{\sqrt{2\pi\sigma^2}} e^{-\frac{(x-\mu)^2}{2\sigma^2}}$, which also shows symmetry about x0.

Normal distribution

In probability theory, the normal (or Gaussian or Gauss or Laplace–Gauss) distribution is a very common continuous probability distribution. Normal distributions are important in statistics and are often used in the natural and social sciences to represent real-valued random variables whose distributions are not known. A random variable with a Gaussian distribution is said to be normally distributed and is called a normal deviate. The normal distribution is useful because of the central limit theorem. In its most general form, under some conditions (which include finite variance), it states that averages of samples of observations of random variables independently drawn from independent distributions converge in distribution to the normal, that is, they become normally distributed when the number of observations is sufficiently large. Physical quantities that are expected to be the sum of many independent processes (such as measurement errors) often have distributions that are nearly normal. Moreover, many results and methods (such as propagation of uncertainty and least squares parameter fitting) can be derived analytically in explicit form when the relevant variables are normally distributed.

The normal distribution is sometimes informally called the bell curve. However, many other distributions are bell-shaped (such as the Cauchy, Student's t-, and logistic distributions).

The probability density of the normal distribution is

$$\sigma^2$$

where

- ìis the mean or expectation of the distribution (and also its median and mode),
- óis the standard deviation, and
- $\mu = 0$ is the variance.

Definition

Standard normal distribution The simplest case of a normal distribution is known as the standard normal distribution. This is a special case when $\sigma = 1$ and $\varphi(x) = \frac{1}{\sqrt{2\pi}} e^{-\frac{1}{2}x^2}$, and it is described by this probability density function:

$$1/\sqrt{2\pi}$$

The factor $\varphi(x)$ in this expression ensures that the total area under the curve $1/\sqrt{2\pi}$ is equal to one.[note 1] The factor 1/2 in the exponent ensures that the distribution has unit variance (i.e. the variance is equal to one), and therefore also unit standard deviation. This function is symmetric around x = 0, where it attains its maximum value $x = +1$ and has inflection points at $x = -1$ and $\sigma^2 = 1/2$. Authors may differ also on which normal distribution should be called the "standard" one. Gauss defined the standard normal as having variance $\varphi(x) = \frac{e^{-x^2}}{\sqrt{\pi}}$, that is $\sigma^2 = 1/(2\pi)$

Stigler goes even further, defining the standard normal with variance $\varphi(x) = e^{-\pi x^2}$:

$$f(x \mid \mu, \sigma^2) = \frac{1}{\sigma}\varphi\left(\frac{x-\mu}{\sigma}\right).$$

General normal distribution

Every normal distribution is a version of the standard normal distribution whose domain has been stretched by a factor ó(the standard deviation) and then translated by ì(the mean value):

$$X = \sigma Z + \mu$$

The probability density must be scaled by 1/ó so that the integral is still 1. If Zis a standard normal deviate, then $Z = (X - \mu)/\sigma$ will have a normal distribution with expected value ìand standard deviation ó.Conversely, if Xis a normal deviate with parameters ìand ó2, then $f(x)=e^{ax^2+bx+c}$ will have a standard normal distribution. This variate is called the standardized form of X. Every normal distribution is the exponential of a quadratic function:

$a<0$

where $c=b^2/(4a)+\ln(-a/\pi)/2$ $\mu=-b/(2a)$. In this form, the mean value is $\sigma^2=-1/(2a)$, and the variance is $a=-1/2$. For the standard normal distribution, $b=0$, $c=-\ln(2\pi)/2$, and $\Sigma=\sigma\sqrt{2}$.

Properties

The normal distribution is the only absolutely continuous distribution whose cumulants beyond the first two (i.e., other than the mean and variance) are zero. It is also the continuous distribution with the maximum entropy for a specified mean and variance. Geary has shown, assuming that the mean and variance are finite, that the normal distribution is the only distribution where the mean and variance calculated from a set of independent draws are independent of each other. The normal distribution is a subclass of the elliptical distributions. The normal distribution is symmetric about its mean, and is non-zero over the entire real line. As such it may not be a suitable model for variables that are inherently positive or strongly skewed, such as the weight of a person or the price of a share. Such variables may be better described by other distributions, such as the log-normal distribution or the Pareto distribution.

The value of the normal distribution is practically zero when the value xlies more than a few standard deviations away from the mean (e.g., a spread of three standard deviations covers all but 0.27% of the total distribution). Therefore, it may not be an appropriate model when one expects a significant fraction of outliers—values that lie many standard deviations away from the mean—and least squares and other statistical inference methods that are optimal for normally distributed variables often become highly unreliable when applied to such data. In those cases, a more heavy-tailed distribution should be assumed and the appropriate robust statistical inference methods applied.

The Gaussian distribution belongs to the family of stable distributions which are the attractors of sums of independent, identically distributed distributions whether or not the mean or variance is finite. Except for the Gaussian which is a limiting case, all stable distributions have heavy tails and infinite variance. It is one of the few distributions that are stable and that have probability density functions that can be expressed analytically, the others being the Cauchy distribution and the Lévy distribution.

Circular error probable

In the military science of ballistics, circular error probable (CEP) (also circular error probability or circle of equal probability) is a measure of a weapon system's precision. It is defined as the radius of a circle, centered on the mean, whose boundary is expected to include the landing points of 50% of the rounds; said otherwise, it is the median error radius. That is, if a given bomb design has a CEP of 100 m, when 100 are targeted at the same point, 50 will fall within a 100 m circle around their average impact point. (The distance between the target point and the average impact point is referred to as bias.) There are associated concepts, such as the DRMS (distance root mean square), which is the square root of the average squared distance error, and R95, which is the radius of the circle where 95% of the values would fall in. The concept of CEP also plays a role when measuring the accuracy of a position obtained by a navigation system, such as GPS or older systems such as LORAN and Loran-C.

Concept of circular error probable

The original concept of CEP was based on a circular bivariate normal distribution (CBN) with CEP as a parameter of the CBN just as ì and ó are parameters of the normal distribution. Munitions with this distribution behavior tend to cluster around the mean impact point, with most reasonably close, progressively fewer and fewer further away, and very few at long distance. That is, if CEP is n metres, 50% of rounds land within n metres of the mean impact, 43.7% between n and 2n, and 6.1% between 2n and 3n metres, and the proportion of rounds that land farther than three times the CEP from the mean is only 0.2%.

CEP is not a good measure of accuracy when this distribution behavior is not met. Precision-guided munitions generally have more "close misses" and so are not normally distributed. Munitions may also have larger standard deviation of range errors than the standard deviation of azimuth (deflection) errors, resulting in an elliptical confidence region. Munition samples may not be exactly on target, that is, the mean vector will not be (0,0). This is referred to as bias. To incorporate accuracy into the CEP concept in these conditions, CEP can be defined as the square root of the mean square error (MSE). The MSE will be the sum of the variance of the range error plus the variance of the azimuth error plus the covariance of the range error with the azimuth error plus the square of the bias. Thus the MSE results from pooling all these sources of error, geometrically corresponding to radius of a circle within which 50% of rounds will land.

Several methods have been introduced to estimate CEP from shot data. Included in these methods are the plug-in approach of Blischke and Halpin (1966), the Bayesian approach of Spall and Maryak (1992), and the maximum likelihood approach of Winkler and Bickert (2012). The Spall and Maryak approach applies when the shot data represent a mixture of different projectile characteristics (e.g., shots from multiple munitions types or from multiple locations directed at one target).

Conversion between CEP, DRMS, 2DRMS, and R95

While 50% is a very common definition for CEP, the circle dimension can be defined for percentages. Percentiles can be determined by recognizing that the horizontal position error is defined by a 2D vector which components are two uncorrelated orthogonal Gaussianrandom variables (one for each axis) each having a standard deviation ó. The distance error is the magnitude of that vector; it is a property of 2D Gaussian vectors that the magnitude follows the Rayleigh distribution, with a standard deviation $Q(F,\sigma) = \sigma\sqrt{-2\ln(1-F/100)}$, which by definition is the DRMS (distance root mean square) value. In turn, the properties of the Rayleigh distributionare, that its percentile at level F" [0%, 100%] is given by the following formula:

$$Q(F,\Sigma) = \Sigma\frac{\sqrt{-2\ln(1-F/100)}}{\sqrt{2}}$$

or, expressed in terms of the DRMS:

Measure of Q	*Probability F (%)*
Distance root mean square ("DRMS")	63.213...
Circular error probability ("CEP", "CEP 50")	50
Twice the distance root mean square ("2DRMS")	98.169...
95% radius ("R95")	95

The relation between Qand Fare given by the following table, where the Fvalues for DRMS and 2DRMS are specific to the Rayleigh distribution and are found numerically, while the CEP and R95 values are definitions:

From $X\downarrow$ to $Y\rightarrow$	RMS (σ)	CEP	DRMS (Σ)	R95	2DRMS (2Σ)
RMS (σ)	-	1.1774	1.4142	2.4477	2.8284
CEP	0.8493	–	1.2011	2.0789	2.4022
DRMS (Σ)	0.7071	0.8326	–	1.7308	2
R95	0.4085	0.4810	0.5778	–	1.1555
2DRMS (2Σ)	0.3536	0.4163	0.5	0.8654	–

We can then derive a conversion table to convert values expressed for one percentile level, to another . Said conversion table, giving the coefficients áto convert Xinto Y = á.X,is given by:

$$\sigma_{\bar{x}} = \frac{\sigma}{\sqrt{n}}$$

Example: a GPS receiver having a 1.25 m DRMS error, will have a 1.25 × 1.73 = 2.16 m R95 radius.

Warning: often, sensor datasheets or other publications state "RMS" values which in general, but not always , stand for "DRMS" values. Also, be wary of habits coming from properties of a 1D normal distribution, such as the 68-95-99.7 rule, in essence trying to say that "R95 = 2DRMS". As shown above, these properties simply do not translate to the distance errors. Finally, mind that these values are obtained for a theoretical distribution; while generally being true for real data, these may be affected by other effects, which the model does not represent.

Standard error

The standard error (SE) of a statistic (usually an estimate of a parameter) is the standard deviation of its sampling distribution or an estimate of that standard deviation. If the parameter or the statistic is the mean, it is called the standard error of the mean (SEM). The sampling distribution of a population mean is generated by repeated sampling and recording of the means obtained. This forms a distribution of different means, and this distribution has its own mean and variance. Mathematically, the variance of the sampling distribution obtained is equal to the variance of the population divided by the sample size.

This is because as the sample size increases, sample means cluster more closely around the population mean. Therefore, the relationship between the standard error and the standard deviation is such that, for a given sample size, the standard error equals the standard deviation divided by the square root of the sample size. In other words, the standard error of the mean is a measure of the dispersion of sample means around the population mean. In regression analysis, the term "standard error" refers either to the square root of the reduced chi-squared statistic or the standard error for a particular regression coefficient (as used in, e.g., confidence intervals).

Standard error of the mean

Population

The standard error of the mean (SEM) can be expressed as:

$$\sigma_{\bar{x}} \approx \frac{s}{\sqrt{n}}$$

where

ó is the standard deviation of the population.

n is the size (number of observations) of the sample.

Estimate

Since the population standard deviation is seldom known, the standard error of the mean is usually estimated as the sample standard deviation divided by the square root of the sample size (assuming statistical independence of the values in the sample).

$$\mathrm{s}_{\bar{x}} = \frac{s}{\sqrt{n}}$$

where

s is the sample standard deviation (i.e., the sample-based estimate of the standard deviation of the population), and n is the size (number of observations) of the sample.

Sample

In those contexts where standard error of the mean is defined not as the standard deviation of the sample mean, but as its estimate, this is the estimate typically given as its value. Thus, it is common to see standard deviation of the mean alternatively defined as:

$$x_1, x_2, \ldots, x_n$$

The standard deviation of the sample mean is equivalent to the standard deviation of the error in the sample mean with respect to the true mean, since the sample mean is an unbiased estimator. Therefore, the standard error of the mean can also be understood as the standard deviation of the error in the sample mean with respect to the true mean (or an estimate of that statistic).

Note: the standard error and the standard deviation of small samples tend to systematically underestimate the population standard error and standard deviation: the standard error of the mean is a biased estimator of the population standard error. With n = 2 the underestimate is about 25%, but for n = 6 the underestimate is only 5%. Gurland and Tripathi (1971) provide a correction and equation for this effect. Sokal and Rohlf (1981) give an equation of the correction factor for small samples of n < 20. See unbiased estimation of standard deviation for further discussion. A practical result: Decreasing the uncertainty in a mean value estimate by a factor of two requires acquiring four times as many observations in the sample. Or decreasing the standard error by a factor of ten requires a hundred times as many observations.

Derivations

The formula may be derived from the variance of a sum of independent random variables.

- If $T = (x_1 + x_2 + \cdots + x_n)$ are nindependent observations from a population that has a mean ìand standard deviation ó, then the variance of the total T / n is nó2.

$$n\left(\frac{\sigma^2}{n^2}\right) = \frac{\sigma^2}{n}.$$

The variance of $\overline{x}$ (the mean) must be

$$\operatorname{var}(\frac{T}{n}) = \frac{1}{n^2}\operatorname{var}(T) = \frac{1}{n^2}n\sigma^2 = \frac{\sigma^2}{n}.$$ Alternatively,

T / n

$$\text{FPC} = \sqrt{\frac{N-n}{N-1}}.$$

- And the standard deviation of $\sigma / \sqrt{n}$ must be

Student approximation when ó value is unknown In many practical applications, the true value of ó is unknown. As a result, we need to use a distribution that takes into account that spread of possible ó's. When the true underlying distribution is known to be Gaussian, although with unknown ó, then the resulting estimated distribution follows the Student t-distribution. The standard error is the standard deviation of the Student t-distribution. T-distributions are slightly different from Gaussian, and vary depending on the size of the sample. Small samples are somewhat more likely to underestimate the population standard deviation and have a mean that differs from the true population mean, and the Student t-distribution accounts for the probability of these events with somewhat heavier tails compared to a Gaussian. To estimate the standard error of a Student t-distribution it is sufficient to use the sample standard deviation "s" instead of ó, and we could use this value to calculate confidence intervals.

Correction for finite population

The formula given above for the standard error assumes that the sample size is much smaller than the population size, so that the population can be considered to be effectively infinite in size. This is usually the case even with finite populations, because most of the time, people are primarily interested in managing the processes that created the existing finite population; this is called an analytic study, following W. Edwards Deming. If people are interested in managing an existing finite population that will not change over time, then it is necessary to adjust for the population size; this is called an enumerative study. When the sampling fraction is large (approximately at 5% or more) in an enumerative study, the estimate of the standard error must be corrected by multiplying by a "finite population correction":

$$\text{FPC} \approx \sqrt{1-\frac{n}{N}}$$

which, for large N:

$$f=\sqrt{\frac{1+\rho}{1-\rho}},$$

to account for the added precision gained by sampling close to a larger percentage of the population. The effect of the FPC is that the error becomes zero when the sample size n is equal to the population size N.

Correction for correlation in the sample

If values of the measured quantity A are not statistically independent but have been obtained from known locations in parameter space x, an unbiased estimate of the true standard error of the mean (actually a correction on the standard deviation part) may be obtained by multiplying the calculated standard error of the sample by the factor f:

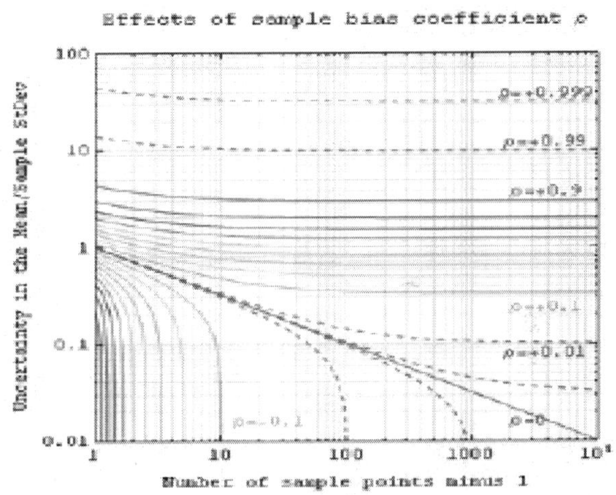

where the sample bias coefficient ñ is the widely used Prais–Winsten estimate of the autocorrelation-coefficient (a quantity between "1 and +1) for all sample point pairs. This approximate formula is for moderate to large sample sizes; the reference gives the exact formulas for any sample size, and can be applied to heavily autocorrelated time series like Wall Street stock quotes. Moreover, this formula works for positive and negative ñ alike. See also unbiased estimation of standard deviation for more discussion.

$$\text{m}\ \{x_i\}_{i\le n}$$

Expected error in the mean of A for a sample of n data points with sample bias coefficient ñ. The unbiased standard error plots as the ñ=0 diagonal line with log-log slope -½.

Relative standard error

The relative standard error of a sample mean is the standard error divided by the mean and expressed as a percentage. It can only be calculated if the mean is a non-zero value.

As an example of the use of the relative standard error, consider two surveys of household income that both result in a sample mean of $50,000. If one survey has a standard error of $10,000 and the other has a standard error of $5,000, then the relative standard errors are 20% and 10% respectively.\

The survey with the lower relative standard error can be said to have a more precise measurement, since it has proportionately less sampling variation around the mean. In fact, data organizations often set reliability standards that their data must reach before publication. For example, the U.S. National Center for Health Statistics typically does not report an estimated mean if its relative standard error exceeds 30%. (NCHS also typically requires at least 30 observations – if not more – for an estimate to be reported.)

Rank correlation

In statistics, a rank correlation is any of several statistics that measure an ordinal association—the relationship between rankings of different ordinal variables or different rankings of the same variable, where a "ranking" is the assignment of the ordering labels "first", "second", "third", etc. to different observations of a particular variable. A rank correlation coefficient measures the degree of similarity between two rankings, and can be used to assess the significance of the relation between them. For example, two common nonparametric methods of significance that use rank correlation are the Mann–Whitney U test and the Wilcoxon signed-rank test.

If, for example, one variable is the identity of a college basketball program and another variable is the identity of a college football program, one could test for a relationship between the poll rankings of the two types of program: do colleges with a higher-ranked basketball program tend to have a higher-ranked football program? A rank correlation coefficient can measure that relationship, and the measure of significance of the rank correlation coefficient can show whether the measured relationship is small enough to likely be a coincidence. If there is only one variable, the identity of a college football program, but it is subject to two different poll rankings (say, one by coaches and one by sportswriters), then the similarity of the two different polls' rankings can be measured with a rank correlation coefficient. As another example, in a contingency table with low income, medium income, and high income in the row variable and educational level—no high school, high school, university—in the column variable), a rank correlation measures the relationship between income and educational level.

Correlation coefficients

Some of the more popular rank correlation statistics include

1. Spearman's ñ
2. Kendall's ô
3. Goodman and Kruskal's ã
4. Somers' D

An increasing rank correlation coefficient implies increasing agreement between rankings. The coefficient is inside the interval ["1, 1] and assumes the value:

- 1 if the agreement between the two rankings is perfect; the two rankings are the same.

- 0 if the rankings are completely independent.
- "1 if the disagreement between the two rankings is perfect; one ranking is the reverse of the other.

Following Diaconis (1988), a ranking can be seen as a permutation of a set of objects. Thus we can look at observed rankings as data obtained when the sample space is (identified with) a symmetric group. We can then introduce a metric, making the symmetric group into a metric space. Different metrics will correspond to different rank correlations.

General correlation coefficient

Kendall showed that his ô(tau) and Spearman's ñ(rho) are particular cases of a general correlation coefficient. Suppose we have a set of nobjects, which are being considered in relation to two properties, represented by xand y, forming the sets of values $\{y_i\}_{i\leq n}$ and $a_{ij} = -a_{ji}$. To any pair of individuals, say the i-th we assign ax-score, denoted by aij, and a y-score, denoted by bij. The only requirement for these functions is that they be anti-symmetric, so $b_{ij} = -b_{ji}$ and $a_{ij} = b_{ij} = 0$. (Note that in particular

$$\Gamma = \frac{\sum_{i,j=1}^{n} a_{ij} b_{ij}}{\sqrt{\sum_{i,j=1}^{n} a_{ij}^2 \sum_{i,j=1}^{n} b_{ij}^2}}$$

if i = j.) Then the generalized correlation coefficient Ã is defined as

$$A = (a_{ij})$$

Equivalently, if all coefficients are collected into matrices $B = (b_{ij})$ and $A^T = -A$, with $B^T = -B$ and $\Gamma = \frac{\langle A, B \rangle_F}{\| A \|_F \| B \|_F}$, then

$$\langle A, B \rangle_F$$

where $\| A \|_F = \sqrt{\langle A, A \rangle_F}$ is the Frobenius inner product and $a_{ij} = r_j - r_i$ the Frobenius norm. In particular, the general correlation coefficient is the cosine of the angle between the matrices Aand B.

Spearman's ñas a particular case

If ri, siare the ranks of the i-member according to the xand the y-quality respectively, we can simply define

$$b_{ij} = s_j - s_i$$

$$\sum a_{ij}^2$$

The sums $\sum b_{ij}^2$ and $\Gamma = \frac{\sum (r_j - r_i)(s_j - s_i)}{\sum (r_j - r_i)^2}$ are equal, since both riand sirange from 1 to n. Then we have:

$$S = \sum_{i=1}^{n} (r_i - s_i)^2 = 2\sum r_i^2 - 2\sum r_i s_i$$

We also have

$$\sum (r_j - r_i)(s_j - s_i) = 2n\sum r_i^2 - \frac{1}{2}n^2(n+1)^2 - nS$$

and hence

$$\sum r_i^2$$

$$\frac{1}{6}n(n+1)(2n+1)$$

being the sum of squares of the first nnaturals equals

$$\sum (r_j - r_i)(s_j - s_i) = \frac{1}{6}n^2(n^2 - 1) - nS$$

. Thus, the last equation reduces to

$$\sum (r_j - r_i)^2 = 2n\sum r_i^2 - 2\sum r_i r_j$$

Further

$$= 2n\sum r_i^2 - 2(\sum r_i)^2 = \frac{1}{6}n^2(n^2 - 1)$$

$$\Gamma_R = 1 - \frac{6\sum d_i^2}{n^3 - n}$$

and thus, substituting into the original formula these results we get

$$d_i = r_i - s_i,$$

where $r = f - u$ is the difference between ranks.

Which is exactly Spearman's rank correlation coefficientñ.

Rank-biserial correlation

Gene Glass noted that the rank-biserial can be derived from Spearman's ñ. "One can derive a coefficient defined on X, the dichotomous variable, and Y, the ranking variable, which estimates Spearman's rho between X and Y in the same way that biserial r estimates Pearson's r between two normal variables" (p. 91). The rank-biserial correlation had been introduced nine years before by Edward Cureton as a measure of rank correlation when the ranks are in two groups.

Kerby simple difference formula

Dave Kerby recommended the rank-biserial as the measure to introduce students to rank correlation, because the general logic can be explained at an introductory level. The rank-biserial is the correlation used with the Mann–Whitney U test, a method commonly covered in introductory college courses on statistics. The data for this test consists of two groups; and for each member of the groups, the outcome is ranked for the study as a whole. Kerby showed that this rank correlation can be expressed in terms of two concepts: the percent of data that support a stated hypothesis, and the percent of data that do not support it. The Kerby simple difference formula states that the rank correlation can be expressed as the difference between the proportion of favorable evidence (f) minus the proportion of unfavorable evidence (u).

$$X_i, Y_i$$

Example and interpretation

To illustrate the computation, suppose a coach trains long-distance runners for one month using two methods. Group A has 5 runners, and Group B has 4 runners. The stated hypothesis is that method A produces faster runners. The race to assess the results finds that the runners from Group A do indeed run faster, with the following ranks: 1, 2, 3, 4, and 6. The slower runners from Group B thus have ranks of 5, 7, 8, and 9.

The analysis is conducted on pairs, defined as a member of one group compared to a member of the other group. For example, the fastest runner in the study is a member of four pairs: (1,5), (1,7), (1,8), and (1,9). All four of these pairs support the hypothesis, because in each pair the runner from Group A is faster than the runner from Group B. There are a total of 20 pairs, and 19 pairs support the hypothesis. The only pair that does not support the hypothesis are the two runners with ranks 5 and 6, because in this pair, the runner from Group B had the faster time. By the Kerby simple difference formula, 95% of the data support the hypothesis (19 of 20 pairs), and 5% do not support (1 of 20 pairs), so the rank correlation is r = .95 - .05 = .90. The maximum value for the correlation is r = 1, which means that 100% of the pairs favor the hypothesis. A correlation of r = 0 indicates that half the pairs favor the hypothesis and half do not; in other words, the sample groups do not differ in ranks, so there is no evidence that they come from two different populations. An effect size of r = 0 can be said to describe no relationship between group membership and the members' ranks.

Spearman's rank correlation coefficient

In statistics, Spearman's rank correlation coefficient or Spearman's rho, named after Charles Spearman and often denoted by the Greek letter ñ(rho) or as rs, is a nonparametric measure of rank correlation (statistical dependence between the rankings of two variables). It assesses how well the relationship between two variables can be described using a monotonic function. The Spearman correlation between two variables is equal to the Pearson correlation between the rank values of those two variables; while Pearson's correlation assesses linear relationships, Spearman's correlation assesses monotonic relationships (whether linear or not). If there are no repeated data values, a perfect Spearman correlation of +1 or "1 occurs when each of the variables is a perfect monotone function of the other.

Intuitively, the Spearman correlation between two variables will be high when observations have a similar (or identical for a correlation of 1) rank (i.e. relative position label of the observations within the variable: 1st, 2nd, 3rd, etc.) between the two variables, and low when observations have a dissimilar (or fully opposed for a correlation of "1) rank between the two variables. Spearman's coefficient is appropriate for both continuous and discrete ordinal variables. Both Spearman's ñ and Kendall's ôcan be formulated as special cases of a more general correlation coefficient.

Definition and calculation

The Spearman correlation coefficient is defined as the Pearson correlation coefficient between the rank variables. For a sample of size n, the nraw scores $\operatorname{rg} X_i, \operatorname{rg} Y_i$ are converted to ranks $r_s = \rho_{\operatorname{rg}_X, \operatorname{rg}_Y} = \frac{\operatorname{cov}(\operatorname{rg}_X, \operatorname{rg}_Y)}{\sigma_{\operatorname{rg}_X} \sigma_{\operatorname{rg}_Y}}$, and rsis computed from:

$$\operatorname{cov}(\operatorname{rg}_X, \operatorname{rg}_Y)$$

where

- ñdenotes the usual Pearson correlation coefficient, but applied to the rank variables.
- $\sigma_{\operatorname{rg}_X}$ is the covariance of the rank variables.
- $\sigma_{\operatorname{rg}_Y}$ and $r_s = 1 - \frac{6\sum d_i^2}{n\ddot{u}n^2 -}.$ are the standard deviations of the rank variables.

Only if all n ranks are distinct integers, it can be computed using the popular formula

$$d_i = \operatorname{rg}(X_i) - \operatorname{rg}(Y_i)$$

where

- $\sigma_{\operatorname{rg}_Y} \sigma_{\operatorname{rg}_Y} = \operatorname{Var} \operatorname{rg}_X = \operatorname{Var} \operatorname{rg}_Y = (n^2 - 1)/12$, is the difference between the two ranks of each observation.
- n is the number of observations

Identical values are usually each assigned fractional ranks equal to the average of their positions in the ascending order of the values, which is equivalent to averaging over all possible permutations. If ties are present in the data set, the simplified formula above yields incorrect results: Only if in both variables all ranks are distinct, then $\sigma_{r_s} = \frac{0.6325}{\sqrt{n-1}}$ (Calculated according to biased variance.). The first equation — normalizing by the standard deviation — may be used even when ranks are normalized to [0, 1] ("relative ranks") because it is insensitive both to translation and linear scaling. The simplified method should also not be used in cases where the data set is truncated; that is, when the Spearman correlation coefficient is desired for the top X records (whether by pre-change rank or post-change rank, or both), the user should use the Pearson correlation coefficient formula given above. The standard error of the coefficient (ó) was determined by Pearson in 1907 and Gosset in 1920. It is

IQ, X_i	Hours of TV per week, Y_i
106	7
86	0
100	27
101	50
99	28
103	29
97	20
113	12
112	6
110	17

Related quantities

There are several other numerical measures that quantify the extent of statistical dependence between pairs of observations. The most common of these is the Pearson product-moment correlation coefficient, which is a similar correlation method to Spearman's rank, that measures the "linear" relationships between the raw numbers rather than between their ranks. An alternative name for the Spearman rank correlation is the "grade correlation"; in this, the "rank" of an observation is replaced by the "grade". In continuous distributions, the grade of an observation is, by convention, always one half less than the rank, and hence the grade and rank correlations are the same in this case. More generally, the "grade" of an observation is proportional to an estimate of the fraction of a population less than a given value, with the half-observation adjustment at observed values. Thus this corresponds to one possible treatment of tied ranks. While unusual, the term "grade correlation" is still in use.

Interpretation

The sign of the Spearman correlation indicates the direction of association between X (the independent variable) and Y (the dependent variable). If Y tends to increase when X increases, the Spearman correlation coefficient is positive. If Y tends to decrease when X increases, the Spearman correlation coefficient is negative. A Spearman correlation of zero indicates that there is no tendency for Y to either increase or decrease when X increases. The Spearman correlation increases in magnitude as X and Y become closer to being perfect monotone functions of each other. When X and Y are perfectly monotonically related, the Spearman correlation coefficient becomes 1. A perfect monotone increasing relationship implies that for any two pairs of data values Xi, Yi and Xj, Yj, that Xi " Xj and Yi " Yj always have the same sign. A perfect monotone decreasing relationship implies that these differences always have opposite signs.

The Spearman correlation coefficient is often described as being "nonparametric". This can have two meanings. First, a perfect Spearman correlation results when X and Y are related by any monotonic function. Contrast this with the Pearson correlation, which only gives a perfect value when X and Y are related by a linear function. The other sense in which the Spearman correlation is nonparametric in that its exact sampling distribution can be obtained without requiring knowledge (i.e., knowing the parameters) of the joint probability distribution of X and Y.

Example

In this example, the raw data in the table below is used to calculate the correlation between the IQ of a person with the number of hours spent in front of TV per week.

$$d_i^2$$

Firstly, evaluate X_i. To do so use the following steps, reflected in the table below.

1. Sort the data by the first column (x_i). Create a new column Y_i and assign it the ranked values 1,2,3,...n.

2. Next, sort the data by the second column (y_i). Create a fourth column d_i and similarly assign it the ranked values 1,2,3,...n.

3. Create a fifth column x_i to hold the differences between the two rank columns (y_i and

IQ, X_i	Hours of TV per week, Y_i	rank x_i	rank y_i	d_i	d_i^2
86	0	1	1	0	0
97	20	2	6	−4	16
99	28	3	8	−5	25
100	27	4	7	−3	9
101	50	5	10	−5	25
103	29	6	9	−3	9
106	7	7	3	4	16
110	17	8	5	3	9
112	6	9	2	7	49
113	12	10	4	6	36

).

4. Create one final column to hold the value of column squared.

d_i^2

With $\sum d_i^2 = 194$ found, add them to find $\rho = 1 - \dfrac{6\sum d_i^2}{n(n^2-1)}$. The value of n is 10. These values can now be substituted back into the equation:

$\rho = 1 - \dfrac{6 \times 194}{10(10^2-1)}$ to give

$$e_i = y_i - f(x_i; \hat{\beta}),$$

which evaluates to ñ = "29/165 = "0.175757575...with a P-value = 0.627188 (using the t distribution). This low value shows that the correlation between IQ and hours spent watching TV is very low, although the negative value suggests that the longer the time spent watching television the lower the IQ. In the case of ties in the original values, this formula should not be used; instead, the Pearson correlation coefficient should be calculated on the ranks (where ties are given ranks, as described above).

Ranking

A ranking is a relationship between a set of items such that, for any two items, the first is either 'ranked higher than', 'ranked lower than' or 'ranked equal to' the second. In mathematics, this is known as a weak order or total preorder of objects. It is not necessarily a total order of objects because two different objects can have the same ranking. The rankings themselves are totally ordered. For example, materials are totally preordered by hardness, while degrees of hardness are totally ordered. If two items are the same in rank it is considered a tie. By reducing detailed measures to a sequence of ordinal numbers, rankings make it possible to evaluate complex information according to certain criteria. Thus, for example, an Internet search engine may rank the pages it finds according to an estimation of their relevance, making it possible for the user quickly to select the pages they are likely to want to see. Analysis of data obtained by ranking commonly requires non-parametric statistics.

Strategies for assigning rankings

It is not always possible to assign rankings uniquely. For example, in a race or competition two (or more) entrants might tie for a place in the ranking. When computing an ordinal measurement, two (or more) of the quantities being ranked might measure equal. In these cases, one of the strategies shown below for assigning the rankings may be adopted. A common shorthand way to distinguish these ranking strategies is by the ranking numbers that would be produced for four items, with the first item ranked ahead of the second and third (which compare equal) which are both ranked ahead of the fourth. These names are also shown below.

Standard competition ranking ("1224" ranking)

In competition ranking, items that compare equal receive the same ranking number, and then a gap is left in the ranking numbers. The number of ranking numbers that are left out in this gap is one less than the number of items that compared equal. Equivalently, each item's ranking number is 1 plus the number of items ranked above it. This ranking strategy is frequently adopted for competitions, as it means that if two (or more) competitors tie for a position in the ranking, the position of all those ranked below them is unaffected (i.e., a competitor only comes second if exactly one person scores better than them, third if exactly two people score better than them, fourth if exactly three people score better than them, etc.). Thus if A ranks ahead of B and C (which compare equal) which are both ranked ahead of D, then A gets ranking number 1 ("first"), B gets ranking number 2 ("joint second"), C also gets ranking number 2 ("joint second") and D gets ranking number 4 ("fourth").

Modified competition ranking ("1334" ranking)

Sometimes, competition ranking is done by leaving the gaps in the ranking numbers before the sets of equal-ranking items (rather than after them as in standard competition ranking).[where?] The number of ranking numbers that are left out in this gap remains one less than the number of items that compared equal. Equivalently, each item's ranking number is equal to the number of items ranked equal to it or above it. This ranking ensures that a competitor only comes second if they score higher than all but one of their opponents, third if they score higher than all but two of their opponents, etc. Thus if A ranks ahead of B and C (which compare equal) which are both ranked head of D, then A gets ranking number 1 ("first"), B gets ranking number 3 ("joint third"), C also gets ranking number 3 ("joint third") and D gets ranking number 4 ("fourth"). In this case, nobody would get ranking number 2 ("second") and that would be left as a gap.

Dense ranking ("1223" ranking)

In dense ranking, items that compare equally receive the same ranking number, and the next item(s) receive the immediately following ranking number. Equivalently, each item's ranking number is 1 plus the number of items ranked above it that are distinct with respect to the ranking order. Thus if A ranks ahead of B and C (which compare equal) which are both ranked ahead of D, then A gets ranking number 1 ("first"), B gets ranking number 2 ("joint second"), C also gets ranking number 2 ("joint second") and D gets ranking number 3 ("Third").

Ordinal ranking ("1234" ranking)

In ordinal ranking, all items receive distinct ordinal numbers, including items that compare equal. The assignment of distinct ordinal numbers to items that compare equal can be done at random, or arbitrarily, but it is generally preferable to use a system that is arbitrary but consistent, as this gives stable results if the ranking is done multiple times. An example of an arbitrary but consistent system would be to incorporate other attributes into the ranking order (such as alphabetical ordering of the competitor's name) to ensure that no two items exactly match. With this strategy, if A ranks ahead of B and C (which compare equal) which are both ranked ahead of D, then A gets ranking number 1 ("first") and D gets ranking number 4 ("fourth"), and either B gets ranking number 2 ("second") and C gets ranking number 3 ("third") or C gets ranking number 2 ("second") and B gets ranking number 3 ("third").

In computer data processing, ordinal ranking is also referred to as "row numbering".

Fractional ranking ("1 2.5 2.5 4" ranking)

Items that compare equal receive the same ranking number, which is the mean of what they would have under ordinal rankings. Equivalently, the ranking number of 1 plus the number of items ranked above it plus half the number of items equal to it. This strategy has the property that the sum of the ranking numbers is the same as under ordinal ranking. For this reason, it is used in computing Borda counts and in statistical tests (see below). Thus if A ranks ahead of B and C (which compare equal) which are both ranked ahead of D, then A gets ranking number 1 ("first"), B and C each get ranking number 2.5 (average of "joint second/third") and D gets ranking number 4 ("fourth"). Here is an example: Suppose you have the data set 1.0, 1.0, 2.0, 3.0, 3.0, 4.0, 5.0, 5.0, 5.0. The ordinal ranks are 1, 2, 3, 4, 5, 6, 7, 8, 9. For $v = 1.0$, the fractional rank is the average of the ordinal ranks: $(1 + 2) / 2 = 1.5$. In a similar manner, for $v = 5.0$, the fractional rank is $(7 + 8 + 9) / 3 = 8.0$. Thus the fractional ranks are: 1.5, 1.5, 3.0, 4.5, 4.5, 6.0, 8.0, 8.0, 8.0

Ranking in statistics

In statistics, "ranking" refers to the data transformation in which numerical or ordinal values are replaced by their rank when the data are sorted. For example, the numerical data 3.4, 5.1, 2.6, 7.3 are observed, the ranks of these data items would be 2, 3, 1 and 4 respectively. For example, the ordinal data hot, cold, warm would be replaced by 3, 1, 2. In these examples, the ranks are assigned to values in ascending order. (In some other cases, descending ranks are used.) Ranks are related to the indexed list of order statistics, which consists of the original dataset rearranged into ascending order. Some kinds of statistical tests employ calculations based on ranks. Examples include:

- Friedman test
- Kruskal–Wallis test
- Rank products
- Spearman's rank correlation coefficient
- Wilcoxon rank-sum test
- Wilcoxon signed-rank test

The distribution of values in decreasing order of rank is often of interest when values vary widely in scale; this is the rank-size distribution (or rank-frequency distribution), for example for city sizes or word frequencies. These often follow a power law. Some ranks can have non-integer values for tied data values. For example, when there is an even number of copies of the same data value, the above described fractional statistical rank of the tied data ends in ½.

Rank function in Excel

Microsoft Excel provides two ranking functions, the Rank.EQ function which assigns competition ranks ("1224") and the Rank.AVG function which assigns fractional ranks ("1 2.5 2.5 4") as described above.

Comparison of rankings

A rank correlation can be used to compare two rankings for the same set of objects. For example, Spearman's rank correlation coefficient is useful to measure the statistical dependence between the rankings of athletes in two tournaments. Another example is the "Rank–rank hypergeometric overlap" approach , which is designed to compare ranking of the genes that are at the "top" of two ordered lists of differentially expressed genes.

Regression validation

In statistics, regression validation is the process of deciding whether the numerical results quantifying hypothesized relationships between variables, obtained from regression analysis, are acceptable as descriptions of the data. The validation process can involve analyzing the goodness of fit of the regression, analyzing whether the regression residuals are random, and checking whether the model's predictive performance deteriorates substantially when applied to data that were not used in model estimation.

Goodness of fit

One measure of goodness of fit is the R2 (coefficient of determination), which in ordinary least squares with an intercept ranges between 0 and 1. While a low R2 implies that the model does not fit the data well, an R2 close to 1 does not guarantee that the model fits the data well: as Anscombe's quartet shows, a high R2 can occur in the presence of misspecification of the functional form of a relationship or in the presence of outliers that distort the true relationship. One problem with the R2 as a measure of model validity is that it can always be increased by adding more variables into the model, except in the unlikely event that the additional variables are exactly uncorrelated with the dependent variable in the data sample being used. This problem can be avoided by doing an F-test of the statistical significance of the increase in the R2, or by instead using the adjusted R2.

Analysis of residuals

The residuals from a fitted model are the differences between the responses observed at each combination of values of the explanatory variables and the corresponding prediction of the response computed using the regression function. Mathematically, the definition of the residual for the ith observation in the data set is written

Variable→	Age	$X_i - \bar{X}$	$(X_i - \bar{X})^2$	← $\bar{X}$ =44.29
	24	-20.29	411.68	
	32	-12.29	151.04	
	32	-12.29	151.04	← squared deviations
	42	-2.29	5.24	
	55	10.71	114.70	
	60	15.71	246.80	
	65	20.71	428.90	
n=	7		1509.43	← $\Sigma(X_i - \bar{X})^2$
		$s^2 = \frac{\Sigma(X_i - \bar{X})^2}{n-1}$	251.57	← sample variance
		$s = \sqrt{\frac{\Sigma(X_i - \bar{X})^2}{n-1}}$	15.86	← sample standard deviation

withyi denoting the ith response in the data set and xi the vector of explanatory variables, each set at the corresponding values found in the ith observation in the data set. If the model fit to the data were correct, the residuals would approximate the random errors that make the relationship between the explanatory variables and the response variable a statistical relationship. Therefore, if the residuals appear to behave randomly, it suggests that the model fits the data well. On the other hand, if non-random structure is evident in the residuals, it is a clear sign that the model fits the data poorly. The next section details the types of plots to use to test different aspects of a model and gives the correct interpretations of different results that could be observed for each type of plot.

Graphical analysis of residuals

A basic, though not quantitatively precise, way to check for problems that render a model inadequate is to conduct a visual examination of the residuals (the mispredictions of the data used in quantifying the model) to look for obvious deviations from randomness. If a visual examination suggests, for example, the possible presence of heteroskedasticity (a relationship between the variance of the model errors and the size of an independent variable's observations), then statistical tests can be performed to confirm or reject this hunch; if it is confirmed, different modeling procedures are called for. Different types of plots of the residuals from a fitted model provide information on the adequacy of different aspects of the model.

1. sufficiency of the functional part of the model: scatter plots of residuals versus predictors
2. non-constant variation across the data: scatter plots of residuals versus predictors; for data collected over time, also plots of residuals against time
3. drift in the errors (data collected over time): run charts of the response and errors versus time

4. independence of errors: lag plot
5. normality of errors: histogram and normal probability plot

Graphical methods have an advantage over numerical methods for model validation because they readily illustrate a broad range of complex aspects of the relationship between the model and the data.

Quantitative analysis of residuals

Numerical methods also play an important role in model validation. For example, the lack-of-fit test for assessing the correctness of the functional part of the model can aid in interpreting a borderline residual plot. One common situation when numerical validation methods take precedence over graphical methods is when the number of parameters being estimated is relatively close to the size of the data set. In this situation residual plots are often difficult to interpret due to constraints on the residuals imposed by the estimation of the unknown parameters. One area in which this typically happens is in optimization applications using designed experiments. Logistic regression with binary data is another area in which graphical residual analysis can be difficult. Serial correlation of the residuals can indicate model misspecification, and can be checked for with the Durbin–Watson statistic. The problem of heteroskedasticity can be checked for in any of several ways.

3

Measures of Variability

Introduction

An average, as a single significant value representing the central tendency of a statistical distribution, is a very useful and important measure, however, the use of a single value to describe the distribution conceals many important facts about it. To understand a statistical distribution fully, we need to calcualte other statistical measures which can reveal those concealed characteristics of the data. A measures of central tendency tells something about the general level of magnitude of the distribution, but it fails to give its complete description. It does not tell how the items in a series are distributed relative to this measure, that is how the items scatter arounded the measure of central tendency. "Each of the values of a variable is sometimes considered to be the same as the average.

The truth is that an average, being just a single figure representing a mass of values and thus serving an important use, conceals the variation among the values". If all the items in a distribution are widely spread and there is no tendency to concentrate around any one value, then clearly no average can adequately summarise or describe the distribution. Two series may have the same average, but the items may scatter widely around the average in one case and be highly congregative in the other. Prof. Neiswanger writes, "Two distribution of statistical data may be symmetrical and have common means, medians and modes, and identical frequencies in the modal class. Yet with these points in common they may differ widely in the scatter or their values about the measures of central tendency." Thus, there is need to get a single figure on variation that would provide a basis for generalizing. Measures of dispersion are measures of scatter about an average, and these measures are sometimes as important as the average itself.

On the basis of measure of central tendency, the structure of statistical series can be of two types:

1. Their averages may be the same, but formation of the items may be very much different.
2. Their averages may be different, but the manner of the distribution of the items may be the same.

Concept of Variation

- Measure of variation is a measure that describes how spread out or scattered a set of data. It is also known as measures of dispersion or measures of spread.

  Examples of Measure of Variation

  There are three measures of variation:

  The range, the variance, and the standard deviation.

Purposes of measuring variations

Measures of variation of dispersion are needed for three basic purposes :

(1) To gauge the reliability of an average. An average will be satisfactory measure of typical size only when it is derived from the data that are homogeneous.A measure of dispersion in conjunction with a measure of central tendency gives a description of the structure of the distribution and the place of individual items in it. In other words, to summarize the characteristics of a distribution, both an average and a measure of dispersion must be presented. Without the average there would be no standard against which to compare the individual values and no useful way of measuring the amount of variation, without an average of differences or deviations between the values and their average, there would be no basis for generalizing about the extent of variability. William A. Spurr and Charles P. Bonini observe, "when dispersion is small, the average is a typical value in that it closely represent the individual values, and it is reliable in that it is a good estimate of the corresponding average in the population, On the other hand, when the dispersion is great, the average is not so typical and, unless the sample is very large, the average may be quite unreliable."

(2) To serve as a basis for control of the variability itself. The second basic purpose of measuring dispersion is to determine the nature and causes of variation in order to control the variation itself. Dispersion is important not as merely supplementary to the average, but because the scatter in a distribution may itself be significant. "In matters of health, variations in body temperature pulse beat and blood pressure are basic guides to diagnosis. Prescribed treatment is designed to control their variation. In industrial production, efficient operation requires control of quality variation, the causes of which are sought through inspection and quality control programmes." In social sciences, the measurement of inequality in the distribution of income and wealth requires the measures of variation.

(3) To compare two or more series with regard to their variability. On the basis of measures of dispersion, the extent of variability between two or more series can be compared. A study of dispersion is useful to find out degree of uniformity or consistency in the two or more sets of data. A greater amount of dispersion means lack of uniformity or consistency in the data.

Properties of a good measure of variation

Measures of Variation

Range: The difference between the highest and lowest score (high-low). It describes the span of scores but cannot be compared to distributions with a different number of observations. In the table below, the range is 41 (65-24).

Variance: The average of the squared deviations between the individual scores and the mean. The larger the variance the more variability there is among the scores. When comparing two samples with the same unit of measurement (age), the variances are comparable even though the sample sizes may be different. Generally, however, smaller samples have greater variability among the scores than larger samples. The sample variance for the data in the table below is 251.57. The formula is almost the same for estimating population variance. See formula in Appendix.

Standard deviation: The square root of variance. It provides a representation of the variation among scores that is directly comparable to the raw scores. The sample standard deviation in the following table is 15.86 years.

$$\sigma^2 = \frac{\Sigma(X-\mu)^2}{N} \textit{ for population data (Definitionb Formula)}$$

Types of Measures of Dispersion

which are:

(a) Absolute Measure of Dispersion

(b) Relative Measure of Dispersion

Absolute Measures of Dispersion : These measures give us an idea about the amount of dispersion in a set of observations. They give the answers in the same units as the units of the original observations. When the observations are in kilograms, the absolute measure is also in kilograms. If we have two sets of observations, we cannot always use the absolute measures to compare their dispersion. We shall explain later as to when the absolute measures can be used for comparison of dispersion in two or more than two sets of data. The absolute measures which are commonly used are:

1. The Range
2. The Quartile Deviation
3. The Mean Deviation
4. The Standard deviation and Variance

Relative Measure of Dispersion: These measures are calculated for the comparison of dispersion in two or more than two sets of observations. These measures are free of the units in which the original data is measured. If the original data is in dollar or kilometers, we do not use these units with relative measure of dispersion. These measures are a sort of ratio and are called coefficients. Each absolute measure of dispersion can be converted into its relative measure. Thus the relative measures of dispersion are:

1. Coefficient of Range or Coefficient of Dispersion.
2. Coefficient of Quartile Deviation or Quartile Coefficient of Dispersion.
3. Coefficient of Mean Deviation or Mean Deviation of Dispersion.
4. Coefficient of Standard Deviation or Standard Coefficient of Dispersion.
5. Coefficient of Variation (a special case of Standard Coefficient of Dispersion)

Measures of Dispersion (Variation or Spread)

- is a measure used to describe the variation of a set of data

II. ABSOLUTE DISPERSION

A. RANGE

Meaning: Range is the difference between the highest and lowest values of the set of data.

Formula for Range :

· Ungrouped Data

R = highest observation minus lowest observation

R = H.V. – L.V.

· Grouped Data

R = highest ucl – lowest lcl

B. VARIANCE and STANDARD DEVIATION

Meaning: Variance is the mean of the squared deviation from the mean.

Standard Deviation is the positive square root of variance.

Formula for Variance and Standard deviation :

$$s^2 = \frac{n\Sigma x^2 - (\Sigma x)^2}{n(n-1)}$$ *computational formula for sample data*

· Ungrouped Data

$$s = \text{standard deviation} = \sqrt{\text{variance}}$$

$$s^2 = \frac{n\Sigma fX^2 - (\Sigma fX)^2}{n(n-1)}$$ *computational formula for sample data*

· Grouped Data

X_i	X_i^2
180	32400
140	19600
85	7225
135	18225
140	19600
90	8100
115	13225
120	14400
145	21025
135	18225
160	25600
99	9801
127	16129
£x = 1671	£x² = 223555

$$\text{variance} = s^2 = \frac{n\Sigma x^2 - (\Sigma x)^2}{n(n-1)}$$

$$s^2 = \frac{13(223{,}555) - (1671)^2}{13(12)}$$

$$s^2 = \frac{113{,}974}{156}$$

$$s^2 = 730.6025641$$

$$s^2 = 730.60$$

$$\text{standard deviation} = s = \sqrt{s^2}$$

$$s = \sqrt{730.6025641} = 27.03$$

Note: final answers are expressed to 2 decimal places.

Example of computation for ungrouped data

Given: Weights of randomly selected students in pounds:

180, 140, 85, 135, 140, 90, 115, 120, 145, 135, 160, 99, 127

a) Computation of Range

R = H.V. – L.V. = 180 – 85

R = 95 pounds

Interpretation: The gap between the heaviest and lightest weights of students is 95 pounds.

b) Computation of Variance and standard deviation

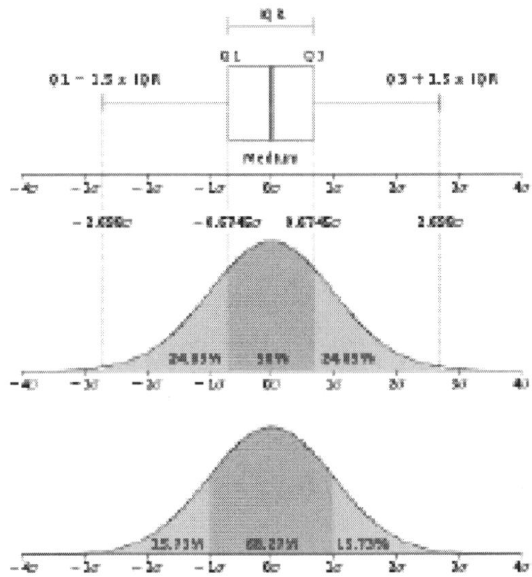

Different Methods of Measuring Dispersion

There are two meanings of dispersion, as explained above. On the basis of these two meanings, there are two mathematical methods of finding dispersion, i.e., methods of limits and methods of moment. Dispersion can also be studied graphically. Thus, the following are the methods of measuring dispersion:

I. Numerical Methods

(i) Metods of Limits

Range

The simplest measures of dispersionn is the range of the data. The range is determined by the two extreme values of the observations and it is simply the difference between the largest and the smallest value in a distribution. Symbolically,

Range (R) = Largest value (L) - Smallest value (S)

or R = L - S

The coefficient of range, which is the relative measure of range, is computed by applying the following formula :

Coefficient of Range (C.R.) = or C. R. =

Example 1

(a) The height of 11 men were 61, 64, 68, 69, 67, 68, 66, 70, 65, 67 and 72 inches. Calculate the range. If the shorest man is omitted, what is the percentage change in the range ?

(b) The weights of 11 forty year old men were 148, 154, 158, 160, 161, 162, 166, 170, 182, 195 and 236 pounds. If the heaviest man is omitted, what is the percentage change in the range?

(c) Mean temperature, deviation from normal (1981) :

Jan.	Feb.	Mar.	Apr.	May	June
+1.5	+2.4	+3.1	-1.5	-0.4	+.3.3
July	Aug.	Sept.	Oct.	Nov.	Dec.
-0.1	-0.6	-1.5	-0.6	-1.9	-6.1

Solution:

(a) Array : 61, 64, 65, 66, 67, 68, 69, 70, 72

Range = Highest Value - Lowest Value = 72 - 61 = 11

When the shorest man (61 inches) is omitted, the range will be = 72 - 64 = 8

Change in the Range = 11 - 8 = 3

Percentage change in range

(b) Array : 148, 154, 158, 160, 161, 162, 166, 170, 182, 195, 236

Range = Highest Value - Lowest Value = 236 - 148 = 88.

When the heaviest man (236 pounds) is omitted, the range will be

= 195 - 148 = 47

Change in the Range = 88 - 47 = 41

Percentage change in the range 41/88x 100

Merits and Demerits of Range

Merits

(1) Range is the simplest measure of dispersion. In other words, it is simple to calculate and easy to understand measure of dispersion. Its use is very common. If it is asked, what is your earnings per month ? or, what is acreage in your field ? etc., the answers will generally be within two limits. If the substance of the reply is ignored, then it is nothing but expression of range in statistical language. Wessell, Willett and Simone observe, "it (Range) is still an important concept. Although it does not consider the measure in Which values are spread out within the distribution but concerns itself only with top and bottom values, the range is still an extremely useful measure."

(2) It gives a broad picture of the data in that it includes the limits within which all of the items occur.

Demerits

(1) It is very much affected by the extreme items. Range is misleading if either of the extreme values is an unusual occurrence. It is not desirable, therefore, to utilise the range, if there is an unusual value in the extreme position.

(2) The range provides no measure of the dispersion of the other values, except that they lie between the two extreme values. It is an unsatisfactory measure because items in a frequency distribution have a tendency towards concentration in the middle of the series.

(3) The range, although it describes variation with a single easy-to-determine manner, does not tell enough because it does not utilise all the information in the set of observations. It does not reflect the distribution of the observations between the extremes. Two sereis may have the same range, but in one, the item may be concentrated at one end of the distribution, and in there other, at the other end of the series. For example, if two series are :

A : 10, 10, 10, 11, 15, B : 10, 12, 15, 15, 15

In A series items are concentrated near the smallest value, while in B series items are concentrated near the largest value, though range of both the distribution is 5. Thus, it is possible to have two distributions with the same range, but whereas in the one the frequencies are fairly evenly distributed throughout the range of the variable, in the other, the majority of values of observations are concentrated about a single values.

(4) It requires only one extreme item at either end of the series to render the range virtually valueless as reliable measure of dispersion. For example, in a factory the range of monthly incomes of a group of workers is, say , 500 -150 = Rs. 350. If a new worker having a monthly income of Rs. 1,000 joins the group, the range will become 1000 - 150 = Rs. 850.

(5) Range is influenced very much by fluctuations of sampling.

In short, dependence on the two extreme items renders the range most unreliable as a guide to the dispersion of the values within a distribution. Its chief merit lies in its simplicity.

Uses of Range

Despite certain limitations, the Range is useful in the following areas:

(1) Quality Control. Range has got a special application in the quality control measures. The control charts are prepared on the basis of range for controlling the quality of products.

(2) Measurement of Fluctuations. Range is a very usefuly measure to study fluctuation of data. Variations in the weather forecasts, movement in the prices of securities etc., can be studied with the help of range.

Inter-Quatile Range

In descriptive statistics, the interquartile range (IQR), also called the midspread or middle fifty, is a measure of statistical dispersion, being equal to the difference between the upper and lower quartiles. IQR = Q3 ” Q1

Use

Unlike (total) range, the interquartile range is a robust statistic, having a breakdown point of 25%, and is thus often preferred to the total range.

The IQR is used to build box plots, simple graphical representations of a probability distribution.

For a symmetric distribution (so the median equals the midhinge, the average of the first and third quartiles), half the IQR equals the median absolute deviation (MAD).

The median is the corresponding measure of central tendency.

Examples

$$Q_1$$

Boxplot (with an interquartile range) and aprobability density function (pdf) of a Normal N(0,1σ2) Population

Data set in a table

i	x[i]	Quartile
1	102	
2	104	
3	105	Q1
4	107	
5	108	
6	109	Q2 (median)
7	110	
8	112	
9	115	Q3
10	116	
11	118	

For the data in this table the interquartile range is IQR = 115 ” 105 = 10.

Data set in a plain-text box plot

```
+——–+-+
o * |——–| | |—|
+——–+-+

+—+—+—+—+—+—+—+—+—+—+—+—+—+ number line
0 1 2 3 4 5 6 7 8 9 10 11 12
```

For the data set in this box plot:

- lower (first) quartile ($x_{.25}$, $Median$) = 7
- median (second quartile) ($x_{.5}$, Q_3) = 8.5
- upper (third) quartile ($x_{.75}$, $IQR = Q_3 - Q_1 = 2$) = 9
- interquartile range, $Q_1 = \text{CDF}^{-1}(0.25)$,

Interquartile range of distributions

The interquartile range of a continuous distribution can be calculated by integrating the probability density function (which yields thecumulative distribution function — any other means of calculating the CDF will also work). The lower quartile, Q1, is a number such that integral of the PDF from -" to Q1 equals 0.25, while the upper quartile, Q3, is such a number that the integral from -" to Q3 equals 0.75; in terms of the CDF, the quartiles can be defined as follows:

$$Q_3 = \text{CDF}^{-1}(0.75),$$

$$Q_1 = (\sigma\, z_1) + X$$

where CDF"1 is the quantile function.

The interquartile range and median of some common distributions are shown below

Distribution	Median	IQR
Normal	μ	2 ϕ–1(0.75) σ 1.349
Laplace	μ	2b ln(2)
Cauchy	μ	2γ

Interquartile range test for normality of distribution

The IQR, mean, and standard deviation of a population P can be used in a simple test of whether or not P is normally distributed, orGaussian. If P is normally distributed, then the standard score of the first quartile, z1, is -0.67, and the standard score of the third quartile, z3, is +0.67. Given mean = X and standard deviation = σ for P, if P is normally distributed, the first quartile

$$Q_3 = (\sigma\, z_3) + X$$

and the third quartile

$$2,\ 4,\ 4,\ 4,\ 5,\ 5,\ 7,\ 9$$

If the actual values of the first or third quartiles differ substantially from the calculated values, P is not normally distributed.

Percentile Range

percentile range is used as a measure of disperson.It is the difference between centile and 10'th percentile.

Mean Deviation or Average Deviation

The most comprehensive description of dispersionn is that which is in terms of an average deviation from some measure of central tendency. The average deviation or mean deviation is a measure of dispersion that is based upon all the items in a distribution whether an array or frequency distribution. Mean or average deviation is the arithmetic mean of the deviations of the data from a measure of central tendency. In other words, the measure obtained by calculating the absolute deviation of each observation from the median or mean and then averaging these deviations by taking their arithmetic mean. In the words of Clark and Schkade, "Average deviation is the average amount of scatter of the items in a distribution from either the mean of the median, ignoring the signs of the deviations. The average that is taken of the scatter is an arithmetic mean, which accounts for the fact that this measure is often called the mean deviation." In deriving mean deviation, absolute deviations, that is deviations in which '+' and '-' signs are ignored. In other words, all the deviations are taken as positive. The reason for ignoring signs is that the sum of the deviations of the values of the items in a series from arithmetic mean is zero and from other averages it is nearly zero, if the distribution is moderately asymmertical. In the process of calculating mean deviation following points should be kept in mind :

(1) Choice of an Average. Theoretically, mean deviation can be computed from any average, i.e., mean or median or mode, but in practice use of median and mean is very popular.

(2) Ignoring Signs. In computing mean deviation, the algebraci signs (plus or minus) of the deviations are ignored, and all the deviations are taken as positive. To indicate the absolute deviations, sign of dev iations, 'd' is sandwitched between two vertical lines called 'Modulus', i.e., . This is called 'mod-d'. This means that deviations are absolute or while finding out deviations, '+' and '-' signs have been ignored..

(3) Mean of the Deviations. Sum of the absolute deviations is divided by the number of items, 'N'. The result is mean deviation of the data.

(4) Formula. Mean deviation is denoted by Greek letter, small Delta . M. D. can also be used for denoting mean deviation. To indicate the average from which mean deviation has been calculated, the sign of average is used as subscript; such as :

(Mean Deviation from Mean)

(Mean Deviation from Median)

(Mean Deviation from Mode)

Coefficient of Mean Deviation. For the purpose of comparing variation among different sets of data, a relative measure is required.. This is essential whenever the sets of data to be compared are expressed in different units or even when the data are in the same units but of different orders of magnitude. A relative measure of dispersion can be obtained by dividing the absolute measure by the average from which deviations were obtained.

Merits and Demerits of Mean Deviation

Merits. Mean deviation possesses the following merits as a measure of dispersion :

(1) Simple and easy to understand. As compared to other calculated measures of

dispersion, mean deviation is easy to calculate and easy to understand. Wessell, Willett and Simone stated, "The outstanding advantage of the average deviation is its relative simplicity. Anyone familiar with the concept of average can readily appreciate the meaning of the average deviation. If a situation requires a measure of dispersion that will be presented to the general public or any group not thoroughly grounded in statistics, the average deviation is very useful."

(2) It is a calculated value. Mean Deviation is a calculated value.

(3) Based on all the items. It takes into account all the items of the series, hence it is affected by every value in the distribution. In the words of Morris Hamburg, "The use of the mean deviation as a measure of dispersion is clearly prefereable to a distance measure such as the range or interquartile range, since the mean deviation takes into account every item in a sset of data. Thus, the mean deviation is a more comprehensive measure of variation than is a distance measure."

(4) Less affected by extreme items. Mean deviation is less affected by extreme items. In smanll samples, which have extreme values, mean deviation is a good measure of variation.

(5) It shows the significance of an average in the distribution.

(6) Mean deviation can be calculated from any average, but use of mean and median is very popular.

(7) In a normal distribution covers nearly 57.5% of the items.

Demerits. The chief demerits of mean deviation are :

(1) The mean deviation suffers from a disadvantage, since algebraic positive and negative signs are ignored in its calculation. This causes the mean deviation to have poor combining properties in so far as its use in more advanced statistical techniques is concerned. That is why, the mean deviation has gained very limited acceptance as regards both in theoretical and applied work in statistics.

(2) Its computation by an arbitrary origin makes the calculation tedius.

(3) It is not a well defined measure, as it can be computed by any aveage. Mean deviation calculated from various averages will not be the same.

Utility

The mean deviation is useful while using small samples. This measure of dispersion is very much used in statistical analysis of economic, business and social phenomena. The National Bureau of Economic Research, U. S. A., computes mean deviation to show how different business cycles vary in duration, intensity and other respects.

The Second Moment of Dispersion

From the mathematical point of view, the practice of ignoring +, - signs of the deviations when computing the mean deviation is quite unjustifiable, and in consequence the mean deviation is unsuitable for use in further calculations. On the other hand, if signs are taken into account, the sum of deviations will he equal to 'zero'.

Standard Deviation

Standard deviation is a widely used measure of variability or diversity used instatistics and probability theory. It shows how much variation or "dispersion" exists from the average (mean, or expected value). A low standard deviation indicates that the data points tend to be very close to the mean, whereas high standard deviation indicates that the data points are spread out over a large range of values.

The standard deviation of a random variable, statistical population, data set, orprobability distribution is the square root of its variance. It is algebraicallysimpler though practically less robust than the average absolute deviation. A useful property of standard deviation is that, unlike variance, it is expressed in the same units as the data.

In addition to expressing the variability of a population, standard deviation is commonly used to measure confidence in statistical conclusions. For example, the margin of error in polling data is determined by calculating the expected standard deviation in the results if the same poll were to be conducted multiple times. The reported margin of error is typically about twice the standard deviation – the radius of a 95 percent confidence interval. Inscience, researchers commonly report the standard deviation of experimental data, and only effects that fall far outside the range of standard deviation are considered statistically significant – normal random error or variation in the measurements is in this way distinguished from causal variation. Standard deviation is also important in finance, where the standard deviation on the rate of return on an investment is a measure of the volatility of the investment.

Basic examples

Consider a population consisting of the following eight values:

$$\frac{2+4+4+4+5+5+7+9}{8} = 5$$

These eight data points have the mean (average) of 5:

$$\begin{array}{ll} (2-5)^2 = (-3)^2 = 9 & (5-5)^2 = 0^2 = 0 \\ (4-5)^2 = (-1)^2 = 1 & (5-5)^2 = 0^2 = 0 \\ (4-5)^2 = (-1)^2 = 1 & (7-5)^2 = 2^2 = 4 \\ (4-5)^2 = (-1)^2 = 1 & (9-5)^2 = 4^2 = 16 \end{array}$$

To calculate the population standard deviation, first compute the difference of each data point from the mean, and square the result of each:

$$\sqrt{\frac{(9+1+1+1+0+0+4+16)}{8}} = 2$$

Next compute the average of these values, and take the square root:

$$\sigma(r) = \sqrt{\frac{1}{N-1}\sum_{i=1}^{N}(x_i - r)^2}.$$

This quantity is the population standard deviation; it is equal to the square root of the variance. The formula is valid only if the eight values we began with form the complete population. If they instead were a random sample, drawn from some larger, "parent" population, then we should have used 7 (which is n " 1) instead of 8 (which is n) in the denominator of the last formula, and then the quantity thus obtained would have been called the sample standard deviation. See the section Estimation below for more details.

A slightly more complicated real life example, the average height for adult men in the United States is about 70", with a standard deviation of around 3". This means that most men (about 68%, assuming a normal distribution) have a height within 3" of the mean (67"–73") — one standard deviation — and almost all men (about 95%) have a height within 6" of the mean (64"–76") — two standard deviations. If the standard deviation were zero, then all men would be exactly 70" tall. If the standard deviation were 20", then men would have much more variable heights, with a typical range of about 50"–90". Three standard deviations account for 99.7% of the sample population being studied, assuming the distribution is normal (bell-shaped).

Relationship between standard deviation and mean

The mean and the standard deviation of a set of data are usually reported together. In a certain sense, the standard deviation is a "natural" measure of statistical dispersion if the center of the data is measured about the mean. This is because the standard deviation from the mean is smaller than from any other point. The precise statement is the following: suppose x1, ..., xn are real numbers and define the function:

$$r = \overline{x}.$$

Using calculus or by completing the square, it is possible to show that σ(r) has a unique minimum at the mean:

$$\sigma_{\text{mean}} = \frac{1}{\sqrt{N}}\sigma$$

Variability can also be measured by the coefficient of variation, which is the ratio of the standard deviation to the mean. It is a dimensionless number.

Often we want some information about the precision of the mean we obtained. We can obtain this by determining the standard deviation of the sampled mean. The standard deviation of the mean is related to the standard deviation of the distribution by:

$$\begin{aligned} \text{var}(X) &\equiv \sigma_X^2 \\ \text{var}(X_1 + X_2) &\equiv \text{var}(X_1) + \text{var}(X_2) \\ \text{var}(cX_1) &\equiv c^2\ \text{var}(X_1) \end{aligned}$$

where N is the number of observation in the sample used to estimate the mean. This can easily be proven with:

$$\begin{aligned} \text{var}(\text{mean}) &= \text{var}\left(\frac{1}{N}\sum_{i=1}^{N} X_i\right) = \frac{1}{N^2}\text{var}\left(\sum_{i=1}^{N} X_i\right) \\ &= \frac{1}{N^2}\sum_{i=1}^{N}\text{var}(X_i) = \frac{N}{N^2}\text{var}(X) = \frac{1}{N}\text{var}(X). \end{aligned}$$

hence

$$\sigma_{\text{mean}} = \frac{\sigma}{\sqrt{N}}.$$

Resulting in:

$$s_j = \sum_{k=1}^{N} x_k^j.$$

Rapid calculation methods

The following two formulas can represent a running (continuous) standard deviation. A set of three power sums s0, s1, s2 are each computed over a set of N values of x, denoted as x1, ..., xN:

$$\sigma = \frac{\sqrt{s_0 s_2 - s_1^2}}{s_0}$$

Note that s0 raises x to the zero power, and since x0 is always 1, s0 evaluates to N.

Given the results of these three running summations, the values s0, s1, s2 can be used at any time to compute the current value of the running standard deviation:

$$s = \sqrt{\frac{s_0 s_2 - s_1^2}{s_0(s_0 - 1)}}.$$

Similarly for sample standard deviation,

$$A_0 = 0$$

$$A_k = A_{k-1} + \frac{x_k - A_{k-1}}{k}$$

In a computer implementation, as the three sj sums become large, we need to consider round-off error, arithmetic overflow, and arithmetic underflow. The method below calculates the running sums method with reduced rounding errors. This is a "one pass" algorithm for calculating variance of n samples without the need to store prior data during the calculation. Applying this method to a time series will result in successive values of standard deviation corresponding to n data points as n grows larger with each new sample, rather than a constant-width sliding window calculation.

For k = 0 ... n:

$$Q_0 = 0$$

$$Q_k = Q_{k-1} + \frac{k-1}{k}(x_k - A_{k-1})^2 = Q_{k-1} + (x_k - A_{k-1})(x_k - A_k)$$

where A is the mean value.

$$s_n^2 = \frac{Q_n}{n-1}$$

Sample variance:

$$\sigma_n^2 = \frac{Q_n}{n}$$

Standard variance:

$$s_j = \sum_{k=1}^{N} w_k x_k^j.$$

Weighted calculation

When the values xi are weighted with unequal weights wi, the power sums s0, s1, s2 are each computed as:

$$W_0 = 0$$

$$W_k = W_{k-1} + w_k$$

And the standard deviation equations remain unchanged. Note that s0 is now the sum of the weights and not the number of samples N.

The incremental method with reduced rounding errors can also be applied, with some additional complexity.

A running sum of weights must be computed for each k from 1 to n:

$$A_0 = 0$$

$$A_k = A_{k-1} + \frac{w_k}{W_k}(x_k - A_{k-1})$$

$$Q_0 = 0$$

$$Q_k = Q_{k-1} + \frac{w_k W_{k-1}}{W_k}(x_k - A_{k-1})^2 = Q_{k-1} + w_k(x_k - A_{k-1})(x_k - A_k)$$

and places where 1/n is used above must be replaced by wi/Wn:

$$\sigma_n^2 = \frac{Q_n}{W_n}$$

In the final division,

$$s_n^2 = \frac{n'}{n' - 1}\sigma_n^2$$

and

$$p = 1/2 \pm \sqrt{1/12}$$

where n is the total number of elements, and n' is the number of elements with non-zero weights. The above formulas become equal to the simpler formulas given above if weights are taken as equal to one.

Quartile Deviation

The quartile deviation is half the difference between the upper and lower quartiles in a distribution. It is a measure of the spread through the middle half of a distribution. It can be useful because it is not influenced by extremely high or extremely low scores. Quartile Deviation is an ordinal statistic and is most often used in conjunction with the median.

Merits of Quartile Deviation:

1. It is easy to calculate and simple to follow.
2. It is not affected by the extreme values and is, therefore, useful in skewed distributions.
3. It is the only method of dispersion applicable in case of 'open-end classes'.

Demerits:

1. Since Quartile Deviation is based on Quartiles, sometimes it is not rigidly defined.
2. It does not take into account all the observations in the series. Hence it is not representative.
3. It is not capable of further algebraic treatment.
4. It is not a stable measure of dispersion as it is affected very much by fluctuations of sampling.
5. In a symmetrical distribution, the value of the median which is the second Quartile of the distribution lies midway between Q1 and Q3. If however, the series in non-symmetrical, Md does not lie midway between Q1 and Q3. If the series is symmetrical md + Q. D should equal Q3 and Q1.

   If it is non-symmetrical md + Q.D will not be equal to Q3 and Q1.

   To that extent Quartile Deviation gives a poor picture of dispersion.

Choice of Suitable Measure of Variation

There are five methods of measuring variation which have been discussed in this chapter : (i) Range, (ii) Mean Deviation, (iii) Standard Deviation (iv) Quartile Deviation, and (v) Lorenz Curve.

Which measure of variation should be used, will depend upon, (1) the characteristics of these measures, (2) nature of data, and (3) the purpose of measuring variation. Range is the simplest measure of variation, because it is the difference between two extreme items. This measure is gainfully employed in quality control and weather forecast areas. Quartile deviation is used to measure variation in open-end distritbution or when it is desirable to rule out the influence of extreme items. In the study of social phenomena, the use of quartile deviation is of great relevance.. The use of the mean d eviation is overshadowed by the use of standard deviation. In correlation, in sampling and in other areas of statistical analysis the standard deviation has become indispensable because of its inherent properties. According to M.M. Blair, "These two measures (Mean and S. D.) are to the statisfician what the axe and cross-cut saw to the woodsman-the basic tools for working upon his raw materials". Hence, in the absence of any special reason, the use of standard deviation as a measure of variation is resorted to.

4

Skewness, Moment & Kurtosis

An average represents the central tendency of the distribution and a measure of variation, degree of deviation around the central value. Skewness is another measure that refers to the amount of symmetry or asymmetry of a distribution. This statistical measure describes the shape of the distribution. Symmetry means that the varieties are equi-distant from the central value on either side. If a distribution is not symmetrical, it is referred to as a skewed or an asymmetrical distribution. A skewed distribution is one which has a pronounced tail in one direction or the other. According to Paden and Lindquist, "a distribution is said to be skewed, if it is lacking symmetry, that is, measures tend to pile up at one end or the other." Skewness denotes the tendency of a distribution to depart from symmetry. In the words of Wessell, Willett and Simone, "Skewness is lack of symmetry. Any measure of skewness indicates the difference between the manner in which items are distributed in a particular distribution compared with a normal distribution." There may be two distributions having the same mean and standard deviation, yet their shapes may be quite different, one may be symmetrical and the other may not be symmetrical.

Types of Frequency Distributions

In general, frequency distributions that form a balanced pattern are called symmetrical distributions, and those that form an unbalanced pattern are called skewed or asymmetrical distributions. In a symmetrical distribution frequencies go on increasing upto a point and then begin to decrease in the same fashion. A special kind of symmetrical distribution is the normal distribution, the pattern formed is not only symmetrical but also has the shape of a bell.

"The concept of skewness and kurtosis are useful since they enable us to more accurately describe a probability distribution."

In a symmetrical distribution, mean, median and mode coincide and they lie at the centre of distribution. As the distribution departs from symmetry these three values are pulled apart.

A distribution in which more than half of the area under the curve is to the right side of the mode, is a positively skewed distribution. In a positively skewed distribution, its right tail is longer than its left tail. Under such a distribution mean is greater than the median, and the median is greater than the mode (X>M>Mo), and the difference between upper quartile and median is greater than the difference between median and lower quartile (Q3-M>M-Q1). In a negatively skewed distribution, more than half of the area under the distribution curve is to the left side of the mode. In such a distribution the elongated tail is to the left and mean is less than the median and median is less than the mode (X<M<Mo), and the difference between upper quartile and median is less than the difference between median and lower quartile (Q3-M<M-Q1).

1. Test of Skewness

In order to find out whether a distribution is symmetrical or skewed, the following facts should be noticed:

(1) Relationship Between Averages. If in a distribution mean, median and mode are not identical, then it is a skewed distribution. The greater is the difference between mean and mode, more will be the skewness in the distribution.

(2) Total of Deviations. If the sum of positive deviations from median or mode is equal to the sum of negative deviation, then there is no skewness in the distribution. The extent of difference between the sums of positive and negative deviations from median or mode will determine the extent of skewness in the data.

(3) The distance of partition values from median. In a symmetrical distribution Q1 and Q2 , D1 and D2, P10 and P90 are equidistant from median. In an asymmetrical distribution it is not so.

(4) The frequencies on either side of the mode. In an asymmetrical distribution, frequencies on either side of the mode are not equal.

(5) The Curve. When the data are plotted on a graph paper, the Curve will not be bell-shaped, or when cut along a vertical line through the centre, two halves will not be identical.

Conversely stated, in the absence of skewness in the distribution:

(i) Values of mean, median and mode will coincide.

(ii) Sum of the positive deviations from the median or mode will be equal to the sum of negative deviations.

(iii) The two quartiles, decile one and nine, and percentile ten and ninety will be equidistant from the median.

(iv) Frequencies on the either side of the mode will be equal.

(v) Data when plotted on a graph paper will take a bell-shaped form.

Measures of Skewness

To find out the direction and the extent of asymmetry in a series statistical measures of skewness are calculated. These measures can be absolute or relative. Absolute measures of skewness tell us the extent of asymmetry and whether it is positive or negative. The absolute skewness can be known by taking the difference between mean and mode. Symbolically,

Absolute SK =– Mo

If the value of mean is greater than the mode (>Mo) skewness will be positive. In case the value of mean is less than the mode (< Mo) skewness will be negative. The greater is the amount of skewness, the more the mean and mode differ because of the influence of extreme items. The reason why the difference between mean and mode is taken for the measure of skewness is that in a symmetrical distribution, both the values alongwith median coincide, but in an asymmetrical distribution, mean moves away from the mode. The more is the skewness in the distribution, greater will be the difference between the mean and he mode.

Thus, the difference between the mean and the mode, whether positive or negative, indicates that the distribution is asymmetrical. However, such an absolute measure of skewness is unsatisfactory, because:

(1) It cannot be used for comparison of skewness in two distributions if they are in different units, because the difference between the mean and the mode will be in terms of the units of distribution.

(2) The difference between the mean and mode may be more in one series and less in another, yet the frequency curves of the two distributions may be similarly skewed.

For comparison, the absolute measures of skewness is changed to relative measures, which is called Coefficient of Skewness.

There are four measures of relative Skewness. They are:

(1) The Karl Pearson's Coefficient of Skewness.

(2) The Bowley' Coefficient of Skewness.

(3) The Kelly's Coefficient of Skewness.

(4) Measure of skewness based on moments.

Karl Pearson's Coefficient of Skewness

Karl Pearson has given a formula, for relative measures of skewness. It is known as Karl Pearson's Coefficient of Skewness or Pearsonian Coefficient of Skewness. The formula is based on the difference between the mean and mode, divided by the standard deviation. The coefficient is represented by J.

If in a particular frequency distribution, it is difficult to determine precisely the mode, or the mode is ill-defined, the coefficient of skewness can be determined by the following changed formula:

This is based on the relationship between different averages in a moderately asymmetrical distribution. In such a distribution:

Mo = X + 3(M–)

or Mo = X – 3(–M)

As Mo = X – 3(–M)

\ – Mo = 3(–M) that is why (– Mo) is replaced by 3(– M)

The Pearsonian coefficient of skewness has the interesting characteristic that it will be positive when the mean the mean is larger than the mode or median, and it will be negative when the arithmetic mean is smaller than the mode or median. In a symmetrical distribution, the value of Pearsonian coefficient of skewness will be zero. There is no theoretical limit to this measure, however, in practice the value given by this formula is rarely very high and usually lies between ±1, The direction of the skewness is given by the algebraic sign of the measure, i.e., if it is plus then the skewness is positive, if it is minus, the skewness is negative. The degree of skewness is obtained by the numerical figure such as .9, 0.4, etc. Thus this formula gives both the direction as well as the degree of skewness.

There is another relative measure of skewness also based on the position of averages. In this, the difference between two averages is divided by the mean deviation.

These formulae are not very much used in practice, because of demerits of mean deviation.

Example 1

Find out the coefficient of skewness for the following:

Wages (Rs.) :	4.5	5.5	6.5	7.5	8.5	9.5	10.5	11.5
No. of Men :	35	40	48	100	125	87	43	22

Solution

X	f	dx=(X–7.5)	fdx	fdx2
4.5	35	–3	–105	315
5.5	40	–2	–80	160
6.5	48	–1	–48	48
7.5	100	0	0	0
8.5	125	+1	+125	125
9.5	87	+2	+174	348
10.5	43	+3	+129	387
11.5	22	+4	+ 88	352
Total	500		+283	1735

Mo=8.5 (Because the highest frequency, i.e., 125, is for this measurement)

Moments

The term 'moment' in mechanics refers to the measure of a force with reference to its tendency to produce rotation. The strength of this tendency is dependent upon the amount of the force and the distance from the origin at which the force is applied. If on both the sides of the origin the force (amount of force x distance) are equal than there will be a balance. At a balanced position the positive product equals the negative product.

The term moment is used in statistics in a quite analogous sense. The class frequencies are looked upon as the forces and the deviations of the different values from the mean (or other point of origin) are taken as distances. In other words, in Statistics, moment is the mean of the first, second, third, fourth, etc., powers of deviations (d1, d2, d3, d4.....) of the different values from the arithmetic mean. The first moment about the mean is zero, because the mean is the centre of gravity of the distribution. It may be recalled here that while calculating mean deviation the algebraic signs (+, –) are ignored, but in computing the first moment these signs are taken into account, therefore it is always zero. The second moment about the mean is the variance or square of standard deviation (σ2).

Kurtosis

In probability theory and statistics, kurtosis is a measure of the shape of the probability distribution of a real-valued random variable. It is closely related to the fourth moment of a distribution (particularly, the fourthstandardized moment), similarly to how the mean, variance and skewness and related to the first, second and third moments of the distribution, respectively.

The exact interpretation is disputed. The "classical" interpretation, which applies only to symmetric distributions (those whose skewness is 0), is that kurtosis measures both the "peakedness" of the distribution and the heaviness of its tail. Various statisticians have proposed other interpretations, such as "lack of shoulders" (where the "shoulder" is defined vaguely as the area between the peak and the tail, or more specifically as the area about one standard deviation from the mean) or "bimodality". Balanda and MacGillivray assert that the standard definition of kurtosis "is a poor measure of the kurtosis, peakedness, or tail weight of a distribution" and instead propose to "define kurtosis vaguely as the location- and scale-free movement of probability mass from the shoulders of a distribution into its center and tails".

From a practical standpoint, it is probably most useful to think of kurtosis as specifically measuring the heaviness of the tail — i.e. the extent to which the distribution of the variable falls off relatively slowly near the extremes, or equivalently the propensity by which a random value in the distribution is likely to fall several standard deviations away from the mean. Heavy-tailed distributions are useful in a wide variety of contexts, e.g. for estimation that is robust to small errors in the model assumptions or to occasional erroneous data points. High-kurtosis distributions do generally have heavy tails, a fact that can be seen directly in the standard formula defining the kurtosis (see below). On the other hand, there are large numbers of exceptional cases where high kurtosis and sharp peaks do not correspond: For example, the pointy-peaked Laplace distribution has an excess kurtosis of 3, whereas the squat, round-peaked Student's t-distribution with degrees of freedomí = 4 has infinite kurtosis. Furthermore, it is not always intuitively obvious what "peakedness" means — particularly as distinguished from low variance.

As with the concept of skewness, there are different ways of defining kurtosis for a theoretical distribution and corresponding ways of estimating it from a sample from a population.

The historically most common measure of kurtosis, originating with Karl Pearson, is defined simply as the fourth standardized moment of the data or population. This standardizes each of the deviations from the mean into a dimensionless number indicating their size relative to thestandard deviation, and then averages their fourth power. Equivalently, each squared deviation is standardized relative to the variance, indicating the relative size compared with the variance, and then the square of these standardized values is averaged. Note that simply directly averaging each standardized squared deviation would produce 1, by the definition of variance. It is not too difficult, then, to see why kurtosis measures tail heaviness: The square of a number increases faster than the number itself when the number is bigger than 1, so the more data points there are whose standardized squared deviation is greater than 1, and the bigger this value is — i.e. the more points there are that fall more than one standard deviation from the mean, and especially that fall many standard deviations from the mean — the higher the kurtosis. This means that kurtosis directly means heavier tails, i.e. more of the variance is the result of infrequent extreme deviations, as opposed to frequent modestly sized deviations.

Terminology and examples

A high kurtosis distribution has longer, fatter tails, and often (but not always) a sharper peak. A low kurtosis distribution has shorter, thinner tails, and often (but not always) a more rounded peak.

Distributions with zero excess kurtosis are called mesokurtic, or mesokurtotic. The most prominent example of a mesokurtic distribution is the normal distribution family, regardless of the values of its parameters. A few other well-known distributions can be mesokurtic, depending on parameter values: for example the binomial distribution is mesokurtic for

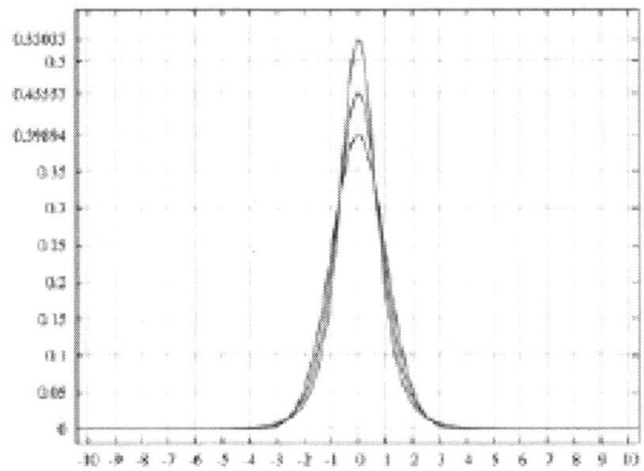

A distribution with positive excess kurtosis is called leptokurtic, or leptokurtotic. "Lepto-" means "slender", ostensibly referring to the peak. In terms of shape, however, a leptokurtic distribution has fatter tails and only sometimes a more acute peak. Examples of leptokurtic distributions include the Cauchy distribution, Student's t-distribution, Rayleigh distribution, Laplace distribution, exponential distribution,Poisson distribution and the logistic distribution. Such distributions are sometimes termed super Gaussian

A distribution with negative excess kurtosis is called platykurtic, or platykurtotic. "Platy-" means "broad" — again, ostensibly referring to the peak. In terms of shape, a platykurtic distribution has thinner tails and only sometimes a lower, wider peak around the mean. Examples of platykurtic distributions include the continuous or discrete uniform distributions, and the raised cosine distribution. The most platykurtic distribution of all is the Bernoulli distribution with p = ½ (for example the number of times one obtains "heads" when flipping a coin once, a coin toss), for which the excess kurtosis is "2. Such distributions are sometimes termed sub Gaussian.

Graphical examples

The Pearson type VII family

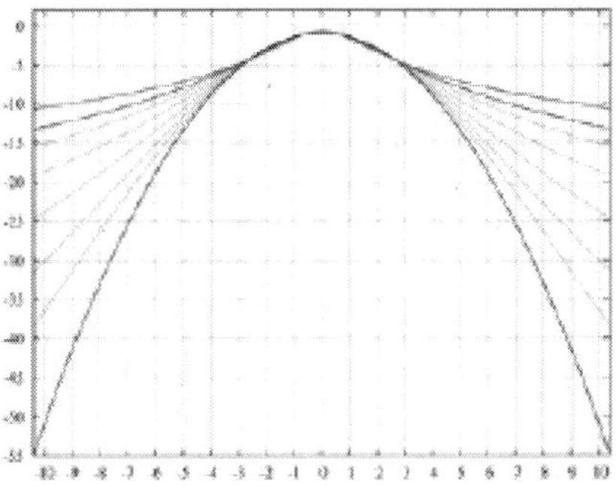

pdf for the Pearson type VII distribution with kurtosis of infinity (red); 2 (blue); and 0 (black)

$$f(x; a, m) = \frac{\Gamma(m)}{a\sqrt{\pi}\,\Gamma(m - 1/2)}\left[1 + \left(\frac{x}{a}\right)^2\right]^{-m},$$

log-pdf for the Pearson type VII distribution with kurtosis of infinity (red); 2 (blue); 1, 1/2, 1/4, 1/8, and 1/16 (gray); and 0 (black)

The effects of kurtosis are illustrated using a parametric family of distributions whose kurtosis can be adjusted while their lower-order moments and cumulants remain constant. Consider the Pearson type VII family, which is a special case of thePearson type IV family restricted to symmetric densities. The probability density function is given by

$$m = 5/2 + 3/\gamma_2$$

where a is a scale parameter and m is a shape parameter.

All densities in this family are symmetric. The kth moment exists providedm > (k + 1)/2. For the kurtosis to exist, we require m > 5/2. Then the mean andskewness exist and are both identically zero. Setting a2 = 2m " 3 makes the variance equal to unity. Then the only free parameter is m, which controls the fourth moment (and cumulant) and hence the kurtosis. One can reparameterize with γ_2, where $g(x;\gamma_2) = f(x;\ a = \sqrt{2 + 6/\gamma_2},\ m = 5/2 + 3/\gamma_2).$ is the kurtosis as defined above. This yields a one-parameter leptokurtic family with zero mean, unit variance, zero skewness, and arbitrary positive kurtosis. The reparameterized density is

$$\gamma_2 \to \infty$$

In the limit as $g(x) = 3\left(2 + x^2\right)^{-5/2}$ ' one obtains the density

$$\gamma_2 \to 0$$

which is shown as the red curve in the images on the right.

In the other direction as $x \mapsto g(x; 2)$ one obtains the standard normal density as the limiting distribution, shown as the black curve.

In the images on the right, the blue curve represents the density $\gamma_2 = \infty$ with kurtosis of 2. The top image shows that leptokurtic densities in this family have a higher peak than the mesokurtic normal density. The comparatively fatter tails of the leptokurtic densities are illustrated in the second image, which plots the natural logarithm of the Pearson type VII densities: the black curve is the logarithm of the standard normal density, which is a parabola. One can see that the normal density allocates little probability mass to the regions far from the mean ("has thin tails"), compared with the blue curve of the leptokurtic Pearson type VII density with kurtosis of 2. Between the blue curve and the black are other Pearson type VII densities with $\gamma 2 = 1, 1/2, 1/4, 1/8$, and $1/16$. The red curve again shows the upper limit of the Pearson type VII family, with

$$g_2 = \frac{m_4}{m_2^2} - 3 = \frac{\frac{1}{n}\sum_{i=1}^{n}(x_i - \overline{x})^4}{\left(\frac{1}{n}\sum_{i=1}^{n}(x_i - \overline{x})^2\right)^2} - 3$$

(which, strictly speaking, means that the fourth moment does not exist). The red curve decreases the slowest as one moves outward from the origin ("has fat tails").

Sample kurtosis

For a sample of n values the sample excess kurtosis is

$$\overline{x}$$

where m4 is the fourth sample moment about the mean, m2 is the second sample moment about the mean (that is, the sample variance), xiis the ith value, and

$$\frac{4[6n(n-1)^2(n+1)]}{(n-3)(n-2)(n+1)(n+3)(n+5)}$$

is the sample mean.

The variance of the sample kurtosis of a sample of size n from the normal distribution is

$$e_i = y_i - f(x_i; \hat{\beta}),$$

An approximate alternative is 24/n but this is inaccurate for small samples.

Measures of Kurtosis

The measure of kurtosis is done by 'Moment ratio', based upon second and fourth moments. Karl Pearson has given the following formulae for measure of kurtosis :

Measure of Kurtosis or $\beta 2$ (Beta-two) or $\alpha 4$ (alpha-four)

In a normal distribution $\beta 2$ will be equal to 3. If it is greater than 3, the curve is more peaked than normal, if less than 3, the curve is flatter at the top than normal.

Thus:

If $\beta 2 = 3$, the curve is normal or Mesokurtic,

If $\beta 2 > 3$, the curve is Leptokurtic or more peaked,

If $\beta 2 < 3$, the curve is Platykurtic or flat topped.

The measure of kurtosis is also represented by $\gamma 2$ (Greek letter gamma two) Therefore if :

$\gamma 2$ or $\beta 2 - 3 = 0$, the curve is Mesokurtic,

$\gamma 2$ is positive, the curve is Leptokurtic,

$\gamma 2$ is negative, the curve is Platykurtic.

Example 18

Find the measure of Kurtosis of the following distribution :

Age in years	No. of Employees	Age in years	No. of Employees
20–25	6	45–50	15
25–30	8	50–55	11
30–35	11	55–60	9
35–40	14	60–65	5
40–45	21		
	Total	100	

Solution

Class	Mid-valuem	f	A = 42.5/i=5	fd'	fd'2	fd'3	fd'4
20–25	22.5	6	–4	–24	96	–384	1536
25–30	27.5	8	–3	–24	72	–216	648
30–35	32.5	11	–2	–22	44	–88	176
35–40	37.5	14	–1	–14	14	–14	14
40–45	42.5	21	0	0	0	0	0
45–50	47.5	15	1	15	15	15	15
50–55	52.5	11	2	22	44	88	176
55–60	57.5	9	3	27	81	243	729
60–65	62.5	5	4	20	80	320	1280
Total		100		0	446	–36	4574

Kelly's Measure of Kurtosis

Kelly has given a measure of kurtosis based on percentiles. His formula is:

if , $\beta 2 > .26315$, the distribution is platykurtic.

$\beta 2 < .26315$, the distribution is leptokurtic.

Utility of Kurtosis. The measure of kurtosis is not of much use in economic and social studies, because in these a normal distribution usually out of question. But it has great importance in biological studies and studies relating to other physical science.

5

Data Collection

Data collection is the process of gathering and measuring information on variables of interest, in an established systematic fashion that enables one to answer stated research questions, test hypotheses, and evaluate outcomes. The data collection component of research is common to all fields of study including physical and social sciences, humanities, business, etc. While methods vary by discipline, the emphasis on ensuring accurate and honest collection remains the same. The goal for all data collection is to capture quality evidence that then translates to rich data analysis and allows the building of a convincing and credible answer to questions that have been posed.

Regardless of the field of study or preference for defining data (quantitative, qualitative), accurate data collection is essential to maintaining the integrity of research. Both the selection of appropriate data collection instruments (existing, modified, or newly developed) and clearly delineated instructions for their correct use reduce the likelihood of errors occurring.

A formal data collection process is necessary as it ensures that data gathered are both defined and accurate and that subsequent decisions based on arguments embodied in the findings are valid. The process provides both a baseline from which to measure and in certain cases a target on what to improve.

Consequences from improperly collected data include:

- Inability to answer research questions accurately.
- Inability to repeat and validate the study.

Distorted findings result in wasted resources and can mislead other researchers to pursue fruitless avenues of investigation. This compromises decisions for public policy, and causes harm to human participants and animal subjects.

While the degree of impact from faulty data collection may vary by discipline and the nature of investigation, there is the potential to cause disproportionate harm when these research results are used to support public policy recommendations.

Observational Study

In epidemiology and statistics, an observational study draws inferences about the possible effect of a treatment on subjects, where the assignment of subjects into a treated group versus a control group is outside the control of the investigator. This is in contrast with experiments, such as randomized controlled trials, where each subject is randomly assigned to a treated group or a control group.

The assignment of treatments may be beyond the control of the investigator for a variety of reasons:

A randomized experiment would violate ethical standards. Suppose one wanted to investigate the abortion - breast cancer hypothesis, which postulates a causal link between induced abortion and the incidence of breast cancer. In a hypothetical controlled experiment, one would start with a large subject pool of pregnant women and divide them randomly into a treatment group (receiving induced abortions) and a control group (bearing children), and then conduct regular cancer screenings for women from both groups. Needless to say, such an experiment would run counter to common ethical principles. (It would also suffer from various confounds and sources of bias, e.g., it would be impossible to conduct it as a blind experiment.) The published studies investigating the abortion-breast cancer hypothesis generally start with a group of women who already have received abortions. Membership in this "treated" group is not controlled by the investigator: the group is formed after the "treatment" has been assigned.

The investigator may simply lack the requisite influence. Suppose a scientist wants to study the public health effects of a community-wide ban on smoking in public indoor areas. In a controlled experiment, the investigator would randomly pick a set of communities to be in the treatment group. However, it is typically up to each community and/or its legislature to enact a smoking ban. The investigator can be expected to lack the political power to cause precisely those communities in the randomly selected treatment group to pass a smoking ban. In an observational study, the investigator would typically start with a treatment group consisting of those communities where a smoking ban is already in effect.

A randomized experiment may be impractical. Suppose a researcher wants to study the suspected link between a certain medication and a very rare group of symptoms arising as a side effect. Setting aside any ethical considerations, a randomized experiment would be impractical because of the rarity of the effect. There may not be a subject pool large enough for the symptoms to be observed in at least one treated subject. An observational study would typically start with a group of symptomatic subjects and work backwards to find those who were given the medication and later developed the symptoms. Thus a subset of the treated group was determined based on the presence of symptoms, instead of by random assignment.

Types of observational studies

Case-control study: study originally developed in epidemiology, in which two existing groups differing in outcome are identified and compared on the basis of some supposed causal attribute.

Cross-sectional study: involves data collection from a population, or a representative subset, at one specific point in time.

Longitudinal study: correlational research study that involves repeated observations of the same variables over long periods of time.

Cohort study or Panel study: a particular form of longitudinal study where a group of patients is closely monitored over a span of time.

Ecological study: an observational study in which at least one variable is measured at the group level.

Degree of usefulness and reliability

Although observational studies cannot be used as reliable sources to make statements of fact about the "safety, efficacy, or effectiveness" of a practice, they can still be of use for some other things:

"They can: 1) provide information on "real world" use and practice; 2) detect signals about the benefits and risks of...[the] use in the general population; 3) help formulate hypotheses to be tested in subsequent experiments; 4) provide part of the community-level data needed to design more informative pragmatic clinical trials; and 5) inform clinical practice."

Discussion

In all of those cases, if a randomized experiment cannot be carried out, the alternative line of investigation suffers from the problem that the decision of which subjects receive the treatment is not entirely random and thus is a potential source of bias. A major challenge in conducting observational studies is to draw inferences that are acceptably free from influences by overt biases, as well as to assess the influence of potential hidden biases.

An observer of an uncontrolled experiment (or process) records potential factors and the data output: the goal is to determine the effects of the factors. Sometimes the recorded factors may not be directly causing the differences in the output. There may be more important factors which were not recorded but are, in fact, causal. Also, recorded or unrecorded factors may be correlated which may yield incorrect conclusions. Finally, as the number of recorded factors increases, the likelihood increases that at least one of the recorded factors will be highly correlated with the data output simply by chance.

In lieu of experimental control, multivariate statistical techniques allow the approximation of experimental control with statistical control, which accounts for the influences of observed factors that might influence a cause-and-effect relationship. In healthcare and the social sciences, investigators may use matching to compare units that nonrandomly received the treatment and control. One common approach is to use propensity score matching in order to reduce confounding.

In 2007, several prominent medical researchers issued the Strengthening the reporting of observational studies in epidemiology (STROBE) statement, in which they called for observational studies to conform to 22 criteria that would make their conclusions easier to understand and generalise.

Simple Random Sample

In statistics, a simple random sample is a subset of individuals (a sample) chosen from a larger set (a population). Each individual is chosen randomly and entirely by chance, such that each individual has the same probability of being chosen at any stage during the sampling process, and each subset of k individuals has the same probability of being chosen for the sample as any other subset of k individuals. This process and technique is known as simple random sampling, and should not be confused with systematic random sampling. A simple random sample is an unbiased surveying technique.

Simple random sampling is a basic type of sampling, since it can be a component of other more complex sampling methods. The principle of simple random sampling is that every object has the same probability of being chosen. For example, suppose N college students want to get a ticket for a basketball game, but there are only X < N tickets for them, so they decide to have a fair way to see who gets to go. Then, everybody is given a number in the range from 0 to N-1, and random numbers are generated, either electronically or from a table of random numbers. Numbers outside the range from 0 to N-1 are ignored, as are any numbers previously selected. The first X numbers would identify the lucky ticket winners.

In small populations and often in large ones, such sampling is typically done "without replacement", i.e., one deliberately avoids choosing any member of the population more than once. Although simple random sampling can be conducted with replacement instead, this is less common and would normally be described more fully as simple random sampling with replacement. Sampling done without replacement is no longer independent, but still satisfies exchangeability, hence many results still hold. Further, for a small sample from a large population, sampling without replacement is approximately the same as sampling with replacement, since the odds of choosing the same individual twice is low.

An unbiased random selection of individuals is important so that if a large number of samples were drawn, the average sample would accurately represent the population. However, this does not guarantee that a particular sample is a perfect representation of the population. Simple random sampling merely allows one to draw externally valid conclusions about the entire population based on the sample. Conceptually, simple random sampling is the simplest of the probability sampling techniques. It requires a complete sampling frame, which may not be available or feasible to construct for large populations. Even if a complete frame is available, more efficient approaches may be possible if other useful information is available about the units in the population.

Advantages are that it is free of classification error, and it requires minimum advance knowledge of the population other than the frame. Its simplicity also makes it relatively easy to interpret data collected in this manner. For these reasons, simple random sampling best suits situations where not much information is available about the population and data collection can be efficiently conducted on randomly distributed items, or where the cost of sampling is small enough to make efficiency less important than simplicity. If these conditions do not hold, stratified sampling or cluster sampling may be a better choice.

Sampling a Dichotomous Population

If the members of the population come in two kinds, say "red" and "black", the number of red elements in a sample of given size will vary by sample and hence is a random variable whose distribution can be studied. That distribution depends on the numbers of red and black elements in the full population. For a simple random sample with replacement, the distribution is a binomial distribution. For a simple random sample without replacement, one obtains a hypergeometric distribution.

Bias in Sampling

In statistics, sampling bias is a bias in which a sample is collected in such a way that some members of the intended population are less likely to be included than others. It results in a biased sample, a non-random sample of a population (or non-human factors) in which all individuals, or instances, were not equally likely to have been selected. If this is not accounted for, results can be erroneously attributed to the phenomenon under study rather than to the method of sampling.

Medical sources sometimes refer to sampling bias as ascertainment bias. Ascertainment bias has basically the same definition, but is still sometimes classified as a separate type of bias.

Distinction from selection bias

Sampling bias is mostly classified as a subtype of selection bias, sometimes specifically termed sample selection bias, but some classify it as a separate type of bias. A distinction, albeit not universally accepted, of sampling bias is that it undermines the external validity of a test (the ability of its results to be generalized to the rest of the population), while selection bias mainly addresses internal validity for differences or similarities found in the sample at hand. In this sense, errors occurring in the process of gathering the sample or cohort cause sampling bias, while errors in any process thereafter cause selection bias.

However, selection bias and sampling bias are often used synonymously.

Types of sampling bias

Selection from a specific real area. For example, a survey of high school students to measure teenage use of illegal drugs will be a biased sample because it does not include home-schooled students or dropouts. A sample is also biased if certain members are underrepresented or overrepresented relative to others in the population. For example, a "man on the street" interview which selects people who walk by a certain location is going to have an overrepresentation of healthy individuals who are more likely to be out of the home than individuals with a chronic illness. This may be an extreme form of biased sampling, because certain members of the population are totally excluded from the sample (that is, they have zero probability of being selected).

Self-selection bias, which is possible whenever the group of people being studied has any form of control over whether to participate. Participants' decision to participate may be correlated with traits that affect the study, making the participants a non-representative sample. For example, people who have strong opinions or substantial knowledge may be more willing to spend time answering a survey than those who do not. Another example is online and phone-in polls, which are biased samples because the respondents are self-selected. Those individuals who are highly motivated to respond, typically individuals who have strong opinions, are overrepresented, and individuals that are indifferent or apathetic are less likely to respond. This often leads to a polarization of responses with extreme perspectives being given a disproportionate weight in the summary. As a result, these types of polls are regarded as unscientific.

Pre-screening of trial participants, or advertising for volunteers within particular groups. For example a study to "prove" that smoking does not affect fitness might recruit at the local fitness center, but advertise for smokers during the advanced aerobics class, and for non-smokers during the weight loss sessions.

Exclusion bias results from exclusion of particular groups from the sample, e.g. exclusion of subjects who have recently migrated into the study area (this may occur when newcomers are not available in a register used to identify the source population). Excluding subjects who move out of the study area during follow-up is rather equivalent of dropout or nonresponse, a selection bias in that it rather affects the internal validity of the study.

Healthy user bias, when the study population is likely healthier than the general population, e.g. workers (i.e. someone in ill-health is unlikely to have a job as manual laborer).

Overmatching, matching for an apparent confounder that actually is a result of the exposure. The control group becomes more similar to the cases in regard to exposure than the general population.

Symptom-based Sampling

The study of medical conditions begins with anecdotal reports. By their nature, such reports only include those referred for diagnosis and treatment. A child who can't function in school is more likely to be diagnosed with dyslexia than a child who struggles but passes. A child examined for one condition is more likely to be tested for and diagnosed with other conditions, skewing comorbidity statistics. As certain diagnoses become associated with behavior problems or intellectual disability, parents try to prevent their children from being stigmatized with those diagnoses, introducing further bias. Studies carefully selected from whole populations are showing that many conditions are much more common and usually much milder than formerly believed.

Truncate Selection in Pedigree Studies

Geneticists are limited in how they can obtain data from human populations. As an example, consider a human characteristic. We are interested in deciding if the characteristic is inherited as a simple Mendelian trait. Following the laws of Mendelian inheritance, if the parents in a family do not have the characteristic, but carry the allele for it, they are carriers (e.g. a non-expressive heterozygote). In this case their children will each have a 25% chance of showing the characteristic. The problem arises because we can't tell which families have both parents as carriers (heterozygous) unless they have a child who exhibits the characteristic. The description follows the textbook by Sutton.

The figure shows the pedigrees of all the possible families with two children when the parents are carriers (Aa).

- Nontruncate selection. In a perfect world we should be able to discover all such families with a gene including those who are simply carriers. In this situation the analysis would be free from ascertainment bias and the pedigrees would be under "nontruncate selection" In practice, most studies identify, and include, families in a study based upon them having affected individuals.
- Truncate selection. When afflicted individuals have an equal chance of being included in a study this is called truncate selection, signifying the inadvertent exclusion (truncation) of families who are carriers for a gene. Because selection is performed on the individual level, families with two or more affected children would have a higher probability of becoming included in the study.

- Complete truncate selection is a special case where each family with an affected child has an equal chance of being selected for the study.

The probabilities of each of the families being selected is given in the figure, with the sample frequency of affected children also given. In this simple case, the researcher will look for a frequency of ?7 or ?8 for the characteristic, depending on the type of truncate selection used.

The caveman effect

An example of selection bias is called the "caveman effect". Much of our understanding of prehistoric peoples comes from caves, such as cave paintings made nearly 40,000 years ago. If there had been contemporary paintings on trees, animal skins or hillsides, they would have been washed away long ago. Similarly, evidence of fire pits, middens, burial sites, etc. are most likely to remain intact to the modern era in caves. Prehistoric people are associated with caves because that is where the data still exists, not necessarily because most of them lived in caves for most of their lives.

Problems caused by sampling bias

A biased sample causes problems because any statistic computed from that sample has the potential to be consistently erroneous. The bias can lead to an over- or underrepresentation of the corresponding parameter in the population. Almost every sample in practice is biased because it is practically impossible to ensure a perfectly random sample. If the degree of underrepresentation is small, the sample can be treated as a reasonable approximation to a random sample. Also, if the group that is underrepresented does not differ markedly from the other groups in the quantity being measured, then a random sample can still be a reasonable approximation.

The word bias has a strong negative connotation. Indeed, biases sometimes come from deliberate intent to mislead or other scientific fraud. In statistical usage, bias merely represents a mathematical property, no matter if it is deliberate or either unconscious or due to imperfections in the instruments used for observation. While some individuals might deliberately use a biased sample to produce misleading results, more often, a biased sample is just a reflection of the difficulty in obtaining a truly representative sample.

Some samples use a biased statistical design which nevertheless allows the estimation of parameters. The U.S. National Center for Health Statistics, for example, deliberately oversamples from minority populations in many of its nationwide surveys in order to gain sufficient precision for estimates within these groups. These surveys require the use of sample weights to produce proper estimates across all ethnic groups. Provided that certain conditions are met (chiefly that the sample is drawn randomly from the entire sample) these samples permit accurate estimation of population parameters.

Historical examples

A classic example of a biased sample and the misleading results it produced occurred in 1936. In the early days of opinion polling, the American Literary Digest magazine collected over two million postal surveys and predicted that the Republican candidate in the U.S. presidential election, Alf Landon, would beat the incumbent president, Franklin Roosevelt, by a large margin. The result was the exact opposite. The Literary Digest survey represented a sample collected from readers of the magazine, supplemented by records of registered automobile owners and telephone users. This sample included an over-representation of individuals who were rich, who, as a group, were more likely to vote for the Republican candidate. In contrast, a poll of only 50 thousand citizens selected by George Gallup's organization successfully predicted the result, leading to the popularity of the Gallup poll.

Another classic example occurred in the 1948 presidential election. On election night, the Chicago Tribune printed the headline DEWEY DEFEATS TRUMAN, which turned out to be mistaken. In the morning the grinning president-elect, Harry S. Truman, was photographed holding a newspaper bearing this headline. The reason the Tribune was mistaken is that their editor trusted the results of a phone survey. Survey research was then in its infancy, and few academics realized that a sample of telephone users was not representative of the general population. Telephones were not yet widespread, and those who had them tended to be prosperous and have stable addresses. (In many cities, the Bell System telephone directory contained the same names as the Social Register.) In addition, the Gallup poll that the Tribune based its headline on was over two weeks old at the time of the printing.

Statistical corrections for a biased sample

If entire segments of the population are excluded from a sample, then there are no adjustments that can produce estimates that are representative of the entire population. But if some groups are underrepresented and the degree of underrepresentation can be quantified, then sample weights can correct the bias.

For example, a hypothetical population might include 10 million men and 10 million women. Suppose that a biased sample of 100 patients included 20 men and 80 women. A researcher could correct for this imbalance by attaching a weight of 2.5 for each male and 0.625 for each female. This would adjust any estimates to achieve the same expected value as a sample that included exactly 50 men and 50 women, unless men and women differed in their likelihood of taking part in the survey.

Design of experiments

In general usage, design of experiments (DOE) or experimental design is the design of any information-gathering exercises where variation is present, whether under the full control of the experimenter or not. However, in statistics, these terms are usually used for controlled experiments. Formal planned experimentation is often used in evaluating physical objects, chemical formulations, structures, components, and materials. Other types of study, and their design, are discussed in the articles on computer experiments, opinion polls and statistical surveys (which are types of observational study), natural experiments and quasi-experiments (for example, quasi-experimental design). See Experiment for the distinction between these types of experiments or studies.

In the design of experiments, the experimenter is often interested in the effect of some process or intervention (the "treatment") on some objects (the "experimental units"), which may be people, parts of people, groups of people, plants, animals, etc. Design of experiments is thus a discipline that has very broad application across all the natural and social sciences and engineering.

History of development

Controlled experimentation on scurvy

In 1747, while serving as surgeon on HMS Salisbury, James Lind carried out a controlled experiment to develop a cure for scurvy.

Lind selected 12 men from the ship, all suffering from scurvy. Lind limited his subjects to men who "were as similar as I could have them", that is he provided strict entry requirements to reduce extraneous variation. He divided them into six pairs, giving each pair different supplements to their basic diet for two weeks. The treatments were all remedies that had been proposed:

- A quart of cider every day
- Twenty five gutts (drops) of elixir vitriol (sulphuric acid) three times a day upon an empty stomach
- One half-pint of seawater every day
- A mixture of garlic, mustard, and horseradish in a lump the size of a nutmeg
- Two spoonfuls of vinegar three times a day
- Two oranges and one lemon every day

The men given citrus fruits recovered dramatically within a week. One of them returned to duty after six days, and the others cared for the rest. The other subjects experienced some improvement, but nothing compared to the subjects who ate the citrus fruits, which proved substantially superior to the other treatments.

Statistical experiments, following Charles S. Peirce

A theory of statistical inference was developed by Charles S. Peirce in "Illustrations of the Logic of Science" (1877-1878) and "A Theory of Probable Inference" (1883), two publications that emphasized the importance of randomization-based inference in statistics.

Randomized experiments

Charles S. Peirce randomly assigned volunteers to a blinded, repeated-measures design to evaluate their ability to discriminate weights. Peirce's experiment inspired other researchers in psychology and education, which developed a research tradition of randomized experiments in laboratories and specialized textbooks in the 1800s.

Optimal designs for regression models

Charles S. Peirce also contributed the first English-language publication on an optimal design for regression models in 1876. A pioneering optimal design for polynomial regression was suggested by Gergonne in 1815. In 1918 Kirstine Smith published optimal designs for polynomials of degree six (and less).

Sequences of experiments

The use of a sequence of experiments, where the design of each may depend on the results of previous experiments, including the possible decision to stop experimenting, is within the scope of Sequential analysis, a field that was pioneered by Abraham Wald in the context of sequential tests of statistical hypotheses. Herman Chernoff wrote an overview of optimal sequential designs, while adaptive designs have been surveyed by S. Zacks. One specific type of sequential design is the "two-armed bandit", generalized to the multi-armed bandit, on which early work was done by Herbert Robbins in 1952.

Principles of experimental design, following Ronald A. Fisher

A methodology for designing experiments was proposed by Ronald A. Fisher, in his innovative books: "The Arrangement of Field Experiments" (1926) and The Design of Experiments (1935). Much of his pioneering work dealt with agricultural applications of statistical methods. As a mundane example, he described how to test the hypothesis that a certain lady could distinguish by flavour alone whether the milk or the tea was first placed in the cup. These methods have been broadly adapted in the physical and social sciences, and are still used in agricultural engineering. The concepts presented here differ from the design and analysis of computer experiments.

Comparison

In some fields of study it is not possible to have independent measurements to a traceable standard. Comparisons between treatments are much more valuable and are usually preferable. Often one compares against a scientific control or traditional treatment that acts as baseline.

Randomization

Random assignment is the process of assigning individuals at random to groups or to different groups in an experiment. The random assignment of individuals to groups (or conditions within a group) distinguishes a rigorous, "true" experiment from an adequate, but less-than-rigorous, "quasi-experiment". There is an extensive body of mathematical theory that explores the consequences of making the allocation of units to treatments by means of some random mechanism such as tables of random numbers, or the use of randomization devices such as playing cards or dice. Provided the sample size is adequate, the risks associated with random allocation (such as failing to obtain a representative sample in a survey, or having a serious imbalance in a key characteristic between a treatment group and a control group) are calculable and hence can be managed down to an acceptable level. Random does not mean haphazard, and great care must be taken that appropriate random methods are used.

Replication

Measurements are usually subject to variation and uncertainty. Measurements are repeated and full experiments are replicated to help identify the sources of variation, to better estimate the true effects of treatments, to further strengthen the experiment's reliability and validity, and to add to the existing knowledge of the topic. However, certain conditions must be met before the replication of the experiment is commenced: the original research question has been published in a peer-reviewed journal or widely cited, the researcher is independent of the original experiment, the researcher must first try to replicate the original findings using the original data, and the write-up should state that the study conducted is a replication study that tried to follow the original study as strictly as possible.

Blocking

Blocking is the arrangement of experimental units into groups (blocks/lots) consisting of units that are similar to one another. Blocking reduces known but irrelevant sources of variation between units and thus allows greater precision in the estimation of the source of variation under study.

Orthogonality

Orthogonality concerns the forms of comparison (contrasts) that can be legitimately and efficiently carried out. Contrasts can be represented by vectors and sets of orthogonal contrasts are uncorrelated and independently distributed if the data are normal. Because of this independence, each orthogonal treatment provides different information to the others. If there are T treatments and T - 1 orthogonal contrasts, all the information that can be captured from the experiment is obtainable from the set of contrasts.

Factorial experiments

Use of factorial experiments instead of the one-factor-at-a-time method. These are efficient at evaluating the effects and possible interactions of several factors (independent variables). Analysis of experiment design is built on the foundation of the analysis of variance, a collection of models that partition the observed variance into components, according to what factors the experiment must estimate or test.

Discussion topics when setting up an experimental design

An experimental design or randomized clinical trial requires careful consideration of several factors before actually doing the experiment. An experimental design is the laying out of a detailed experimental plan in advance of doing the experiment. Some of the following topics have already been discussed in the principles of experimental design section:

1. How many factors does the design have? and are the levels of these factors fixed or random?
2. Are control conditions needed, and what should they be?
3. Manipulation checks; did the manipulation really work?
4. What are the background variables?
5. What is the sample size. How many units must be collected for the experiment to be generalisable and have enough power?
6. What is the relevance of interactions between factors?
7. What is the influence of delayed effects of substantive factors on outcomes?
8. How do response shifts affect self-report measures?
9. How feasible is repeated administration of the same measurement instruments to the same units at different occasions, with a post-test and follow-up tests?

10. What about using a proxy pretest?
11. Are there lurking variables?
12. Should the client/patient, researcher or even the analyst of the data be blind to conditions?
13. What is the feasibility of subsequent application of different conditions to the same units?
14. How many of each control and noise factors should be taken into account?

Statistical Control

It is best that a process be in reasonable statistical control prior to conducting designed experiments. When this is not possible, proper blocking, replication, and randomization allow for the careful conduct of designed experiments. To control for nuisance variables, researchers institute control checks as additional measures. Investigators should ensure that uncontrolled influences (e.g., source credibility perception) are measured do not skew the findings of the study. A manipulation check is one example of a control check. Manipulation checks allow investigators to isolate the chief variables to strengthen support that these variables are operating as planned.

One of the most important requirements of experimental research designs is the necessity of eliminating the effects of spurious, intervening, and antecedent variables. In the most basic model, cause (X) leads to effect (Y). But there could be a third variable (Z) that influences (Y), and X might not be the true cause at all. Z is said to be a spurious variable and must be controlled for. The same is true for intervening variables (a variable in between the supposed cause (X) and the effect (Y)), and anteceding variables (a variable prior to the supposed cause (X) that is the true cause). When a third variable is involved and has not been controlled for, the relation is said to be a zero order relationship. In most practical applications of experimental research designs there are several causes (X1, X2, X3). In most designs, only one of these causes is manipulated at a time.

Experimental designs after Fisher

Some efficient designs for estimating several main effects were found independently and in near succession by Raj Chandra Bose and K. Kishen in 1940 at the Indian Statistical Institute, but remained little known until the Plackett-Burman designs were published in Biometrika in 1946. About the same time, C. R. Rao introduced the concepts of orthogonal arrays as experimental designs. This concept played a central role in the development of Taguchi methods by Genichi Taguchi, which took place during his visit to Indian Statistical Institute in early 1950s. His methods were successfully applied and adopted by Japanese and Indian industries and subsequently were also embraced by US industry albeit with some reservations.

In 1950, Gertrude Mary Cox and William Gemmell Cochran published the book Experimental Designs, which became the major reference work on the design of experiments for statisticians for years afterwards.

Developments of the theory of linear models have encompassed and surpassed the cases that concerned early writers. Today, the theory rests on advanced topics in linear algebra, algebra and combinatorics.

As with other branches of statistics, experimental design is pursued using both frequentist and Bayesian approaches: In evaluating statistical procedures like experimental designs, frequentist statistics studies the sampling distribution while Bayesian statistics updates a probability distribution on the parameter space.

Human participant experimental design constraints

Laws and ethical considerations preclude some carefully designed experiments with human subjects. Legal constraints are dependent on jurisdiction. Constraints may involve institutional review boards, informed consent and confidentiality affecting both clinical (medical) trials and behavioral and social science experiments. In the field of toxicology, for example, experimentation is performed on laboratory animals with the goal of defining safe exposure limits for humans. Balancing the constraints are views from the medical field. Regarding the randomization of patients, "... if no one knows which therapy is better, there is no ethical imperative to use one therapy or another." Regarding experimental design, "... it is clearly not ethical to place subjects at risk to collect data in a poorly designed study when this situation can be easily avoided...".

6

Descriptive Statistics for Numerical Variables

Descriptive statistics is the discipline of quantitatively describing the main features of a collection of information, or the quantitative description itself. Descriptive statistics are distinguished from inferential statistics (or inductive statistics), in that descriptive statistics aim to summarize a sample, rather than use the data to learn about the population that the sample of data is thought to represent. This generally means that descriptive statistics, unlike inferential statistics, are not developed on the basis of probability theory. Even when a data analysis draws its main conclusions using inferential statistics, descriptive statistics are generally also presented. For example in a paper reporting on a study involving human subjects, there typically appears a table giving the overall sample size, sample sizes in important subgroups (e.g., for each treatment or exposure group), and demographic or clinical characteristics such as the average age, the proportion of subjects of each sex, and the proportion of subjects with related comorbidities.

Some measures that are commonly used to describe a data set are measures of central tendency and measures of variability or dispersion. Measures of central tendency include the mean, median and mode, while measures of variability include the standard deviation (or variance), the minimum and maximum values of the variables, kurtosis and skewness.

Use in Statistical Analysis

Descriptive statistics provides simple summaries about the sample and about the observations that have been made. Such summaries may be either quantitative, i.e. summary statistics, or visual, i.e. simple-to-understand graphs. These summaries may either form the basis of the initial description of the data as part of a more extensive statistical analysis, or they may be sufficient in and of themselves for a particular investigation.

For example, the shooting percentage in basketball is a descriptive statistic that summarizes the performance of a player or a team. This number is the number of shots made divided by the number of shots taken. For example, a player who shoots 33% is making approximately one shot in every three. The percentage summarizes or describes multiple discrete events. Consider also the grade point average. This single number describes the general performance of a student across the range of their course experiences.

The use of descriptive and summary statistics has an extensive history and, indeed, the simple tabulation of populations and of economic data was the first way the topic of statistics appeared. More recently, a collection of summarisation techniques has been formulated under the heading of exploratory data analysis: an example of such a technique is the box plot. In the business world, descriptive statistics provides a useful summary of many types of data. For example, investors and brokers may use a historical account of return behavior by performing empirical and analytical analyses on their investments in order to make better investing decisions in the future.

Univariate analysis

Univariate analysis involves describing the distribution of a single variable, including its central tendency (including the mean, median, and mode) and dispersion (including the range and quantiles of the data-set, and measures of spread such as the variance and standard deviation). The shape of the distribution may also be described via indices such as skewness and kurtosis. Characteristics of a variable's distribution may also be depicted in graphical or tabular format, including histograms and stem-and-leaf display.

Bivariate analysis

When a sample consists of more than one variable, descriptive statistics may be used to describe the relationship between pairs of variables. In this case, descriptive statistics include:

- Cross-tabulations and contingency tables
- Graphical representation via scatterplots
- Quantitative measures of dependence
- Descriptions of conditional distributions

The main reason for differentiating univariate and bivariate analysis is that bivariate analysis is not only simple descriptive analysis, but also it describes the relationship between two different variables. Quantitative measures of dependence include correlation (such as Pearson's r when both variables are continuous, or Spearman's rho if one or both are not) and covariance (which reflects the scale variables are measured on). The slope, in regression analysis, also reflects the relationship between variables. The unstandardised slope indicates the unit change in the criterion variable for a one unit change in the predictor. The standardised slope indicates this change in standardised (z-score) units. Highly skewed data are often transformed by taking logarithms. Use of logarithms makes graphs more symmetrical and look more similar to the normal distribution, making them easier to interpret intuitively. Central tendency

In statistics, a central tendency (or, more commonly, a measure of central tendency) is a central value or a typical value for a probability distribution. It is occasionally called an average or just the center of the distribution. The most common measures of central tendency are the arithmetic mean, the median and the mode. A central tendency can be calculated for either a finite set of values or for a theoretical distribution, such as the normal distribution. Occasionally authors use central tendency (or centrality), to mean "the tendency of quantitative data to cluster around some central value." This meaning might be expected from the usual dictionary definitions of the words tendency and centrality. Those authors may judge whether data has a strong or a weak central tendency based on the statistical dispersion, as measured by the standard deviation or something similar.

The term "central tendency" dates from the late 1920s.

Measures of Central Tendency

The following may be applied to one-dimensional data. Depending on the circumstances, it may be appropriate to transform the data before calculating a central tendency. Examples are squaring the values or taking logarithms. Whether a transformation is appropriate and what it should be depend heavily on the data being analyzed.

- Arithmetic mean (or simply, mean) – the sum of all measurements divided by the number of observations in the data set
- Median – the middle value that separates the higher half from the lower half of the data set. The median and the mode are the only measures of central tendency that can be used for ordinal data, in which values are ranked relative to each other but are not measured absolutely.
- Mode – the most frequent value in the data set. This is the only central tendency measure that can be used with nominal data, which have purely qualitative category assignments.
- Geometric mean – the *n*th root of the product of the data values, where there are *n* of these. This measure is valid only for data that are measured absolutely on a strictly positive scale.
- Harmonic mean – the reciprocal of the arithmetic mean of the reciprocals of the data values. This measure too is valid only for data that are measured absolutely on a strictly positive scale.
- Weighted mean – an arithmetic mean that incorporates weighting to certain data elements
- Truncated mean – the arithmetic mean of data values after a certain number or proportion of the highest and lowest data values have been discarded.
- Interquartile mean (a type of truncated mean)
- Midrange – the arithmetic mean of the maximum and minimum values of a data set.
- Midhinge – the arithmetic mean of the two quartiles.
- Trimean – the weighted arithmetic mean of the median and two quartiles.
- Winsorized mean – an arithmetic mean in which extreme values are replaced by values closer to the median.

Any of the above may be applied to each dimension of multi-dimensional data, but the results may not be invariant to rotations of the multi-dimensional space. In addition, there is the

- Geometric median - which minimizes the sum of distances to the data points. This is the same as the median when applied to one-dimensional data, but it is not the same as taking the median of each dimension independently. It is not invariant to different rescaling of the different dimensions.

The Quadratic mean (often known as the root mean square) is useful in engineering, but is not often used in statistics. This is because it is not a good indicator of the center of the distribution when the distribution includes negative values.

Solutions to Variational Problems

Several measures of central tendency can be characterized as solving a variational problem, in the sense of the calculus of variations, namely minimizing variation from the center. That is, given a measure of statistical dispersion, one asks for a measure of central tendency that minimizes variation: such that variation from the center is minimal among all choices of center. In a quip, "dispersion precedes location". In the sense of L spaces, the correspondence is:

Thus standard deviation about the mean is lower than standard deviation about any other point, and the maximum deviation about the midrange is lower than the maximum deviation about any other point. The uniqueness of this characterization of mean follows from convex optimization. Indeed, for a given (fixed) data set x, the function

$$f_2(c) = \|x - c\|_2$$

represents the dispersion about a constant value c relative to the L norm. Because the function $f2$ is a strictly convex coercive function, the minimizer exists and is unique.

Note that the median in this sense is not in general unique, and in fact any point between the two central points of a discrete distribution minimizes average absolute deviation. The dispersion in the L norm, given by

$$f_1(c) = \|x - c\|_1$$

is not strictly convex, whereas strict convexity is needed to ensure uniqueness of the minimizer. In spite of this, the minimizer is unique for the L norm.

Relationships between the mean, median and mode

For unimodal distributions the following bounds are known and are sharp:

$$\frac{|\theta - \mu|}{\sigma} \leq \sqrt{3},$$

$$\frac{|\nu - \mu|}{\sigma} \leq \sqrt{0.6},$$

$$\frac{|\theta - \nu|}{\sigma} \leq \sqrt{3},$$

where μ is the mean, v is the median, θ is the mode, and σ is the standard deviation.

For every distribution,

$$\frac{|\nu - \mu|}{\sigma} \leq 1.$$

Statistical dispersion

In statistics, dispersion (also called variability, scatter, or spread) denotes how stretched or squeezed is a distribution (theoretical or that underlying a statistical sample). Common examples of measures of statistical dispersion are the variance, standard deviation and interquartile range.

Dispersion is contrasted with location or central tendency, and together they are the most used properties of distributions.

Measures of statistical dispersion

A measure of statistical dispersion is a nonnegative real number that is zero if all the data are the same and increases as the data become more diverse.

Most measures of dispersion have the same units as the quantity being measured. In other words, if the measurements are in metres or seconds, so is the measure of dispersion. Such measures of dispersion include:

- Sample standard deviation
- Interquartile range (IQR) or Interdecile range
- Range
- Mean difference
- Median absolute deviation (MAD)
- Average absolute deviation (or simply called average deviation)
- Distance standard deviation

These are frequently used (together with scale factors) as estimators of scale parameters, in which capacity they are called estimates of scale. Robust measures of scale are those unaffected by a small number of outliers, and include the IQR and MAD.

All the above measures of statistical dispersion have the useful property that they are location-invariant, as well as linear in scale. So if a random variable X has a dispersion of SX then a linear transformation $Y = aX + b$ for real a and b should have dispersion $SY = |a|SX$.

Other measures of dispersion are **dimensionless**. In other words, they have no units even if the variable itself has units. These include:

- Coefficient of variation
- Quartile coefficient of dispersion
- Relative mean difference, equal to twice the Gini coefficient

There are other measures of dispersion:

- Variance (the square of the standard deviation) — location-invariant but not linear in scale.
- Variance-to-mean ratio — mostly used for count data when the term coefficient of dispersion is used and when this ratio is dimensionless, as count data are themselves dimensionless, not otherwise.

Some measures of dispersion have specialized purposes, among them the Allan variance and the Hadamard variance.

For categorical variables, it is less common to measure dispersion by a single number; see qualitative variation. One measure that does so is the discrete entropy.

Sources of statistical dispersion

In the physical sciences, such variability may result from random measurement errors: instrument measurements are often not perfectly precise, i.e., reproducible, and there is additional inter-rater variability in interpreting and reporting the measured results. One may assume that the quantity being measured is stable, and that the variation between measurements is due to observational error. A system of a large number of particles is characterized by the mean values of a relatively few number of macroscopic quantities such as temperature, energy, and density. The standard deviation is an important measure in Fluctuation theory, which explains many physical phenomena, including why the sky is blue.

In the biological sciences, the quantity being measured is seldom unchanging and stable, and the variation observed might additionally be *intrinsic* to the phenomenon: It may be due to *inter-individual variability*, that is, distinct members of a population differing from each other. Also, it may be due to *intra-individual variability*, that is, one and the same subject differing in tests taken at different times or in other differing conditions. Such types of variability are also seen in the arena of manufactured products; even there, the meticulous scientist finds variation.

In economics, finance, and other disciplines, regression analysis attempts to explain the dispersion of a dependent variable, generally measured by its variance, using one or more independent variables each of which itself has positive dispersion. The fraction of variance explained is called the coefficient of determination.

A partial ordering of dispersion

A mean-preserving spread (MPS) is a change from one probability distribution A to another probability distribution B, where B is formed by spreading out one or more portions of A's probability density function while leaving the mean (the expected value) unchanged. The concept of a mean-preserving spread provides a partial ordering of probability distributions according to their dispersions: of two probability distributions, one may be ranked as having more dispersion than the other, or alternatively neither may be ranked as having more dispersion.

Shape of the distribution

In statistics, the concept of the shape of the distribution refers to the shape of a probability distribution and it most often arises in questions of finding an appropriate distribution to use to model the statistical properties of a population, given a sample from that population. The shape of a distribution may be considered either descriptively, using terms such as "J-shaped", or numerically, using quantitative measures such as skewness and kurtosis.

Considerations of the shape of a distribution arise in statistical data analysis, where simple quantitative descriptive statistics and plotting techniques such as histograms can lead on to the selection of a particular family of distributions for modelling purposes.

Descriptions of shape

The shape of a distribution will fall somewhere in a continuum where a flat distribution might be considered central and where types of departure from this include: mounded (or unimodal), U-shaped, J-shaped, reverse-J shaped and multi-modal. A bimodal distribution would have two high points rather than one. The shape of a distribution is sometimes characterised by the behaviours of the tails (as in a long or short tail). For example a flat distribution can be said either to have no tails, or to have short tails. A normal distribution is usually regarded as having short tails, while an exponential distribution has exponential tails and a Pareto distribution has long tails.

7

Probability

Probability is a measure of the likeliness that an event will occur. Probability is used to quantify an attitude of mind towards some proposition of whose truth we are not certain. The proposition of interest is usually of the form "Will a specific event occur?" The attitude of mind is of the form "How certain are we that the event will occur?" The certainty we adopt can be described in terms of a numerical measure and this number, between 0 and 1 (where 0 indicates impossibility and 1 indicates certainty), we call probability. Thus the higher the probability of an event, the more certain we are that the event will occur. A simple example would be the toss of a fair coin. Since the 2 outcomes are deemed equiprobable, the probability of "heads" equals the probability of "tails" and each probability is 1/2 or equivalently a 50% chance of either "heads" or "tails".

These concepts have been given an axiomatic mathematical derivation in probability theory, which is used widely in such areas of study as mathematics, statistics, finance, gambling, science (in particular physics), artificial intelligence/machine learning, computer science, and philosophy to, for example, draw inferences about the expected frequency of events. Probability theory is also used to describe the underlying mechanics and regularities of complex systems.In some areas, such as mathematics or logic, results of some process can be known with certainty (e.g., 2+3=5). Most real life situations, however, involve variability and uncertainty. For example, it is uncertain whether it will rain tomorrow; the price of a given stock a week from today is uncertain Note_1 ; the number of claims that a car insurance policy holder will make over a one-year period is uncertain. Uncertainty or "randomness" (meaning variability of results) is usually due to some mixture of two factors: (1) variability in populations consisting of animate or inanimate objects (e.g., people vary in size, weight, blood type etc.), and (2) variability in processes or phenomena (e.g., the random selection of 6 numbers from 49 in a lottery draw can lead to a very large number of different outcomes; stock or currency prices fluctuate substantially over time).

Variability and uncertainty make it more difficult to plan or to make decisions. Although they cannot usually be eliminated, it is however possible to describe and to deal with variability and uncertainty, by using the theory of probability. This course develops both the theory and applications of probability.

Classical Definition

What does "equally likely" mean? This appears to use the concept of probability while trying to define it! We could remove the phrase "provided all outcomes are equally likely", but then the definition would clearly be unusable in many settings where the outcomes in S did not tend to occur equally often.

Relative Frequency Definition

Since we can never repeat an experiment or process indefinitely, we can never know the probability of any event from the relative frequency definition. In many cases we can't even obtain a long series of repetitions due to time, cost, or other limitations. For example, the probability of rain today can't really be obtained by the relative frequency definition since today can't be repeated again.

Interpretations

When dealing with experiments that are random and well-defined in a purely theoretical setting (like tossing a fair coin), probabilities describe the statistical number of outcomes considered divided by the number of all outcomes (tossing a fair coin twice will yield head-head with probability 1/4, because the four outcomes head-head, head-tails, tails-head and tails-tails are equally likely to occur). When it comes to practical application however there are two major competing categories of probability interpretations, whose adherents possess different views about the fundamental nature of probability:

1. Objectivists assign numbers to describe some objective or physical state of affairs. The most popular version of objective probability is frequentist probability, which claims that the probability of a random event denotes the *relative frequency of occurrence* of an experiment's outcome, when repeating the experiment. This interpretation considers probability to be the relative frequency "in the long run" of outcomes. A modification of this is propensity probability, which interprets probability as the tendency of some experiment to yield a certain outcome, even if it is performed only once.
2. Subjectivists assign numbers per subjective probability, i.e., as a degree of belief. The degree of belief has been interpreted as, "the price at which you would buy or sell a bet that pays 1 unit of utility if E, 0 if not E." The most popular version of subjective probability is Bayesian probability, which includes expert knowledge as well as experimental data to produce probabilities. The expert knowledge is represented by some (subjective) prior probability distribution. The data is incorporated in a likelihood function. The product of the prior and the likelihood, normalized, results in a posterior probability distribution that incorporates all the information known to date. Starting from arbitrary, subjective probabilities for a group of agents, some Bayesians claim that all agents will eventually have sufficiently similar assessments of probabilities, given enough evidence.

Etymology

The word *Probability* derives from the Latin *probabilitas*, which can also mean *probity*, a measure of the authority of a witness in a legal case in Europe, and often correlated with the witness's nobility. In a sense, this differs much from the modern meaning of *probability*, which, in contrast, is a measure of the weight of empirical evidence, and is arrived at from inductive reasoning and statistical inference.

History

The scientific study of probability is a modern development. Gambling shows that there has been an interest in quantifying the ideas of probability for millennia, but exact mathematical descriptions arose much later. There are reasons of course, for the slow development of the mathematics of probability. Whereas games of chance provided the impetus for the mathematical study of probability, fundamental issues are still obscured by the superstitions of gamblers.

According to Richard Jeffrey, "Before the middle of the seventeenth century, the term 'probable' (Latin *probabilis*) meant *approvable*, and was applied in that sense, univocally, to opinion and to action. A probable action or opinion was one such as sensible people would undertake or hold, in the circumstances." However, in legal contexts especially, 'probable' could also apply to propositions for which there was good evidence.

Aside from elementary work by Gerolamo Cardano in the 16th century, the doctrine of probabilities dates to the correspondence of Pierre de Fermat and Blaise Pascal (1654). Christiaan Huygens (1657) gave the earliest known scientific treatment of the subject. Jakob Bernoulli's *Ars Conjectandi* (posthumous, 1713) and Abraham de Moivre's *Doctrine of Chances* (1718) treated the subject as a branch of mathematics. See Ian Hacking's *The Emergence of Probability* and James Franklin's *The Science of Conjecture* for histories of the early development of the very concept of mathematical probability.

The theory of errors may be traced back to Roger Cotes's *Opera Miscellanea* (posthumous, 1722), but a memoir prepared by Thomas Simpson in 1755 (printed 1756) first applied the theory to the discussion of errors of observation. The reprint (1757) of this memoir lays down the axioms that positive and negative errors are equally probable, and that certain assignable limits define the range of all errors. Simpson also discusses continuous errors and describes a probability curve.

The first two laws of error that were proposed both originated with Pierre-Simon Laplace. The first law was published in 1774 and stated that the frequency of an error could be expressed as an exponential function of the numerical magnitude of the error, disregarding sign. The second law of error was proposed in 1778 by Laplace and stated that the frequency of the error is an exponential function of the square of the error. The second law of error is called the normal distribution or the Gauss law. "It is difficult historically to attribute that law to Gauss, who in spite of his well-known precocity had probably not made this discovery before he was two years old."

Daniel Bernoulli (1778) introduced the principle of the maximum product of the probabilities of a system of concurrent errors.

Adrien-Marie Legendre (1805) developed the method of least squares, and introduced it in his *Nouvelles méthodes pour la détermination des orbites des comètes* (*New Methods for Determining the Orbits of Comets*). In ignorance of Legendre's contribution, an Irish-American writer, Robert Adrain, editor of "The Analyst" (1808), first deduced the law of facility of error,

$$\phi(x) = ce^{-h^2 x^2},$$

where h is a constant depending on precision of observation, and c is a scale factor ensuring that the area under the curve equals 1. He gave two proofs, the second being essentially the same as John Herschel's (1850). Gauss gave the first proof that seems to have been known in Europe (the third after Adrain's) in 1809. Further proofs were given by Laplace (1810, 1812), Gauss (1823), James Ivory (1825, 1826), Hagen (1837), Friedrich Bessel (1838), W. F. Donkin (1844, 1856), and Morgan Crofton (1870). Other contributors were Ellis (1844),

De Morgan (1864), Glaisher (1872), and Giovanni Schiaparelli (1875). Peters's (1856) formula for *r*, the probable error of a single observation, is well known.

In the nineteenth century authors on the general theory included Laplace, Sylvestre Lacroix (1816), Littrow (1833), Adolphe Quetelet (1853), Richard Dedekind (1860), Helmert (1872), Hermann Laurent (1873), Liagre, Didion, and Karl Pearson. Augustus De Morgan and George Boole improved the exposition of the theory.

Andrey Markov introduced the notion of Markov chains (1906), which played an important role in stochastic processes theory and its applications. The modern theory of probability based on the measure theory was developed by Andrey Kolmogorov (1931).

On the geometric side contributors to *The Educational Times* were influential (Miller, Crofton, McColl, Wolstenholme, Watson, and Artemas Martin).

Theory

Like other theories, the theory of probability is a representation of probabilistic concepts in formal terms—that is, in terms that can be considered separately from their meaning. These formal terms are manipulated by the rules of mathematics and logic, and any results are interpreted or translated back into the problem domain.

There have been at least two successful attempts to formalize probability, namely the Kolmogorov formulation and the Cox formulation. In Kolmogorov's formulation, sets are interpreted as events and probability itself as a measure on a class of sets. In Cox's theorem, probability is taken as a primitive (that is, not further analyzed) and the emphasis is on constructing a consistent assignment of probability values to propositions. In both cases, the laws of probability are the same, except for technical details.

There are other methods for quantifying uncertainty, such as the Dempster–Shafer theory or possibility theory, but those are essentially different and not compatible with the laws of probability as usually understood.

Applications

Probability theory is applied in everyday life in risk assessment and in trade on financial markets. Governments apply probabilistic methods in environmental regulation, where it is called pathway analysis. A good example is the effect of the perceived probability of any widespread Middle East conflict on oil prices—which have ripple effects in the economy as a whole. An assessment by a commodity trader that a war is more likely vs. less likely sends prices up or down, and signals other traders of that opinion. Accordingly, the probabilities are neither assessed independently nor necessarily very rationally. The theory of behavioral finance emerged to describe the effect of such groupthink on pricing, on policy, and on peace and conflict.

The discovery of rigorous methods to assess and combine probability assessments has changed society. It is important for most citizens to understand how probability assessments are made, and how they contribute to decisions.

Another significant application of probability theory in everyday life is reliability. Many consumer products, such as automobiles and consumer electronics, use reliability theory in product design to reduce the probability of failure. Failure probability may influence a manufacturer's decisions on a product's warranty.

The cache language model and other statistical language models that are used in natural language processing are also examples of applications of probability theory.

Relation to Randomness

In a deterministic universe, based on Newtonian concepts, there would be no probability if all conditions were known (Laplace's demon), (but there are situations in which sensitivity to initial conditions exceeds our ability to measure them, i.e. know them). In the case of a roulette wheel, if the force of the hand and the period of that force are known, the number on which the ball will stop would be a certainty (though as a practical matter, this would likely be true only of a roulette wheel that had not been exactly levelled - as Thomas A. Bass' Newtonian Casino revealed). Of course, this also assumes knowledge of inertia and friction of the wheel, weight, smoothness and roundness of the ball, variations in hand speed during the turning and so forth. A probabilistic description can thus be more useful than Newtonian mechanics for analyzing the pattern of outcomes of repeated rolls of a roulette wheel. Physicists face the same situation in kinetic theory of gases, where the system, while deterministic in principle, is so complex (with the number of molecules typically the order of magnitude of Avogadro constant 6.02·10) that only a statistical description of its properties is feasible.

Probability theory is required to describe quantum phenomena. A revolutionary discovery of early 20th century physics was the random character of all physical processes that occur at sub-atomic scales and are governed by the laws of quantum mechanics. The objective wave function evolves deterministically but, according to the Copenhagen interpretation, it deals with probabilities of observing, the outcome being explained by a wave function collapse when an observation is made. However, the loss of determinism for the sake of instrumentalism did not meet with universal approval. Albert Einstein famously remarked in a letter to Max Born: "I am convinced that God does not play dice". Like Einstein, Erwin Schrödinger, who discovered the wave function, believed quantum mechanics is a statistical approximation of an underlying deterministic reality. In modern interpretations, quantum decoherence accounts for subjectively probabilistic behavior.

Subjective Probability

This definition gives no rational basis for people to agree on a right answer. There is some controversy about when, if ever, to use subjective probability except for personal decision-making. It will not be used in Stat 230.

These difficulties can be overcome by treating probability as a mathematical system defined by a set of axioms. In this case we do not worry about the numerical values of probabilities until we consider a specific application. This is consistent with the way that other branches of mathematics are defined and then used in specific applications (e.g., the way calculus and real-valued functions are used to model and describe the physics of gravity and motion).

The mathematical approach that we will develop and use in the remaining chapters assumes the following:

- probabilities are numbers between 0 and 1 that apply to outcomes, termed ``events",
- each event may or may not occur in a given setting.

Exercises:

1. Try to think of examples of probabilities you have encountered which might have been obtained by each of the three ``definitions".
2. Which definitions do you think could be used for obtaining the following probabilities?
3. You have a claim on your car insurance in the next year.
4. There is a meltdown at a nuclear power plant during the next 5 years.
5. A person's birthday is in April.
6. Give examples of how probability applies to each of the following areas.
    - o Lottery draws
    - o Auditing of expense items in a financial statement
    - o Disease transmission (e.g. measles, tuberculosis, STD's)
    - o Public opinion polls
7. Mathematical Probability Models

Sample Spaces and Probability

Consider some phenomenon or process which is repeatable, at least in theory, and suppose that certain events (outcomes) A1, A2, A3,... are defined. We will often term the phenomenon or process an "experiment" and refer to a single repetition of the experiment as a "trial". Then the probability of an event A, denoted $P(A)$, is a number between 0 and 1.

If probability is to be a useful mathematical concept, it should possess some other properties. For example, if our "experiment" consists of tossing a coin with two sides, Head and Tail, then we might wish to consider the events A_1 = "Head turns up" and A_2 = "Tail turns up". It would clearly not be desirable to allow, say, $P(A_1) = 0.6$ and $P(A_2) = 0.6$, so that $P(A_1) + P(A_2) > 1$. (Think about why this is so.) To avoid this sort of thing we begin with the following definition.

Definition

A sample space S is a set of distinct outcomes for an experiment or process, with the property that in a single trial, one and only one of these outcomes occurs. The outcomes that make up the sample space are called sample points.

A sample space is part of the probability model in a given setting. It is not necessarily unique, as the following example shows.

Example: Roll a 6-sided die, and define the events

$$a_i = \quad (i = 1,2,3,4,5,6)$$

Then we could take the sample space as $S = \{a_1, a_2, a_3, a_4, a_5, a_6\}$. However, we could also define events

E = even number turns up

O = odd number turns up

and take $S = \{E, O\}$. Both sample spaces satisfy the definition, and which one we use would depend on what we wanted to use the probability model for. In most cases we would use the first sample space.

Sample spaces may be either discrete or non-discrete; S is discrete if it consists of a finite or countably infinite set of simple events. The two sample spaces in the preceding example are discrete. A sample space $S = \{1, 2, 3, \ldots\}$ consisting of all the positive integers is also, for example, discrete, but a sample space $S = \{x : x > 0\}$ consisting of all positive real numbers is not. For the next few chapters we consider only discrete sample spaces. This makes it easier to define mathematical probability, as follows.

Definition

Let $S = \{a_1, a_2, a_3, \ldots\}$ be a discrete sample space. Then probabilities $P(a_i)$ are numbers attached to the a_i's $(i = 1, 2, 3, \ldots)$ such that the following two conditions hold:

1. $0 \leq P(a_i) \leq 1$
2. $\sum_i P(a_i) = 1$

The set of values $\{P(a_i),\ i = 1, 2, \ldots\}$ is called a probability distribution on *S*.

Definition

An event in a discrete sample space is a subset $A \subset S$. If the event contains only one point, e.g. $A_1 = \{a_1\}$ we call it a simple event. An event A made up of two or more simple events such as $A = \{a_1, a_2\}$ is called a compound event.

Our notation will often not distinguish between the point a_i and the simple event $A_i = \{a_i\}$ which has this point as its only element, although they differ as mathematical objects. The condition (2) in the definition above reflects the idea that when the process or experiment happens, some event in must occur. The probability of a more general event (not necessarily a simple event) is then defined as follows:

Definition

The probability $P(A)$ of an event A is the sum of the probabilities for all the simple events that make up .

For example, the probability of the compound event $A = \{a_1, a_2, a_3\} = P(a_1) + P(a_2) + P(a_3)$. The definition of probability does not say what numbers to assign to the simple events for a given setting, only what properties the numbers must possess. In an actual situation, we try to specify numerical values that make the model useful; this usually means that we try to specify numbers that are consistent with one or more of the empirical "definitions" of Chapter 1.

Example: Suppose a 6-sided die is rolled, and let the sample space be $S = \{1,2,3,4,5,6\}$, where 1 means the number 1 occurs, and so on. If the die is an ordinary one, we would find it useful to define probabilities as $P(i) = 1/6 \quad i = 1,2,3,4,5,6,$ because if the die were tossed repeatedly (as in some games or gambling situations) then each number would occur close to $1/6$ of the time. However, if the die were weighted in some way, these numerical values would not be so useful.

Note that if we wish to consider some compound event, the probability is easily obtained. For example, if A = "even number" then because $A = \{2,4,6\}$ we get $P(A) = P(2) + P(4) + P(6) = 1/2$.

We now consider some additional examples, starting with some simple "toy" problems involving cards, coins and dice and then considering a more scientific example.

Remember that in using probability we are actually constructing mathematical models. We can approach a given problem by a series of three steps:

1. Specify a sample space S.
2. Assign numerical probabilities to the simple events in .
3. For any compound event , find by adding the probabilities of all the simple events that make up .

Many probability problems are stated as "Find the probability that ...". To solve the problem you should then carry out step (2) above by assigning probabilities that reflect long run relative frequencies of occurrence of the simple events in repeated trials, if possible.

Some Examples

When S has few points, one of the easiest methods for finding the probability of an event is to list all outcomes. In many problems a sample space with equally probable simple events can be used, and the first few examples are of this type.

Example: Draw 1 card from a standard well-shuffled deck (13 cards of each of 4 suits - spades, hearts, diamonds, clubs). Find the probability the card is a club.

Solution 1: Let S = { spade, heart, diamond, club}. (The points of are generally listed between brackets {}.) Then has 4 points, with 1 of them being "club", so (club) = .

Solution 2: Let = {each of the 52 cards}. Then 13 of the 52 cards are clubs, so

Note 1: A sample space is not necessarily unique, as mentioned earlier. The two solutions illustrate this. Note that in the first solution the event A = "the card is a club" is a simple event, but in the second it is a compound event.

Note 2: In solving the problem we have assumed that each simple event in S is equally probable. For example in Solution 1 each simple event has probability $1/4$. This seems to be the only sensible choice of numerical value in this setting. (Why?)

Note 3: The term "odds" is sometimes used. The odds of an event is the probability it occurs divided by the probability it does not occur. In this card example the odds in favour of clubs are 1:3; we could also say the odds against clubs are 3:1.

Example: Toss a coin twice. Find the probability of getting 1 head. (In this course, 1 head is taken to mean **exactly** 1 head. If we meant at least 1 head we would say so.)

Solution 1: Let $S = \{HH, HT, TH, TT\}$ and assume the simple events each have probability $\frac{1}{4}$. (If your notation is not obvious, please explain it. For example, HT means head on the 1st toss and tails on the 2nd.) Since 1 head occurs for simple events and , we get (1 head) = $\frac{2}{4} = \frac{1}{2}$

Solution 2: Let S = { 0 heads, 1 head, 2 heads } and assume the simple events each have probability $\frac{1}{3}$. Then P(1 head) = $\frac{1}{3}$.

Which solution is right? Both are mathematically "correct". However, we want a solution that is useful in terms of the probabilities of events reflecting their relative frequency of occurrence in repeated trials. In that sense, the points in solution 2 are not equally likely. The outcome 1 head occurs more often than either 0 or 2 heads in actual repeated trials. You can experiment to verify this (for example of the nine replications of the experiment in Figure coins, 2 heads occurred 2 of the nine times, 1 head occurred 6 of the 9 times. For more certainty you should replicate this experiment many times. You can do this without benefit of coin at http://shazam.econ.ubc.ca/flip/index.html). So we say solution 2 is incorrect for ordinary physical coins though a better term might be "incorrect model". If we were determined to use the sample space in solution 2, we could do it by assigning appropriate probabilities to each point. From solution 1, we can see that 0 heads would have a probability of $\frac{1}{4}$, 1 head $\frac{1}{2}$, and 2 heads . However, there seems to be little point using a sample space whose points are not equally probable when one with equally probable points is readily available.

Example: Roll a red die and a green die. Find the probability the total is 5.

Solution: Let (x, y) represent getting x on the red die and y on the green die.

Then, with these as simple events, the sample space is

$$S = \{ \begin{array}{cccccc} (1,1) & (1,2) & (1,3) & \cdots & (1,6) \\ (2,1) & (2,2) & (2,3) & \cdots & (2,6) \\ (3,1) & (3,2) & (3,3) & \cdots & (3,6) \\ & -- & -- & -- & \\ (6,1) & (6,2) & (6,3) & \cdots & (6,6)\} \end{array}$$

The sample points giving a total of 5 are (1,4) (2,3) (3,2), and (4,1).

Therefore P(total is 5) = $\frac{4}{36}$

Example: Suppose the 2 dice were now identical red dice. Find the probability the total is 5.

Solution 1: Since we can no longer distinguish between (x,y) and (y,x), the only distinguishable points in S are :

$$S = \{ \begin{array}{ccccc} (1,1) & (1,2) & (1,3) & \cdots & (1,6) \\ & (2,2) & (2,3) & \cdots & (2,6) \\ & & (3,3) & \cdots & (3,6) \\ & & & .. & .. \\ & & & & (6,6)\} \end{array}$$

Using this sample space, we get a total of 5 from points $(1,4)$ and $(2,3)$ only. If we assign equal probability $\frac{1}{21}$ to each point (simple event) then we get P(total is 5) = $\frac{2}{21}$.

At this point you should be suspicious since $\frac{2}{21} \neq \frac{4}{36}$. The colour of the dice shouldn't have any effect on what total we get, so this answer must be wrong. The problem is that the 21 points in S here are not equally likely. If this experiment is repeated, the point (1, 2) occurs twice as often in the long run as the point (1,1). The only sensible way to use this sample space would be to assign probability weights $\frac{1}{36}$ to the points (x,x) and $\frac{2}{36}$ to the points (x,y) for $x \neq y$. Of course we can compare these probabilities with experimental evidence. On the website http://www.math.duke.edu/education/postcalc/probability/dice/index.html you may throw dice up to 10,000 times and record the results. For example on 1000 throws of two dice (see Figure 2dice), there were 121 occasions when the sum of the values on the dice was 5, indicating the probability is around 121/1000 or 0.121 This compares with the true probability

Solution 2: Pretend the dice can be distinguished even though they can't. (Imagine, for example, that we put a white dot on one die, or label one of them 1 and the other as 2.) We then get the same 36 sample points as in the example with the red die and the green die. Hence $P(\text{total is } 5) = \frac{4}{36}$ But, you argue, the dice were identical, and you cannot distinguish them! The laws determining the probabilities associated with these two dice do not, of course, know whether your eyesight is so keen that you can or cannot distinguish the dice. These probabilities must be the same in either case. In many cases, when objects are indistinguishable and we are interested in calculating a probability, the calculation is made easier by pretending the objects can be distinguished.

This illustrates a common pitfall in using probability. When treating objects in an experiment as distinguishable leads to a different answer from treating them as identical, the points in the sample space for identical objects are usually not "equally likely" in terms of their long run relative frequencies. It is generally safer to pretend objects can be distinguished even when they can't be, in order to get equally likely sample points.

While the method of finding probability by listing all the points in S can be useful, it isn't practical when there are a lot of points to write out (e.g., if 3 dice were tossed there would be 216 points in). We need to have more efficient ways of figuring out the number of outcomes in or in a compound event without having to list them all. Chapter 3 considers ways to do this, and then Chapter 4 develops other ways to manipulate and calculate probabilities.

To conclude this chapter, we remark that in some settings we rely on previous repetitions of an experiment, or on scientific data, to assign numerical probabilities to events. Problems 2.6 and 2.7 below illustrate this. Although we often use "toy" problems involving things such as coins, dice and simple games for examples, probability is used to deal with a huge variety of practical problems. Problems 2.6 and 2.7, and many others to be discussed later, are of this type.

8

Probability Distributions

In probability and statistics, a probability distribution assigns a probability to each measurable subset of the possible outcomes of a random experiment, survey, or procedure of statistical inference. Examples are found in experiments whose sample space is non-numerical, where the distribution would be a categorical distribution; experiments whose sample space is encoded by discrete random variables, where the distribution can be specified by a probability mass function; and experiments with sample spaces encoded by continuous random variables, where the distribution can be specified by a probability density function. More complex experiments, such as those involving stochastic processes defined in continuous time, may demand the use of more general probability measures.

In applied probability, a probability distribution can be specified in a number of different ways, often chosen for mathematical convenience:

- by supplying a valid probability mass function or probability density function
- by supplying a valid cumulative distribution function or survival function
- by supplying a valid hazard function
- by supplying a valid characteristic function
- by supplying a rule for constructing a new random variable from other random variables whose joint probability distribution is known.

A probability distribution can either be univariate or multivariate. A univariate distribution gives the probabilities of a single random variable taking on various alternative values; a multivariate distribution (a joint probability distribution) gives the probabilities of a random vector—a set of two or more random variables—taking on various combinations of values. Important and commonly encountered univariate probability distributions include the binomial distribution, the hypergeometric distribution, and the normal distribution. The multivariate normal distribution is a commonly encountered multivariate distribution.

Introduction

To define probability distributions for the simplest cases, one needs to distinguish between discrete and continuous random variables. In the discrete case, one can easily assign a probability to each possible value: for example, when throwing a fair die, each of the six values *1* to *6* has the probability 1/6. In contrast, when a random variable takes values from a continuum, probabilities can be nonzero only if they refer to intervals: in quality control one might demand that the probability of a "500 g" package containing between 490 g and 510 g should be no less than 98%.

If the random variable is real-valued (or more generally, if a total order is defined for its possible values), the cumulative distribution function (CDF) gives the probability that the random variable is no larger than a given value; in the real-valued case, the CDF is the integral of the probability density function (pdf) provided that this function exists.

Terminology

As probability theory is used in quite diverse applications, terminology is not uniform and sometimes confusing. The following terms are used for non-cumulative probability distribution functions:

- Probability mass, Probability mass function, p.m.f.: for discrete random variables.
- Categorical distribution: for discrete random variables with a finite set of values.
- Probability density, Probability density function, p.d.f: most often reserved for continuous random variables.

The following terms are somewhat ambiguous as they can refer to non-cumulative or cumulative distributions, depending on authors' preferences:

- Probability distribution function: continuous or discrete, non-cumulative or cumulative.
- Probability function: even more ambiguous, can mean any of the above or other things.

Finally

- Probability distribution: sometimes the same as probability distribution function, but usually refers to the more complete assignment of probabilities to all measurable subsets of outcomes, not just to specific outcomes or ranges of outcomes.

Basic terms

- Mode: for a discrete random variable, the value with highest probability (the location at which the probability mass function has its peak); for a continuous random variable, the location at which the probability density function has its peak.
- Support: the smallest closed set whose complement has probability zero.
- Head: the range of values where the pmf or pdf is relatively high.
- Tail: the complement of the head within the support; the large set of values where the pmf or pdf is relatively low.
- Expected value or mean: the weighted average of the possible values, using their probabilities as their weights; or the continuous analog thereof.
- Median: the value such that the set of values less than the median has a probability of one-half.
- Variance: the second moment of the pmf or pdf about the mean; an important measure of the dispersion of the distribution.
- Standard deviation: the square root of the variance, and hence another measure of dispersion.
- Symmetry: a property of some distributions in which the portion of the distribution to the left of a specific value is a mirror image of the portion to its right.
- Skewness: a measure of the extent to which a pmf or pdf "leans" to one side of its mean.

Cumulative distribution function

Because a probability distribution Pr on the real line is determined by the probability of a scalar random variable *X* being in a half-open interval (-", *x*], the probability distribution is completely characterized by its cumulative distribution function:

$$F(x) = \Pr[X \leq x] \qquad \text{for all } x \in \mathbb{R}.$$

Discrete probability distribution

A discrete probability distribution shall be understood as a *probability distribution* characterized by a probability mass function. Thus, the distribution of a random variable *X* is discrete, and *X* is then called a discrete random variable, if

$$\sum_u \Pr(X = u) = 1$$

as *u* runs through the set of all possible values of *X*. It follows that such a random variable can assume only a finite or countably infinite number of values. For the number of potential values to be countably infinite even though their probabilities sum to 1 requires that the probabilities decline to zero fast enough: for example, if $\Pr(X = n) = \frac{1}{2^n}$ for $n =$ 1, 2, ..., we have the sum of probabilities 1/2 + 1/4 + 1/8 + ... = 1.

Among the most well-known discrete probability distributions that are used for statistical modeling are the Poisson distribution, the Bernoulli distribution, the binomial distribution, the geometric distribution, and the negative binomial distribution. In addition, the discrete uniform distribution is commonly used in computer programs that make equal-probability random selections between a number of choices.

Cumulative density

Equivalently to the above, a discrete random variable can be defined as a random variable whose cumulative distribution function (cdf) increases only by jump discontinuities—that is, its cdf increases only where it "jumps" to a higher value, and is constant between those jumps. The points where jumps occur are precisely the values which the random variable may take.

Delta-function representation

Consequently, a discrete probability distribution is often represented as a generalized probability density function involving Dirac delta functions, which substantially unifies the treatment of continuous and discrete distributions. This is especially useful when dealing with probability distributions involving both a continuous and a discrete part.

Indicator-function representation

For a discrete random variable *X*, let *u*0, *u*1, ... be the values it can take with non-zero probability. Denote

$$\Omega_i = \{\omega : X(\omega) = u_i\},\ i = 0, 1, 2, \dots$$

These are disjoint sets, and by formula (1)

$$\Pr\left(\bigcup_i \Omega_i\right) = \sum_i \Pr(\Omega_i) = \sum_i \Pr(X = u_i) = 1.$$

It follows that the probability that *X* takes any value except for *u*0, *u*1, ... is zero, and thus one can write *X* as

$$X = \sum_i u_i 1_{\Omega_i}$$

except on a set of probability zero, where 1_A is the indicator function of *A*. This may serve as an alternative definition of discrete random variables.

Continuous probability distribution

A continuous probability distribution is a *probability distribution* that has a probability density function. Mathematicians also call such a distribution absolutely continuous, since its cumulative distribution function is absolutely continuous with respect to the Lebesgue measure λ. If the distribution of *X* is continuous, then *X* is called a continuous random variable. There are many examples of continuous probability distributions: normal, uniform, chi-squared, and others.

Intuitively, a continuous random variable is the one which can take a continuous range of values — as opposed to a discrete distribution, where the set of possible values for the random variable is at most countable. While for a discrete distribution an event with probability zero is impossible (e.g. rolling 3½ on a standard die is impossible, and has probability zero), this is not so in the case of a continuous random variable. For example, if one measures the width of an oak leaf, the result of 3½ cm is possible, however it has probability zero because there are uncountably many other potential values even between 3 cm and 4 cm. Each of these individual outcomes has probability zero, yet the probability that the outcome will fall into the interval (3 cm, 4 cm) is nonzero. This apparent paradox is resolved by the fact that the probability that *X* attains some value within an infinite set, such as an interval, cannot be found by naively adding the probabilities for individual values. Formally, each value has an infinitesimally small probability, which statistically is equivalent to zero.

Formally, if *X* is a continuous random variable, then it has a probability density function *f*(*x*), and therefore its probability of falling into a given interval, say [*a*, *b*] is given by the integral

$$\Pr[a \leq X \leq b] = \int_a^b f(x)\,dx$$

In particular, the probability for *X* to take any single value *a* (that is *a* d" *X* d" *a*) is zero, because an integral with coinciding upper and lower limits is always equal to zero.

The definition states that a continuous probability distribution must possess a density, or equivalently, its cumulative distribution function be absolutely continuous. This requirement is stronger than simple continuity of the cumulative distribution function, and there is a special class of distributions, singular distributions, which are neither continuous nor discrete nor a mixture of those. An example is given by the Cantor distribution. Such singular distributions however are never encountered in practice.

Note on terminology: some authors use the term "continuous distribution" to denote the distribution with continuous cumulative distribution function. Thus, their definition includes both the (absolutely) continuous and singular distributions.

By one convention, a probability distribution μ is called *continuous* if its cumulative distribution function $F(x) = \mu(-\infty, x]$ is continuous and, therefore, the probability measure of singletons $\mu\{x\} = 0$ for all x. Another convention reserves the term *continuous probability distribution* for absolutely continuous distributions. These distributions can be characterized by a probability density function: a non-negative Lebesgue integrable function f defined on the real numbers such that

$$F(x) = \mu(-\infty, x] = \int_{-\infty}^{x} f(t)\, dt.$$

Discrete distributions and some continuous distributions (like the Cantor distribution) do not admit such a density.

Some properties

- The probability distribution of the sum of two independent random variables is the convolution of each of their distributions.
- Probability distributions are not a vector space—they are not closed under linear combinations, as these do not preserve non-negativity or total integral 1—but they are closed under convex combination, thus forming a convex subset of the space of functions (or measures).

Kolmogorov definition

In the measure-theoretic formalization of probability theory, a random variable is defined as a measurable function *X* from a probability space $(\Omega, \mathcal{F}, P)$ to measurable space $(\mathcal{X}, \mathcal{A})$. A probability distribution is the pushforward measure, P, satisfying *X**P = P*X* on .

Random number generation

A frequent problem in statistical simulations (the Monte Carlo method) is the generation of pseudo-random numbers that are distributed in a given way. Most algorithms are based on a pseudorandom number generator that produces numbers *X* that are uniformly distributed in the interval [0,1). These random variates *X* are then transformed via some algorithm to create a new random variate having the required probability distribution.

Applications

The concept of the probability distribution and the random variables which they describe underlies the mathematical discipline of probability theory, and the science of statistics. There is spread or variability in almost any value that can be measured in a population (e.g. height of people, durability of a metal, sales growth, traffic flow, etc.); almost all measurements are made with some intrinsic error; in physics many processes are described probabilistically, from the kinetic properties of gases to the quantum mechanical description of fundamental particles. For these and many other reasons, simple numbers are often inadequate for describing a quantity, while probability distributions are often more appropriate.

As a more specific example of an application, the cache language models and other statistical language models used in natural language processing to assign probabilities to the occurrence of particular words and word sequences do so by means of probability distributions.

Common Probability Distributions

The following is a list of some of the most common probability distributions, grouped by the type of process that they are related to. For a more complete list, see list of probability distributions, which groups by the nature of the outcome being considered (discrete, continuous, multivariate, etc.)

Note also that all of the univariate distributions below are singly peaked; that is, it is assumed that the values cluster around a single point. In practice, actually observed quantities may cluster around multiple values. Such quantities can be modeled using a mixture distribution.

Related to real-valued quantities that grow linearly (e.g. errors, offsets)

- Normal distribution (Gaussian distribution), for a single such quantity; the most common continuous distribution

Related to positive real-valued quantities that grow exponentially (e.g. prices, incomes, populations):

- Log-normal distribution, for a single such quantity whose log is normally distributed
- Pareto distribution, for a single such quantity whose log is exponentially distributed; the prototypical power law distribution.

Related to real-valued quantities that are assumed to be uniformly distributed over a (possibly unknown) region

- Discrete uniform distribution, for a finite set of values (e.g. the outcome of a fair die)
- Continuous uniform distribution, for continuously distributed values

Related to Bernoulli trials (yes/no events, with a given probability)

- Basic distributions:
  - Bernoulli distribution, for the outcome of a single Bernoulli trial (e.g. success/failure, yes/no)
  - Binomial distribution, for the number of "positive occurrences" (e.g. successes, yes votes, etc.) given a fixed total number of independent occurrences
  - Negative binomial distribution, for binomial-type observations but where the quantity of interest is the number of failures before a given number of successes occurs
  - Geometric distribution, for binomial-type observations but where the quantity of interest is the number of failures before the first success; a special case of the negative binomial distribution
- Related to sampling schemes over a finite population:
  - Hypergeometric distribution, for the number of "positive occurrences" (e.g. successes, yes votes, etc.) given a fixed number of total occurrences, using sampling without replacement

  - Beta-binomial distribution, for the number of "positive occurrences" (e.g. successes, yes votes, etc.) given a fixed number of total occurrences, sampling using a Polya urn scheme (in some sense, the "opposite" of sampling without replacement)

Related to categorical outcomes (events with K possible outcomes, with a given probability for each outcome)

- Categorical distribution, for a single categorical outcome (e.g. yes/no/maybe in a survey); a generalization of the Bernoulli distribution
- Multinomial distribution, for the number of each type of categorical outcome, given a fixed number of total outcomes; a generalization of the binomial distribution
- Multivariate hypergeometric distribution, similar to the multinomial distribution, but using sampling without replacement; a generalization of the hypergeometric distribution

Related to events in a Poisson process (events that occur independently with a given rate)

- Poisson distribution, for the number of occurrences of a Poisson-type event in a given period of time
- Exponential distribution, for the time before the next Poisson-type event occurs
- Gamma distribution, for the time before the next k Poisson-type events occur

Related to the absolute values of vectors with normally distributed components

- Rayleigh distribution, for the distribution of vector magnitudes with Gaussian distributed orthogonal components. Rayleight distributions are found in RF signals with Gaussian real and imaginary components.
- Rice distribution, a generalization of the Rayleigh distributions for where there is a stationary background signal component. Found in Rician fading of radio signals due to multipath propagation and in MR images with noise corruption on non-zero NMR signals.

Related to normally distributed quantities operated with sum of squares (for hypothesis testing)

- Chi-squared distribution, the distribution of a sum of squared standard normal variables; useful e.g. for inference regarding the sample variance of normally distributed samples
- Student's t distribution, the distribution of the ratio of a standard normal variable and the square root of a scaled chi squared variable; useful for inference regarding the mean of normally distributed samples with unknown variance
- F-distribution, the distribution of the ratio of two scaled chi squared variables; useful e.g. for inferences that involve comparing variances or involving R-squared (the squared correlation coefficient)

Useful as conjugate prior distributions in Bayesian inference

- Beta distribution, for a single probability (real number between 0 and 1); conjugate to the Bernoulli distribution and binomial distribution
- Gamma distribution, for a non-negative scaling parameter; conjugate to the rate parameter of a Poisson distribution or exponential distribution, the precision (inverse variance) of a normal distribution, etc.

- Dirichlet distribution, for a vector of probabilities that must sum to 1; conjugate to the categorical distribution and multinomial distribution; generalization of the beta distribution
- Wishart distribution, for a symmetric non-negative definite matrix; conjugate to the inverse of the covariance matrix of a multivariate normal distribution; generalization of the gamma distribution

Binomial distribution

"Binomial model" redirects here. For the binomial model in options pricing, see Binomial options pricing model.

In probability theory and statistics, the binomial distribution is the discrete probability distribution of the number of successes in a sequence of n independent yes/no experiments, each of which yields success with probability p. Such a success/failure experiment is also called a Bernoulli experiment or Bernoulli trial; when $n = 1$, the binomial distribution is a Bernoulli distribution. The binomial distribution is the basis for the popular binomial test of statistical significance.

The binomial distribution is frequently used to model the number of successes in a sample of size n drawn with replacement from a population of size N. If the sampling is carried out without replacement, the draws are not independent and so the resulting distribution is a hypergeometric distribution, not a binomial one. However, for N much larger than n, the binomial distribution is a good approximation, and widely used.

Specification

Probability mass function

In general, if the random variable X follows the binomial distribution with parameters n and p, we write $X \sim B(n, p)$. The probability of getting exactly k successes in n trials is given by the probability mass function:

$$f(k;n,p) = \Pr(X = k) = \binom{n}{k} p^k (1-p)^{n-k}$$

for k = 0, 1, 2, ..., n, where

$$\binom{n}{k} = \frac{n!}{k!(n-k)!}$$

is the binomial coefficient, hence the name of the distribution. The formula can be understood as follows: we want k successes (p) and n " k failures (1 " p). However, the k successes can occur anywhere among the n trials, and there are $\binom{n}{k}$ different ways of distributing k successes in a sequence of n trials.

In creating reference tables for binomial distribution probability, usually the table is filled in up to $n/2$ values. This is because for $k > n/2$, the probability can be calculated by its complement as

$$f(k,n,p) = f(n-k,n,1-p).$$

Looking at the expression $f(k, n, p)$ as a function of k, there is a k value that maximizes it. This k value can be found by calculating

$$\frac{f(k+1,n,p)}{f(k,n,p)} = \frac{(n-k)p}{(k+1)(1-p)}$$

and comparing it to 1. There is always an integer M that satisfies

$$(n+1)p-1 \leq M < (n+1)p.$$

$f(k, n, p)$ is monotone increasing for $k < M$ and monotone decreasing for $k > M$, with the exception of the case where $(n + 1)p$ is an integer. In this case, there are two values for which f is maximal: $(n + 1)p$ and $(n + 1)p$ " 1. M is the *most probable* (*most likely*) outcome of the Bernoulli trials and is called the mode. Note that the probability of it occurring can be fairly small.

Recurrence relation

$$\{p(n-k)\text{Prob}(k) + (k+1)(p-1)\text{Prob}(k+1) = 0, \text{Prob}(0) = (1-p)^n\}$$

Cumulative distribution function: The cumulative distribution function can be expressed as:

$$F(k;n,p) = \Pr(X \leq k) = \sum_{i=0}^{\lfloor k \rfloor} \binom{n}{i} p^i (1-p)^{n-i}$$

where $\lfloor k \rfloor$ is the "floor" under k, i.e. the greatest integer less than or equal to k.

It can also be represented in terms of the regularized incomplete beta function, as follows:

$$\begin{aligned} F(k;n,p) &= \Pr(X \leq k) \\ &= I_{1-p}(n-k, k+1) \\ &= (n-k)\binom{n}{k} \int_0^{1-p} t^{n-k-1}(1-t)^k \, dt. \end{aligned}$$

Some closed-form bounds for the cumulative distribution function are given below.

Example

Suppose a biased coin comes up heads with probability 0.3 when tossed. What is the probability of achieving 0, 1,..., 6 heads after six tosses?

$$\Pr(0 \text{ heads}) = f(0) = \Pr(X=0) = \binom{6}{0} 0.3^0 (1-0.3)^{6-0} \approx 0.1176$$

$$\Pr(1 \text{ head}) = f(1) = \Pr(X=1) = \binom{6}{1} 0.3^1 (1-0.3)^{6-1} \approx 0.3025$$

$$\Pr(2 \text{ heads}) = f(2) = \Pr(X=2) = \binom{6}{2} 0.3^2 (1-0.3)^{6-2} \approx 0.3241$$

$$\Pr(3 \text{ heads}) = f(3) = \Pr(X=3) = \binom{6}{3} 0.3^3 (1-0.3)^{6-3} \approx 0.1852$$

$$\Pr(4 \text{ heads}) = f(4) = \Pr(X = 4) = \binom{6}{4} 0.3^4 (1 - 0.3)^{6-4} \approx 0.0595$$

$$\Pr(5 \text{ heads}) = f(5) = \Pr(X = 5) = \binom{6}{5} 0.3^5 (1 - 0.3)^{6-5} \approx 0.0102$$

$$\Pr(6 \text{ heads}) = f(6) = \Pr(X = 6) = \binom{6}{6} 0.3^6 (1 - 0.3)^{6-6} \approx 0.0007$$

Mean and variance

If $X \sim B(n, p)$, that is, X is a binomially distributed random variable, n being the total number of experiments and p the probability of each experiment yielding a successful result, then the expected value of X is

$$\mathrm{E}[X] = np,_{\mathrm{Z}}$$

(For example, if n=100, and p=25/100, then 25% of the results are likely to be successful. It is expected that 25 results are successful even though it is not certain.)

and the variance

$$\mathrm{Var}[X] = np(1 - p).$$

Mode and Median

Usually the mode of a binomial $B(n, p)$ distribution is equal to $\lfloor (n+1)p \rfloor$, where $\lfloor \cdot \rfloor$ is the floor function. However when $(n + 1)p$ is an integer and p is neither 0 nor 1, then the distribution has two modes: $(n + 1)p$ and $(n + 1)p$ ” 1. When p is equal to 0 or 1, the mode will be 0 and n correspondingly. These cases can be summarized as follows:

$$\text{mode} = \begin{cases} \lfloor (n+1)p \rfloor & \text{if } (n+1)p \text{ is } 0 \text{ or a noninteger}, \\ (n+1)p \ \text{ and } \ (n+1)p - 1 & \text{if } (n+1)p \in \{1, \dots, n\}, \\ n & \text{if } (n+1)p = n+1. \end{cases}$$

In general, there is no single formula to find the median for a binomial distribution, and it may even be non-unique. However several special results have been established:

- If np is an integer, then the mean, median, and mode coincide and equal np.
- Any median m must lie within the interval #*np*# d” *m* d” #*np* #.
- A median m cannot lie too far away from the mean: |*m* “ *np*| d” min{ ln 2, max{*p*, 1 “ *p*}}.
- The median is unique and equal to m = round(np) in cases when either *p* d” 1 “ ln 2 or *p* e” ln 2 or |*m* ” *np*| d” min{*p*, 1 ” *p*} (except for the case when p = ½ and n is odd).
- When $p = 1/2$ and n is odd, any number m in the interval ½(*n* ” 1) d” *m* d” ½(*n* + 1) is a median of the binomial distribution. If $p = 1/2$ and n is even, then $m = n/2$ is the unique median.

Covariance between two binomials

If two binomially distributed random variables X and Y are observed together, estimating their covariance can be useful. Using the definition of covariance, in the case $n = 1$ (thus being Bernoulli trials) we have

$$\mathrm{Cov}(X, Y) = \mathrm{E}(XY) - \mu_X\mu_Y.$$

The first term is non-zero only when both X and Y are one, and μX and μY are equal to the two probabilities. Defining pB as the probability of both happening at the same time, this gives

$$\mathrm{Cov}(X, Y) = p_B - p_X p_Y,$$

and for n independent pairwise trials

$$\mathrm{Cov}(X, Y)_n = n(p_B - p_X p_Y).$$

If X and Y are the same variable, this reduces to the variance formula given above.

Related distributions

Sums of binomials

If $X \sim \mathrm{B}(n, p)$ and $Y \sim \mathrm{B}(m, p)$ are independent binomial variables with the same probability p, then $X + Y$ is again a binomial variable; its distribution is

$$X + Y \sim B(n + m, p).$$

Conditional binomials

If $X \sim \mathrm{B}(n, p)$ and, conditional on X, $Y \sim \mathrm{B}(X, q)$, then Y is a simple binomial variable with distribution

$$Y \sim B(n,pq).$$

Bernoulli distribution

The Bernoulli distribution is a special case of the binomial distribution, where $n = 1$. Symbolically, $X \sim \mathrm{B}(1, p)$ has the same meaning as $X \sim \mathrm{Bern}(p)$. Conversely, any binomial distribution, $\mathrm{B}(n, p)$, is the distribution of the sum of n Bernoulli trials, $\mathrm{Bern}(p)$, each with the same probability p.

Poisson binomial distribution

The binomial distribution is a special case of the Poisson binomial distribution, which is a sum of n independent non-identical Bernoulli trials $\mathrm{Bern}(pi)$. If X has the Poisson binomial distribution with $p1 = \ldots = pn = p$ then $X \sim \mathrm{B}(n, p)$.

Normal approximation

If n is large enough, then the skew of the distribution is not too great. In this case a reasonable approximation to $\mathrm{B}(n, p)$ is given by the normal distribution

$$\mathcal{N}(np,\, np(1 - p)),$$

and this basic approximation can be improved in a simple way by using a suitable continuity correction. The basic approximation generally improves as n increases (at least

20) and is better when p is not near to 0 or 1. Various rules of thumb may be used to decide whether n is large enough, and p is far enough from the extremes of zero or one:

One rule is that both x=np and n(1 ? p) must be greater than 5. However, the specific number varies from source to source, and depends on how good an approximation one wants; some sources give 10 which gives virtually the same results as the following rule for large n until n is very large (ex: x=11, n=7752).

A second rule is that for $n > 5$ the normal approximation is adequate if

$$\left|\left(\frac{1}{\sqrt{n}}\right)\left(\sqrt{\frac{1-p}{p}}-\sqrt{\frac{p}{1-p}}\right)\right| < 0.3$$

Another commonly used rule holds that the normal approximation is appropriate only if everything within 3 standard deviations of its mean is within the range of possible values, that is if

$$\mu \pm 3\sigma = np \pm 3\sqrt{np(1-p)} \in [0, n].$$

The following is an example of applying a continuity correction. Suppose one wishes to calculate Pr(*X* d" 8) for a binomial random variable *X*. If *Y* has a distribution given by the normal approximation, then Pr(*X* d" 8) is approximated by Pr(*Y* d" 8.5). The addition of 0.5 is the continuity correction; the uncorrected normal approximation gives considerably less accurate results.

This approximation, known as de Moivre–Laplace theorem, is a huge time-saver when undertaking calculations by hand (exact calculations with large *n* are very onerous); historically, it was the first use of the normal distribution, introduced in Abraham de Moivre's book *The Doctrine of Chances* in 1738. Nowadays, it can be seen as a consequence of the central limit theorem since B(*n*, *p*) is a sum of *n* independent, identically distributed Bernoulli variables with parameter *p*. This fact is the basis of a hypothesis test, a "proportion z-test", for the value of *p* using *x/n*, the sample proportion and estimator of *p*, in a common test statistic.

For example, suppose one randomly samples *n* people out of a large population and ask them whether they agree with a certain statement. The proportion of people who agree will of course depend on the sample. If groups of *n* people were sampled repeatedly and truly randomly, the proportions would follow an approximate normal distribution with mean equal to the true proportion *p* of agreement in the population and with standard deviation σ = (*p*(1 " *p*)/*n*). Large sample sizes *n* are good because the standard deviation, as a proportion of the expected value, gets smaller, which allows a more precise estimate of the unknown parameter *p*.

Poisson approximation

The binomial distribution converges towards the Poisson distribution as the number of trials goes to infinity while the product *np* remains fixed. Therefore the Poisson distribution with parameter $\lambda = np$ can be used as an approximation to B(*n*, *p*) of the binomial distribution if *n* is sufficiently large and *p* is sufficiently small. According to two rules of thumb, this approximation is good if *n* e" 20 and *p* d" 0.05, or if *n* e" 100 and *np* d" 10.

Limiting distributions

Poisson limit theorem: As *n* approaches “ and *p* approaches 0 while *np* remains fixed at ë > 0 or at least *np* approaches ë > 0, then the Binomial(*n*, *p*) distribution approaches the Poisson distribution with expected value ë.

de Moivre–Laplace theorem: As *n* approaches “ while *p* remains fixed, the distribution of

$$\frac{X - np}{\sqrt{np(1-p)}}$$

approaches the normal distribution with expected value 0 and variance 1. This result is sometimes loosely stated by saying that the distribution of *X* is asymptotically normal with expected value *np* and variance *np*(1 ” *p*). This result is a specific case of the central limit theorem.

Beta distribution

Beta distributions provide a family of conjugate prior probability distributions for binomial distributions in Bayesian inference. The domain of the beta distribution can be viewed as a probability, and in fact the beta distribution is often used to describe the distribution of a probability value *p*:

$$P(p;\alpha,\beta) = \frac{p^{\alpha-1}(1-p)^{\beta-1}}{\mathrm{B}(\alpha,\beta)}$$

Confidence intervals

Even for quite large values of *n*, the actual distribution of the mean is significantly nonnormal. Because of this problem several methods to estimate confidence intervals have been proposed.

Let *n*1 be the number of successes out of *n*, the total number of trials, and let

$$\hat{p} = \frac{n_1}{n}$$

be the proportion of successes. Let *z*α/2 be the 100(1 “ α/2)th percentile of the standard normal distribution.

Wald method

$$\hat{p} \pm z_{\frac{\alpha}{2}} \sqrt{\frac{\hat{p}(1-\hat{p})}{n}}.$$

A continuity correction of 0.5/*n* may be added.

Agresti-Coull method

$$\tilde{p} \pm z_{\frac{\alpha}{2}} \sqrt{\frac{\tilde{p}(1-\tilde{p})}{n + z_{\frac{\alpha}{2}}^2}}.$$

Here the estimate of p is modified to

$$\tilde{p} = \frac{n_1 + \frac{1}{2}z^2_{\frac{\alpha}{2}}}{n + z^2_{\frac{\alpha}{2}}}$$

ArcSine method

$$\sin^2\left(\arcsin\left(\sqrt{\hat{p}}\right) \pm \frac{z}{2\sqrt{n}}\right)$$

Wilson (score) method

$$\frac{\hat{p} + \frac{1}{2n}z^2_{1-\frac{\alpha}{2}} \pm \frac{1}{2n}z_{1-\frac{\alpha}{2}}\sqrt{4n\hat{p}(1-\hat{p}) + z^2_{1-\frac{\alpha}{2}}}}{1 + \frac{1}{n}z^2_{1-\frac{\alpha}{2}}}.$$

The exact (Clopper-Pearson) method is the most conservative. The Wald method although commonly recommended in the text books is the most biased.

Generating binomial random variates

Methods for random number generation where the marginal distribution is a binomial distribution are well-established. One way to generate random samples from a binomial distribution is to use an inversion algorithm. To do so, one must calculate the probability that P(X=k) for all values k from 0 through n. (These probabilities should sum to a value close to one, in order to encompass the entire sample space.) Then by using a Linear congruential generator to generate samples uniform between 0 and 1, one can transform the calculated samples U[0,1] into discrete numbers by using the probabilities calculated in step one.

Normal distribution

In probability theory, the normal (or Gaussian) distribution is a very commonly occurring continuous probability distribution—a function that tells the probability that any real observation will fall between any two real limits or real numbers, as the curve approaches zero on either side. Normal distributions are extremely important in statistics and are often used in the natural and social sciences for real-valued random variables whose distributions are not known.

The normal distribution is immensely useful because of the central limit theorem, which states that, under mild conditions, the mean of many random variables independently drawn from the same distribution is distributed approximately normally, irrespective of the form of the original distribution: physical quantities that are expected to be the sum of many independent processes (such as measurement errors) often have a distribution very close to the normal. Moreover, many results and methods (such as propagation of uncertainty and least squares parameter fitting) can be derived analytically in explicit form when the relevant variables are normally distributed.

The Gaussian distribution is sometimes informally called the bell curve. However, many other distributions are bell-shaped (such as Cauchy's, Student's, and logistic). The terms Gaussian function and Gaussian bell curve are also ambiguous because they sometimes refer to multiples of the normal distribution that cannot be directly interpreted in terms of probabilities.

A normal distribution is $$f(x,\mu,\sigma) = \frac{1}{\sigma\sqrt{2\pi}}e^{-\frac{(x-\mu)^2}{2\sigma^2}}$$

The parameter μ in this definition is the *mean* or *expectation* of the distribution (and also its median and mode). The parameter σ is its standard deviation; its variance is therefore σ . A random variable with a Gaussian distribution is said to be normally distributed and is called a normal deviate.

If $\mu = 0$ and $\sigma = 1$, the distribution is called the standard normal distribution or the unit normal distribution, and a random variable with that distribution is a standard normal deviate.

The normal distribution is the only absolutely continuous distribution all of whose cumulants beyond the first two (i.e., other than the mean and variance) are zero. It is also the continuous distribution with the maximum entropy for a given mean and variance.

The normal distribution is a subclass of the elliptical distributions. The normal distribution is symmetric about its mean, and is non-zero over the entire real line. As such it may not be a suitable model for variables that are inherently positive or strongly skewed, such as the weight of a person or the price of a share. Such variables may be better described by other distributions, such as the log-normal distribution or the Pareto distribution. The value of the normal distribution is practically zero when the value x lies more than a few standard deviations away from the mean. Therefore, it may not be an appropriate model when one expects a significant fraction of outliers—values that lie many standard deviations away from the mean — and least squares and other statistical inference methods that are optimal for normally distributed variables often become highly unreliable when applied to such data. In those cases, a more heavy-tailed distribution should be assumed and the appropriate robust statistical inference methods applied.

The Gaussian distribution belongs to the family of stable distributions which are the attractors of sums of independent, identically distributed distributions whether or not the mean or variance is finite. Except for the Gaussian which is a limiting case, all stable distributions have heavy tails and infinite variance.

Definition

Standard normal distribution

The simplest case of a normal distribution is known as the *standard normal distribution*. This is a special case where μ=0 and σ=1, and it is described by this probability density function:

$$\phi(x) = \frac{e^{-\frac{1}{2}x^2}}{\sqrt{2\pi}}$$

The factor $1/\sqrt{2\pi}$ in this expression ensures that the total area under the curve Õ(x) is equal to one. The 1/2 in the exponent ensures that the distribution has unit variance (and therefore also unit standard deviation). This function is symmetric around x=0, where it attains its maximum value $1/\sqrt{2\pi}$; and has inflection points at +1 and "1.

Authors may differ also on which normal distribution should be called the "standard" one. Gauss himself defined the standard normal as having variance σ = 1/2, that is

$$\phi(x) = \frac{e^{-x^2}}{\sqrt{\pi}}$$

Stigler goes even further, defining the standard normal with variance $\sigma = 1/2\pi$:

$$\phi(x) = e^{-\pi x^2}$$

General normal distribution

Any normal distribution is a version of the standard normal distribution whose domain has been stretched by a factor σ (the standard deviation) and then translated by μ (the mean value):

$$f(x, \mu, \sigma) = \frac{1}{\sigma}\phi\left(\frac{x - \mu}{\sigma}\right).$$

The probability density must be scaled by $1/\sigma$ so that the integral is still 1.

If Z is a standard normal deviate, then $X = Z\sigma + \mu$ will have a normal distribution with expected value μ and standard deviation σ. Conversely, if X is a general normal deviate, then Z = (X" μ)/σ will have a standard normal distribution.

Every normal distribution is the exponential of a quadratic function:

$$f(x) = e^{ax^2+bx+c}$$

where a is negative and c is $-\ln(-4a\pi)/2$. In this form, the mean value μ is "b/a, and the variance σ is "1/(2a). For the standard normal distribution, a is "1/2, b is zero, and c is $-\ln(2\pi)/2$.

Notation

The standard Gaussian distribution (with zero mean and unit variance) is often denoted with the Greek letter Õ (phi). The alternative form of the Greek phi letter, φ, is also used quite often. The normal distribution is also often denoted by $N(\mu, \sigma)$. Thus when a random variable X is distributed normally with mean μ and variance σ, we write

$$X \sim \mathcal{N}(\mu, \sigma^2).$$

Alternative parametrizations

Some authors advocate using the precision τ as the parameter defining the width of the distribution, instead of the deviation σ or the variance σ. The precision is normally defined as the reciprocal of the variance, $1/\sigma$. The formula for the distribution then becomes

$$f(x) = \sqrt{\frac{\tau}{2\pi}}\, e^{\frac{-\tau(x-\mu)^2}{2}}.$$

This choice is claimed to have advantages in numerical computations when σ is very close to zero and simplify formulas in some contexts, such as in the Bayesian inference of variables with multivariate normal distribution. Occasionally, the precision τ is $1/\sigma$, the reciprocal of the standard deviation; so that

$$f(x) = \frac{\tau}{\sqrt{2\pi}}\, e^{\frac{-\tau^2(x-\mu)^2}{2}}.$$

According to Stigler, this formulation is advantageous because of a much simpler and easier-to-remember formula, the fact that the pdf has unit height at zero, and simple approximate formulas for the quantiles of the distribution.

Properties

Symmetries and derivatives

The normal distribution $f(x)$, with any mean μ and any positive deviation σ, has the following properties:

- It is symmetric around the point x = ì, which is at the same time the mode, the median and the mean of the distribution.
- It is unimodal: its first derivative is positive for x < ì, negative for x > ì, and zero only at x = ì.
- It has two inflection points (where the second derivative of f is zero and changes sign), located one standard deviation away from the mean, namely at x = ì " ó and x = ì + ó.
- It is log-concave.
- It is infinitely differentiable, indeed supersmooth of order 2.

Furthermore, the standard normal distribution Õ (with $\mu = 0$ and $\sigma = 1$) also has the following properties:

- Its first derivative Õ2 (x) is "xÕ(x).
- Its second derivative Õ2 2 (x) is (x " 1)Õ(x)
- More generally, its n-th derivative Õ(x) is (-1)$Hn(x)$Õ(x), where Hn is the Hermite polynomial of order n.

Differential equation

$$\left\{\sigma^2 f'(x) + f(x)(x-\mu) = 0,\ f(0) = \frac{e^{-\frac{\mu^2}{2\sigma^2}}}{\sqrt{2\pi}\sigma}\right\}$$

$$\left\{f'(x) + \tau f(x)(x-\mu) = 0,\ f(0) = \frac{\sqrt{\tau}e^{-\frac{\mu^2\tau}{2}}}{\sqrt{2\pi}}\right\}$$

Moments

The plain and absolute moments of a variable X are the expected values of X and $|X|$,respectively. If the expected value μ of X is zero, these parameters are called *central moments*. Usually we are interested only in moments with integer order p.

If X has a normal distribution, these moments exist and are finite for any p whose real part is greater than "1. For any non-negative integer p, the plain central moments are

$$\mathrm{E}\left[X^p\right] = \begin{cases} 0 & \text{if } p \text{ is odd,} \\ \sigma^p\,(p-1)!! & \text{if } p \text{ is even.} \end{cases}$$

Here $n!!$ denotes the double factorial, that is, the product of every odd number from n to 1.

The central absolute moments coincide with plain moments for all even orders, but are nonzero for odd orders. For any non-negative integer p,

$$\mathrm{E}\left[|X|^p\right] = \sigma^p\,(p-1)!! \cdot \begin{Bmatrix} \sqrt{\frac{2}{\pi}} & \text{if } p \text{ is odd} \\ 1 & \text{if } p \text{ is even} \end{Bmatrix} = \sigma^p \cdot \frac{2^{\frac{p}{2}}\Gamma\left(\frac{p+1}{2}\right)}{\sqrt{\pi}}$$

The last formula is valid also for any non-integer p > "1.

When the mean μ is not zero, the plain and absolute moments can be expressed in terms of confluent hypergeometric functions $1F1$ and U.

$$\mathrm{E}\left[X^p\right] = \sigma^p \cdot \left(-i\sqrt{2}\,\mathrm{sgn}\,\mu\right)^p U\left(-\frac{1}{2}p, \frac{1}{2}, -\frac{1}{2}(\mu/\sigma)^2\right),$$

$$\mathrm{E}\left[|X|^p\right] = \sigma^p \cdot 2^{\frac{p}{2}}\frac{\Gamma\left(\frac{1+p}{2}\right)}{\sqrt{\pi}}\,{}_1F_1\left(-\frac{1}{2}p, \frac{1}{2}, -\frac{1}{2}(\mu/\sigma)^2\right).$$

Zero-variance limit

In the limit when σ tends to zero, the probability density $f(x)$ eventually tends to zero at any x "" μ, but grows without limit if $x = \mu$, while its integral remains equal to 1. Therefore, the normal distribution cannot be defined as an ordinary function when $\sigma = 0$.

However, one can define the normal distribution with zero variance as a generalized function; specifically, as Dirac's "delta function" δ translated by the mean μ, that is $f(x) = \delta(x"\mu)$. Its CDF is then the Heaviside step function translated by the mean μ, namely

$$F(x) = \begin{cases} 0 & \text{if } x < \mu \\ 1 & \text{if } x \geq \mu \end{cases}$$

The central limit theorem

The central limit theorem states that under certain (fairly common) conditions, the sum of many random variables will have an approximately normal distribution. More specifically, where X1, …, Xn are independent and identically distributed random variables with the same arbitrary distribution, zero mean, and variance ?; and Z is their mean scaled by $\sqrt{n}$

$$Z = \sqrt{n}\left(\frac{1}{n}\sum_{i=1}^{n} X_i\right)$$

Then, as n increases, the probability distribution of Z will tend to the normal distribution with zero mean and variance σ.

The theorem can be extended to variables Xi that are not independent and/or not identically distributed if certain constraints are placed on the degree of dependence and the moments of the distributions.

Many test statistics, scores, and estimators encountered in practice contain sums of certain random variables in them, and even more estimators can be represented as sums of random variables through the use of influence functions. The central limit theorem implies that those statistical parameters will have asymptotically normal distributions.

The central limit theorem also implies that certain distributions can be approximated by the normal distribution, for example:

- The binomial distribution $B(n, p)$ is approximately normal with mean np and variance $np(1"p)$ for large n and for p not too close to zero or one.
- The Poisson distribution with parameter *ë* is approximately normal with mean *ë* and variance *ë*, for large values of *ë*.
- The chi-squared distribution ÷(k) is approximately normal with mean k and variance $2k$, for large k.
- The Student's t-distribution *t*(*í*) is approximately normal with mean 0 and variance 1 when *í* is large.

Whether these approximations are sufficiently accurate depends on the purpose for which they are needed, and the rate of convergence to the normal distribution. It is typically the case that such approximations are less accurate in the tails of the distribution.

A general upper bound for the approximation error in the central limit theorem is given by the Berry–Esseen theorem, improvements of the approximation are given by the Edgeworth expansions.

Operations on normal deviates

The family of normal distributions is closed under linear transformations: if X is normally distributed with mean μ and deviation σ, then the variable $Y = aX + b$, for any real numbers a and b, is also normally distributed, with mean $a\mu + b$ and deviation $a\sigma$.

Also if $X1$ and $X2$ are two independent normal random variables, with means $\mu 1$, $\mu 2$ and standard deviations $\sigma 1$, $\sigma 2$, then their sum $X1 + X2$ will also be normally distributed, with mean $\mu 1 + \mu 2$ and variance $\sigma_1^2 + \sigma_2^2$.

In particular, if X and Y are independent normal deviates with zero mean and variance σ, then $X + Y$ and X " Y are also independent and normally distributed, with zero mean and variance 2σ. This is a special case of the polarization identity.

Also, if $X1$, $X2$ are two independent normal deviates with mean μ and deviation σ, and a, b are arbitrary real numbers, then the variable

$$X_3 = \frac{aX_1 + bX_2 - (a+b)\mu}{\sqrt{a^2 + b^2}} + \mu$$

is also normally distributed with mean μ and deviation σ. It follows that the normal distribution is stable (with exponent $\alpha = 2$).

More generally, any linear combination of independent normal deviates is a normal deviate.

Infinite divisibility and Cramér's theorem

For any positive integer n, any normal distribution with mean μ and variance σ is the distribution of the sum of n independent normal deviates, each with mean μ/n and variance σ/n. This property is called infinite divisibility.

Conversely, if *X*1 and *X*2 are independent random variables and their sum *X*1 + *X*2 has a normal distribution, then both *X*1 and *X*2 must be normal deviates.

This result is known as Cramér's decomposition theorem, and is equivalent to saying that the convolution of two distributions is normal if and only if both are normal. Cramér's theorem implies that a linear combination of independent non-Gaussian variables will never have an exactly normal distribution, although it may approach it arbitrarily close.

Bernstein's theorem

Bernstein's theorem states that if *X* and *Y* are independent and *X* + *Y* and *X* " *Y* are also independent, then both *X* and *Y* must necessarily have normal distributions.

More generally, if *X*1, ..., *Xn* are independent random variables, then two distinct linear combinations "*akXk* and "*bkXk* will be independent if and only if all *Xk*'s are normal and "*akbkσ* 2

k = 0, where *σ* 2

k denotes the variance of *Xk*.

Other properties

1. If the characteristic function *öX* of some random variable *X* is of the form *öX*(*t*) = *e*, where *Q*(*t*) is a polynomial, then the Marcinkiewicz theorem (named after Józef Marcinkiewicz) asserts that *Q* can be at most a quadratic polynomial, and therefore *X* a normal random variable. The consequence of this result is that the normal distribution is the only distribution with a finite number (two) of non-zero cumulants.
2. If *X* and *Y* are jointly normal and uncorrelated, then they are independent. The requirement that *X* and *Y* should be *jointly* normal is essential, without it the property does not hold. For non-normal random variables uncorrelatedness does not imply independence.
3. The Kullback–Leibler divergence of one normal distributions *X*1 <" *N*(ì1, ó1)from another *X*2 <" *N*(ì2, ó2)is given by:

$$D_{KL}(X_1 \,\|\, X_2) = \frac{(\mu_1 - \mu_2)^2}{2\sigma_2^2} + \frac{1}{2}\left(\frac{\sigma_1^2}{\sigma_2^2} - 1 - \ln\frac{\sigma_1^2}{\sigma_2^2}\right).$$

The Hellinger distance between the same distributions is equal to

$$H^2(X_1, X_2) = 1 - \sqrt{\frac{2\sigma_1\sigma_2}{\sigma_1^2 + \sigma_2^2}}\, e^{-\frac{1}{4}\frac{(\mu_1-\mu_2)^2}{\sigma_1^2+\sigma_2^2}}.$$

4. The Fisher information matrix for a normal distribution is diagonal and takes the form

$$\mathcal{I} = \begin{pmatrix} \frac{1}{\sigma^2} & 0 \\ 0 & \frac{1}{2\sigma^4} \end{pmatrix}$$

5. Normal distributions belongs to an exponential family with natural parameters $\theta_1 = \frac{\mu}{\sigma^2}$ and $\theta_2 = \frac{-1}{2\sigma^2}$, and natural statistics *x* and *x*. The dual, expectation parameters for normal distribution are ç1 = ì and ç2 = ì + ó.
6. The conjugate prior of the mean of a normal distribution is another normal distribution. Specifically, if *x*1, ..., *xn* are iid *N*(ì, ó) and the prior is ì ~ *N*(ì0, ó20), then the posterior distribution for the estimator of ì will be

$$\mu|x_1,\ldots,x_n \sim \mathcal{N}\left(\frac{\frac{\sigma^2}{n}\mu_0 + \sigma_0^2\bar{x}}{\frac{\sigma^2}{n} + \sigma_0^2}, \left(\frac{n}{\sigma^2} + \frac{1}{\sigma_0^2}\right)^{-1}\right)$$

7. Of all probability distributions over the reals with mean ì and variance ó, the normal distribution *N*(ì, ó) is the one with the maximum entropy.
8. The family of normal distributions forms a manifold with constant curvature "1. The same family is flat with respect to the (±1)-connections " and ".

Related distributions

Operations on a single random variable

If *X* is distributed normally with mean μ and variance σ, then

- The exponential of *X* is distributed log-normally: *e* ~ ln(*N* (ì, ó)).
- The absolute value of *X* has folded normal distribution: |*X*| ~ *Nf* (ì, ó). If ì = 0 this is known as the half-normal distribution.
- The square of *X*/ó has the noncentral chi-squared distribution with one degree of freedom: *X*/ó ~ ÷1(ì/ó). If ì = 0, the distribution is called simply chi-squared.
- The distribution of the variable *X* restricted to an interval [*a*, *b*] is called the truncated normal distribution.
- (*X*" ì) has a Lévy distribution with location 0 and scale ó.

Combination of two independent random variables

If *X*1 and *X*2 are two independent standard normal random variables with mean 0 and variance 1, then

- Their sum and difference is distributed normally with mean zero and variance two: *X*1 ± *X*2 <" *N*(0, 2).
- Their product *Z* = *X*1·*X*2 follows the "product-normal" distribution with density function *fZ*(*z*) = ð*K*0(|*z*|), where *K*0 is the modified Bessel function of the second kind. This

distribution is symmetric around zero, unbounded at $z = 0$, and has the characteristic function $\ddot{o}Z(t) = (1 + t)$.

- Their ratio follows the standard Cauchy distribution: $X1 \div X2$ <" Cauchy(0, 1).
- Their Euclidean norm $\sqrt{X_1^2 + X_2^2}$ has the Rayleigh distribution.

Operations on the density function

The split normal distribution is most directly defined in terms of joining scaled sections of the density functions of different normal distributions and rescaling the density to integrate to one. The truncated normal distribution results from rescaling a section of a single density function.

Extensions

The notion of normal distribution, being one of the most important distributions in probability theory, has been extended far beyond the standard framework of the univariate (that is one-dimensional) case (Case 1). All these extensions are also called *normal* or *Gaussian* laws, so a certain ambiguity in names exists.

The multivariate normal distribution describes the Gaussian law in the k-dimensional Euclidean space. A vector X" R is multivariate-normally distributed if any linear combination of its components "k

j=1aj Xj has a (univariate) normal distribution. The variance of X is a $k \times k$ symmetric positive-definite matrix V. The multivariate normal distribution is a special case of the elliptical distributions. As such, its iso-density loci in the $k = 2$ case are ellipses and in the case of arbitrary k are ellipsoids.

Rectified Gaussian distribution a rectified version of normal distribution with all the negative elements reset to 0

Complex normal distribution deals with the complex normal vectors. A complex vector X " **C** is said to be normal if both its real and imaginary components jointly possess a $2k$-dimensional multivariate normal distribution. The variance-covariance structure of X is described by two matrices: the *variance* matrix Ã, and the *relation* matrix C. Matrix normal distribution describes the case of normally distributed matrices.

Gaussian processes are the normally distributed stochastic processes. These can be viewed as elements of some infinite-dimensional Hilbert space H, and thus are the analogues of multivariate normal vectors for the case k = ". A random element h " H is said to be normal if for any constant a " H the scalar product (a, h) has a (univariate) normal distribution. The variance structure of such Gaussian random element can be described in terms of the linear *covariance operator K: H '! H*. Several Gaussian processes became popular enough to have their own names:

- Brownian motion,
- Brownian bridge,
- Ornstein–Uhlenbeck process.

Gaussian q-distribution is an abstract mathematical construction that represents a "q-analogue" of the normal distribution.

The q-Gaussian is an analogue of the Gaussian distribution, in the sense that it maximises the Tsallis entropy, and is one type of Tsallis distribution. Note that this distribution is different from the Gaussian q-distribution above.

One of the main practical uses of the Gaussian law is to model the empirical distributions of many different random variables encountered in practice. In such case a possible extension would be a richer family of distributions, having more than two parameters and therefore being able to fit the empirical distribution more accurately. The examples of such extensions are:

Pearson distribution— a four-parametric family of probability distributions that extend the normal law to include different skewness and kurtosis values.

Normality tests

Normality tests assess the likelihood that the given data set {*x*1, ..., *xn*} comes from a normal distribution. Typically the null hypothesis *H*0 is that the observations are distributed normally with unspecified mean μ and variance σ, versus the alternative *Ha* that the distribution is arbitrary. Many tests (over 40) have been devised for this problem, the more prominent of them are outlined below:

"Visual" tests are more intuitively appealing but subjective at the same time, as they rely on informal human judgement to accept or reject the null hypothesis.

Q-Q plot— is a plot of the sorted values from the data set against the expected values of the corresponding quantiles from the standard normal distribution. That is, it's a plot of point of the form (Ö(*pk*), *x*(*k*)), where plotting points *pk* are equal to *pk* = (*k* " *á*)/(*n* + 1 " 2*á*) and *á* is an adjustment constant, which can be anything between 0 and 1. If the null hypothesis is true, the plotted points should approximately lie on a straight line.

P-P plot— similar to the Q-Q plot, but used much less frequently. This method consists of plotting the points (Ö(*z*(*k*)), *pk*), where $z_{(k)}=(x_{(k)}-\hat{\mu})/\hat{\sigma}$. For normally distributed data this plot should lie on a 45° line between (0, 0) and (1, 1).

Shapiro-Wilk test employs the fact that the line in the Q-Q plot has the slope of *ó*. The test compares the least squares estimate of that slope with the value of the sample variance, and rejects the null hypothesis if these two quantities differ significantly.

Normal probability plot (rankit plot):

- Moment tests:
  - o D'Agostino's K-squared test
  - o Jarque–Bera test
- Empirical distribution function tests:
  - o Lilliefors test (an adaptation of the Kolmogorov–Smirnov test)
  - o Anderson–Darling test

Estimation of parameters: It is often the case that we don't know the parameters of the normal distribution, but instead want to estimate them. That is, having a sample (*x*1, ..., *xn*) from a normal *N*(μ, σ) population we would like to learn the approximate values of parameters μ and σ. The standard approach to this problem is the maximum likelihood method, which requires maximization of the *log-likelihood function*:

$$\ln \mathcal{L}(\mu, \sigma^2) = \sum_{i=1}^{n} \ln f(x_i; \mu, \sigma^2) = -\frac{n}{2}\ln(2\pi) - \frac{n}{2}\ln\sigma^2 - \frac{1}{2\sigma^2}\sum_{i=1}^{n}(x_i - \mu)^2.$$

Taking derivatives with respect to μ and σ and solving the resulting system of first order conditions yields the *maximum likelihood estimates*:

$$\hat{\mu} = \overline{x} \equiv \frac{1}{n}\sum_{i=1}^{n} x_i, \qquad \hat{\sigma}^2 = \frac{1}{n}\sum_{i=1}^{n}(x_i - \overline{x})^2.$$

Estimator $\hat{\mu}$is called the *sample mean*, since it is the arithmetic mean of all observations. The statistic $\overline{x}$is complete and sufficient for μ, and therefore by the Lehmann–Scheffé theorem, is the uniformly minimum variance unbiased (UMVU) estimator. In finite samples it is distributed normally:

$$\hat{\mu} \sim \mathcal{N}(\mu, \sigma^2/n).$$

The variance of this estimator is equal to the $\mu\mu$-element of the inverse Fisher information matrix $\mathcal{I}^{-1}$. This implies that the estimator is finite-sample efficient. Of practical importance is the fact that the standard error of $\hat{\mu}$is proportional to $1/\sqrt{n}$, that is, if one wishes to decrease the standard error by a factor of 10, one must increase the number of points in the sample by a factor of 100. This fact is widely used in determining sample sizes for opinion polls and the number of trials in Monte Carlo simulations.

From the standpoint of the asymptotic theory, is consistent, that is, it converges in probability to μ as *n* '! ". The estimator is also asymptotically normal, which is a simple corollary of the fact that it is normal in finite samples:

$$\sqrt{n}(\hat{\mu} - \mu) \xrightarrow{d} \mathcal{N}(0, \sigma^2).$$

The estimator $\hat{\sigma}^2$is called the *sample variance*, since it is the variance of the sample (*x*1, …, *xn*). In practice, another estimator is often used instead of the . This other estimator is denoted *s*, and is also called the *sample variance*, which represents a certain ambiguity in terminology; its square root *s* is called the *sample standard deviation*. The estimator *s* differs from by having (*n* " 1) instead of *n* in the denominator (the so-called Bessel's correction):

$$s^2 = \frac{n}{n-1}\hat{\sigma}^2 = \frac{1}{n-1}\sum_{i=1}^{n}(x_i - \overline{x})^2.$$

The difference between *s* and $\hat{\sigma}^2$becomes negligibly small for large *n*'s. In finite samples however, the motivation behind the use of *s* is that it is an unbiased estimator of the underlying parameter σ, whereas is biased. Also, by the Lehmann–Scheffé theorem the estimator *s* is uniformly minimum variance unbiased (UMVU), which makes it the "best" estimator among all unbiased ones. However it can be shown that the biased estimator is "better" than the *s* in terms of the mean squared error (MSE) criterion. In finite samples both *s* and have scaled chi-squared distribution with (*n* " 1) degrees of freedom:

$$s^2 \sim \frac{\sigma^2}{n-1}\cdot\chi^2_{n-1}, \qquad \hat{\sigma}^2 \sim \frac{\sigma^2}{n}\cdot\chi^2_{n-1}.$$

The first of these expressions shows that the variance of *s* is equal to 2σ/(*n*"1), which is slightly greater than the $\sigma\sigma$-element of the inverse Fisher information matrix $\mathcal{I}^{-1}$. Thus,

s is not an efficient estimator for σ, and moreover, since s is UMVU, we can conclude that the finite-sample efficient estimator for σ does not exist.

Applying the asymptotic theory, both estimators s and $\hat{\sigma}^2$are consistent, that is they converge in probability to σ as the sample size n '! ". The two estimators are also both asymptotically normal:

$$\sqrt{n}(\hat{\sigma}^2 - \sigma^2) \simeq \sqrt{n}(s^2 - \sigma^2) \xrightarrow{d} \mathcal{N}(0, 2\sigma^4).$$

In particular, both estimators are asymptotically efficient for σ.

By Cochran's theorem, for normal distributions the sample mean $\hat{\mu}$and the sample variance s are independent, which means there can be no gain in considering their joint distribution. There is also a reverse theorem: if in a sample the sample mean and sample variance are independent, then the sample must have come from the normal distribution. The independence between and s can be employed to construct the so-called *t-statistic*:

$$t = \frac{\hat{\mu} - \mu}{s/\sqrt{n}} = \frac{\overline{x} - \mu}{\sqrt{\frac{1}{n(n-1)}\sum(x_i - \overline{x})^2}} \sim t_{n-1}$$

This quantity t has the Student's t-distribution with (n " 1) degrees of freedom, and it is an ancillary statistic (independent of the value of the parameters). Inverting the distribution of this t-statistics will allow us to construct the confidence interval for μ; similarly, inverting the χ distribution of the statistic s will give us the confidence interval for σ:

$$\mu \in \left[\hat{\mu} + t_{n-1,\alpha/2}\frac{1}{\sqrt{n}}s,\ \hat{\mu} + t_{n-1,1-\alpha/2}\frac{1}{\sqrt{n}}s\right] \approx \left[\hat{\mu} - |z_{\alpha/2}|\frac{1}{\sqrt{n}}s,\ \hat{\mu} + |z_{\alpha/2}|\frac{1}{\sqrt{n}}s\right],$$

$$\sigma^2 \in \left[\frac{(n-1)s^2}{\chi^2_{n-1,1-\alpha/2}},\ \frac{(n-1)s^2}{\chi^2_{n-1,\alpha/2}}\right] \approx \left[s^2 - |z_{\alpha/2}|\frac{\sqrt{2}}{\sqrt{n}}s^2,\ s^2 + |z_{\alpha/2}|\frac{\sqrt{2}}{\sqrt{n}}s^2\right],$$

where *tk,p* and χ 2

k,p are the p quantiles of the t- and χ-distributions respectively. These confidence intervals are of the *level* 1 " α, meaning that the true values μ and σ fall outside of these intervals with probability α. In practice people usually take α = 5%, resulting in the 95% confidence intervals. The approximate formulas in the display above were derived from the asymptotic distributions of $\hat{\mu}$and s. The approximate formulas become valid for large values of n, and are more convenient for the manual calculation since the standard normal quantiles *zα/2* do not depend on n. In particular, the most popular value of α = 5%, results in |*z*0.025| = 1.96.

Bayesian analysis of the normal distribution

Bayesian analysis of normally distributed data is complicated by the many different possibilities that may be considered:

- Either the mean, or the variance, or neither, may be considered a fixed quantity.
- When the variance is unknown, analysis may be done directly in terms of the variance, or in terms of the precision, the reciprocal of the variance. The reason for expressing the formulas in terms of precision is that the analysis of most cases is simplified.
- Both univariate and multivariate cases need to be considered.

- Either conjugate or improper prior distributions may be placed on the unknown variables.
- An additional set of cases occurs in Bayesian linear regression, where in the basic model the data is assumed to be normally distributed, and normal priors are placed on the regression coefficients. The resulting analysis is similar to the basic cases of independent identically distributed data, but more complex.

The formulas for the non-linear-regression cases are summarized in the conjugate prior article.

With unknown mean and unknown variance

For a set of i.i.d. normally distributed data points **X** of size *n* where each individual point *x* follows $x \sim \mathcal{N}(\mu, \sigma^2)$ with unknown mean μ and unknown variance σ, a combined (multivariate) conjugate prior is placed over the mean and variance, consisting of a normal-inverse-gamma distribution. Logically, this originates as follows:

1. From the analysis of the case with unknown mean but known variance, we see that the update equations involve sufficient statistics computed from the data consisting of the mean of the data points and the total variance of the data points, computed in turn from the known variance divided by the number of data points.
2. From the analysis of the case with unknown variance but known mean, we see that the update equations involve sufficient statistics over the data consisting of the number of data points and sum of squared deviations.
3. Keep in mind that the posterior update values serve as the prior distribution when further data is handled. Thus, we should logically think of our priors in terms of the sufficient statistics just described, with the same semantics kept in mind as much as possible.
4. To handle the case where both mean and variance are unknown, we could place independent priors over the mean and variance, with fixed estimates of the average mean, total variance, number of data points used to compute the variance prior, and sum of squared deviations. Note however that in reality, the total variance of the mean depends on the unknown variance, and the sum of squared deviations that goes into the variance prior (appears to) depend on the unknown mean. In practice, the latter dependence is relatively unimportant: Shifting the actual mean shifts the generated points by an equal amount, and on average the squared deviations will remain the same. This is not the case, however, with the total variance of the mean: As the unknown variance increases, the total variance of the mean will increase proportionately, and we would like to capture this dependence.
5. This suggests that we create a *conditional prior* of the mean on the unknown variance, with a hyperparameter specifying the mean of the pseudo-observations associated with the prior, and another parameter specifying the number of pseudo-observations. This number serves as a scaling parameter on the variance, making it possible to control the overall variance of the mean relative to the actual variance parameter. The prior for the variance also has two hyperparameters, one specifying the sum of squared deviations of the pseudo-observations associated with the prior, and another specifying once again

the number of pseudo-observations. Note that each of the priors has a hyperparameter specifying the number of pseudo-observations, and in each case this controls the relative variance of that prior. These are given as two separate hyperparameters so that the variance (aka the confidence) of the two priors can be controlled separately.

6. This leads immediately to the normal-inverse-gamma distribution, which is the product of the two distributions just defined, with conjugate priors used (an inverse gamma distribution over the variance, and a normal distribution over the mean, *conditional* on the variance) and with the same four parameters just defined.

   The priors are normally defined as follows:

$$p(\mu|\sigma^2;\mu_0,n_0) \sim \mathcal{N}(\mu_0,\sigma^2/n_0)$$

$$p(\sigma^2;\nu_0,\sigma_0^2) \sim I\chi^2(\nu_0,\sigma_0^2) = IG(\nu_0/2,\nu_0\sigma_0^2/2)$$

   The update equations can be derived, and look as follows:

$$\bar{x} = \frac{1}{n}\sum_{i=1}^{n} x_i$$

$$\mu_0' = \frac{n_0\mu_0 + n\bar{x}}{n_0 + n}$$

$$n_0' = n_0 + n$$

$$\nu_0' = \nu_0 + n$$

$$\nu_0'\sigma_0^{2'} = \nu_0\sigma_0^2 + \sum_{i=1}^{n}(x_i - \bar{x})^2 + \frac{n_0 n}{n_0 + n}(\mu_0 - \bar{x})^2$$

The respective numbers of pseudo-observations add the number of actual observations to them. The new mean hyperparameter is once again a weighted average, this time weighted by the relative numbers of observations. Finally, the update for $\nu_0'\sigma_0^{2'}$ is similar to the case with known mean, but in this case the sum of squared deviations is taken with respect to the observed data mean rather than the true mean, and as a result a new "interaction term" needs to be added to take care of the additional error source stemming from the deviation between prior and data mean.

Occurrence

The occurrence of normal distribution in practical problems can be loosely classified into three categories:

1. Exactly normal distributions;
2. Approximately normal laws, for example when such approximation is justified by the central limit theorem; and
3. Distributions modeled as normal – the normal distribution being the distribution with maximum entropy for a given mean and variance.

Exact normality

Certain quantities in physics are distributed normally, as was first demonstrated by James Clerk Maxwell. Examples of such quantities are:

- Velocities of the molecules in the ideal gas. More generally, velocities of the particles in any system in thermodynamic equilibrium will have normal distribution, due to the maximum entropy principle.
- Probability density function of a ground state in a quantum harmonic oscillator.
- The position of a particle that experiences diffusion. If initially the particle is located at a specific point (that is its probability distribution is the dirac delta function), then after time *t* its location is described by a normal distribution with variance *t*, which satisfies the diffusion equation "/"*t f*(*x*,*t*) = 1/2 "/"*x f*(*x*,*t*). If the initial location is given by a certain density function *g*(*x*), then the density at time *t* is the convolution of *g* and the normal PDF.

Approximate normality

Approximately normal distributions occur in many situations, as explained by the central limit theorem. When the outcome is produced by many small effects acting *additively and independently*, its distribution will be close to normal. The normal approximation will not be valid if the effects act multiplicatively (instead of additively), or if there is a single external influence that has a considerably larger magnitude than the rest of the effects.

In counting problems, where the central limit theorem includes a discrete-to-continuum approximation and where infinitely divisible and decomposable distributions are involved, such as

- Binomial random variables, associated with binary response variables;
- Poisson random variables, associated with rare events;

Thermal light has a Bose–Einstein distribution on very short time scales, and a normal distribution on longer timescales due to the central limit theorem.

Assumed normality

I can only recognize the occurrence of the normal curve – the Laplacian curve of errors – as a very abnormal phenomenon. It is roughly approximated to in certain distributions; for this reason, and on account for its beautiful simplicity, we may, perhaps, use it as a first approximation, particularly in theoretical investigations.

—Pearson (1901)

There are statistical methods to empirically test that assumption, see the above Normality tests section.

In biology, the *logarithm* of various variables tend to have a normal distribution, that is, they tend to have a log-normal distribution (after separation on male/female subpopulations), with examples including:

- Measures of size of living tissue (length, height, skin area, weight);

- The *length* of *inert* appendages (hair, claws, nails, teeth) of biological specimens, *in the direction of growth*; presumably the thickness of tree bark also falls under this category;
- Certain physiological measurements, such as blood pressure of adult humans.

In finance, in particular the Black–Scholes model, changes in the *logarithm* of exchange rates, price indices, and stock market indices are assumed normal (these variables behave like compound interest, not like simple interest, and so are multiplicative). Some mathematicians such as Benoît Mandelbrot have argued that log-Levy distributions, which possesses heavy tails would be a more appropriate model, in particular for the analysis for stock market crashes.

Measurement errors in physical experiments are often modeled by a normal distribution. This use of a normal distribution does not imply that one is assuming the measurement errors are normally distributed, rather using the normal distribution produces the most conservative predictions possible given only knowledge about the mean and variance of the errors.

In standardized testing, results can be made to have a normal distribution by either selecting the number and difficulty of questions (as in the IQ test) or transforming the raw test scores into "output" scores by fitting them to the normal distribution. For example, the SAT's traditional range of 200–800 is based on a normal distribution with a mean of 500 and a standard deviation of 100.

Many scores are derived from the normal distribution, including percentile ranks ("percentiles" or "quantiles"), normal curve equivalents, stanines, z-scores, and T-scores. Additionally, some behavioral statistical procedures assume that scores are normally distributed; for example, t-tests and ANOVAs. Bell curve grading assigns relative grades based on a normal distribution of scores.

In hydrology the distribution of long duration river discharge or rainfall, e.g. monthly and yearly totals, is often thought to be practically normal according to the central limit theorem. The blue picture illustrates an example of fitting the normal distribution to ranked October rainfalls showing the 90% confidence belt based on the binomial distribution. The rainfall data are represented by plotting positions as part of the cumulative frequency analysis.

Generating values from normal distribution

In computer simulations, especially in applications of the Monte-Carlo method, it is often desirable to generate values that are normally distributed. The algorithms listed below all generate the standard normal deviates, since a $N(\mu, \sigma 2)$ can be generated as $X = \mu + \sigma Z$, where Z is standard normal. All these algorithms rely on the availability of a random number generator U capable of producing uniform random variates.

The most straightforward method is based on the probability integral transform property: if U is distributed uniformly on (0,1), then Ö(U) will have the standard normal distribution. The drawback of this method is that it relies on calculation of the probit function Ö, which cannot be done analytically. Some approximate methods are described in Hart (1968) and in the erf article. Wichura gives a fast algorithm for computing this function to 16 decimal places, which is used by R to compute random variates of the normal distribution.

An easy to program approximate approach, that relies on the central limit theorem, is as follows: generate 12 uniform $U(0,1)$ deviates, add them all up, and subtract 6 – the resulting random variable will have approximately standard normal distribution. In truth, the distribution will be Irwin–Hall, which is a 12-section eleventh-order polynomial approximation to the normal distribution. This random deviate will have a limited range of (“6, 6).

The Box–Muller method uses two independent random numbers *U* and *V* distributed uniformly on (0,1). Then the two random variables *X* and *Y*

$$X = \sqrt{-2 \ln U} \cos(2\pi V), \qquad Y = \sqrt{-2 \ln U} \sin(2\pi V).$$

will both have the standard normal distribution, and will be independent. This formulation arises because for a bivariate normal random vector (*X Y*) the squared norm *X* + *Y* will have the chi-squared distribution with two degrees of freedom, which is an easily generated exponential random variable corresponding to the quantity “2ln(*U*) in these equations; and the angle is distributed uniformly around the circle, chosen by the random variable *V*.

Marsaglia polar method is a modification of the Box–Muller method algorithm, which does not require computation of functions `sin()` and `cos()`. In this method *U* and *V* are drawn from the uniform (“1,1) distribution, and then *S* = *U* + *V* is computed. If *S* is greater or equal to one then the method starts over, otherwise two quantities

$$X = U\sqrt{\frac{-2 \ln S}{S}}, \qquad Y = V\sqrt{\frac{-2 \ln S}{S}}$$

are returned. Again, *X* and *Y* will be independent and standard normally distributed. The Ratio method is a rejection method. The algorithm proceeds as follows:

- Generate two independent uniform deviates *U* and *V*;
- Compute *X* = “8/*e* (*V* “ 0.5)/*U*;
- Optional: if *X* d” 5 “ 4*eU* then accept *X* and terminate algorithm;
- Optional: if *X* e” 4*e*/*U* + 1.4 then reject *X* and start over from step 1;
- If *X* d” “4 ln*U* then accept *X*, otherwise start over the algorithm.

The ziggurat algorithm is faster than the Box–Muller transform and still exact. In about 97% of all cases it uses only two random numbers, one random integer and one random uniform, one multiplication and an if-test. Only in 3% of the cases, where the combination of those two falls outside the “core of the ziggurat” (a kind of rejection sampling using logarithms), do exponentials and more uniform random numbers have to be employed.

There is also some investigation into the connection between the fast Hadamard transform and the normal distribution, since the transform employs just addition and subtraction and by the central limit theorem random numbers from almost any distribution will be transformed into the normal distribution. In this regard a series of Hadamard transforms can be combined with random permutations to turn arbitrary data sets into a normally distributed data.

Numerical approximations for the normal CDF

The standard normal CDF is widely used in scientific and statistical computing. The values Φ(*x*) may be approximated very accurately by a variety of methods, such as numerical integration, Taylor series, asymptotic series and continued fractions. Different approximations are used depending on the desired level of accuracy.

Zelen & Severo (1964) give the approximation for Ö(x) for $x > 0$ with the absolute error |$\mathring{a}(x)$| < 7.5·10 (algorithm 26.2.17):

$$\Phi(x) = 1 - \phi(x)\left(b_1 t + b_2 t^2 + b_3 t^3 + b_4 t^4 + b_5 t^5\right) + \varepsilon(x), \qquad t = \frac{1}{1 + b_0 x},$$

where Õ(x) is the standard normal PDF, and $b0$ = 0.2316419, $b1$ = 0.319381530, $b2$ = "0.356563782, $b3$ = 1.781477937, $b4$ = "1.821255978, $b5$ = 1.330274429.

Hart (1968) lists almost a hundred of rational function approximations for the `erfc()` function. His algorithms vary in the degree of complexity and the resulting precision, with maximum absolute precision of 24 digits. An algorithm by West (2009) combines Hart's algorithm 5666 with a continued fraction approximation in the tail to provide a fast computation algorithm with a 16-digit precision.

Cody (1969) after recalling Hart68 solution is not suited for *erf*, gives a solution for both *erf* and *erfc*, with maximal relative error bound, via Rational Chebyshev Approximation.

Marsaglia (2004) suggested a simple algorithm based on the Taylor series expansion

$$\Phi(x) = \frac{1}{2} + \phi(x)\left(x + \frac{x^3}{3} + \frac{x^5}{3\cdot 5} + \frac{x^7}{3\cdot 5\cdot 7} + \frac{x^9}{3\cdot 5\cdot 7\cdot 9} + \cdots\right)$$

for calculating Ö(x) with arbitrary precision. The drawback of this algorithm is comparatively slow calculation time (for example it takes over 300 iterations to calculate the function with 16 digits of precision when x = 10).

The GNU Scientific Library calculates values of the standard normal CDF using Hart's algorithms and approximations with Chebyshev polynomials.

History

Development

Some authors attribute the credit for the discovery of the normal distribution to de Moivre, who in 1738 published in the second edition of his "*The Doctrine of Chances*" the study of the coefficients in the binomial expansion of (a + b). De Moivre proved that the middle term in this expansion has the approximate magnitude of $2/\sqrt{2\pi n}$, and that "If m or ½n be a Quantity infinitely great, then the Logarithm of the Ratio, which a Term distant from the middle by the Interval –*!*, has to the middle Term, is $-\frac{2\ell\ell}{n}$." Although this theorem can be interpreted as the first obscure expression for the normal probability law, Stigler points out that de Moivre himself did not interpret his results as anything more than the approximate rule for the binomial coefficients, and in particular de Moivre lacked the concept of the probability density function.

In 1809 Gauss published his monograph "*Theoria motus corporum coelestium in sectionibus conicis solem ambientium*" where among other things he introduces several important statistical concepts, such as the method of least squares, the method of maximum likelihood, and the *normal distribution*. Gauss used M, M2 , M2 2 , … to denote the measurements of some unknown quantity V, and sought the "most probable" estimator: the one that maximizes the probability $\varphi(M''V)$ · φ(M2 "V) · φ(M2 2 "V) · … of obtaining the observed experimental results. In his notation $\varphi\Delta$ is the probability law of the measurement errors of magnitude Δ. Not knowing what the function φ is, Gauss requires that his method should reduce to the well-known answer: the arithmetic mean of the measured values. Starting from these principles, Gauss demonstrates that the only law that rationalizes the choice of arithmetic mean as an estimator of the location parameter, is the normal law of errors:

$$\varphi\Delta = \frac{h}{\sqrt{\pi}}\, e^{-\mathrm{hh}\Delta\Delta},$$

where h is "the measure of the precision of the observations". Using this normal law as a generic model for errors in the experiments, Gauss formulates what is now known as the non-linear weighted least squares (NWLS) method.

Although Gauss was the first to suggest the normal distribution law, Laplace made significant contributions. It was Laplace who first posed the problem of aggregating several observations in 1774, although his own solution led to the Laplacian distribution. It was Laplace who first calculated the value of the integral +" *edt* = "π in 1782, providing the normalization constant for the normal distribution. Finally, it was Laplace who in 1810 proved and presented to the Academy the fundamental central limit theorem, which emphasized the theoretical importance of the normal distribution.

It is of interest to note that in 1809 an American mathematician Adrain published two derivations of the normal probability law, simultaneously and independently from Gauss. His works remained largely unnoticed by the scientific community, until in 1871 they were "rediscovered" by Abbe.

In the middle of the 19th century Maxwell demonstrated that the normal distribution is not just a convenient mathematical tool, but may also occur in natural phenomena: "The number of particles whose velocity, resolved in a certain direction, lies between x and $x + dx$ is

$$\mathrm{N}\, \frac{1}{\alpha\sqrt{\pi}}\, e^{-\frac{x^2}{\alpha^2}}\, dx$$

Naming

Since its introduction, the normal distribution has been known by many different names: the law of error, the law of facility of errors, Laplace's second law, Gaussian law, etc. Gauss himself apparently coined the term with reference to the "normal equations" involved in its applications, with normal having its technical meaning of orthogonal rather than "usual". However, by the end of the 19th century some authors had started using the name *normal distribution*, where the word "normal" was used as an adjective – the term now being seen as a reflection of the fact that this distribution was seen as typical, common – and thus "normal". Peirce (one of those authors) once defined "normal" thus: "...the 'normal' is not the average (or any other kind of mean) of what actually occurs, but of what *would*, in the long run, occur under certain circumstances." Around the turn of the 20th century Pearson popularized the term *normal* as a designation for this distribution.

Many years ago I called the Laplace–Gaussian curve the *normal* curve, which name, while it avoids an international question of priority, has the disadvantage of leading people to believe that all other distributions of frequency are in one sense or another 'abnormal'.

—Pearson (1920)

Also, it was Pearson who first wrote the distribution in terms of the standard deviation σ as in modern notation. Soon after this, in year 1915, Fisher added the location parameter to the formula for normal distribution, expressing it in the way it is written nowadays:

$$df = \frac{1}{\sigma\sqrt{2\pi}} e^{-\frac{(x-m)^2}{2\sigma^2}} dx$$

The term "standard normal", which denotes the normal distribution with zero mean and unit variance came into general use around 1950s, appearing in the popular textbooks by P.G. Hoel (1947) "*Introduction to mathematical statistics*" and A.M. Mood (1950) "*Introduction to the theory of statistics*".

When the name is used, the "Gaussian distribution" was named after Carl Friedrich Gauss, who introduced the distribution in 1809 as a way of rationalizing the method of least squares as outlined above. Among English speakers, both "normal distribution" and "Gaussian distribution" are in common use, with different terms preferred by different communities.

Discrete probability distribution

In probability theory and statistics, a discrete probability distribution is a probability distribution characterized by a probability mass function. Thus, the distribution of a random variable *X* is discrete, and *X* is then called a discrete random variable, if as *u* runs through the set of all possible values of *X*. It follows that such a random variable can assume only a finite or countably infinite number of values. That is, the possible values might be listed, although the list might be infinite. For example, count observations such as the numbers of birds in flocks comprise only natural number values {0, 1, 2, ...}. By contrast, continuous observations such as the weights of birds comprise real number values and would typically be modeled by a continuous probability distribution such as the normal.

In cases more frequently considered, this set of possible values is a topologically discrete set in the sense that all its points are isolated points. But there are discrete random variables for which this countable set is dense on the real line (for example, a distribution over rational numbers).

Among the most well-known discrete probability distributions that are used for statistical modeling are the Poisson distribution, the Bernoulli distribution, the binomial distribution, the geometric distribution, and the negative binomial distribution. In addition, the discrete uniform distribution is commonly used in computer programs that make equal-probability random selections between a number of choices.

Alternative description

Equivalently to the above, a discrete random variable can be defined as a random variable whose cumulative distribution function (cdf) increases only by jump discontinuities—that is, its cdf increases only where it "jumps" to a higher value, and is constant between those jumps. The points where jumps occur are precisely the values which the random variable may take. The number of such jumps may be finite or countably infinite. The set of locations of such jumps need not be topologically discrete; for example, the cdf might jump at each rational number.

Consequently, a discrete probability distribution is often represented as a generalized probability density function involving Dirac delta functions, which substantially unifies the treatment of continuous and discrete distributions. This is especially useful when dealing with probability distributions involving both a continuous and a discrete part.

Representation in terms of indicator functions

For a discrete random variable *X*, let *u*0, *u*1, ... be the values it can take with non-zero probability. Denote These are disjoint sets, and by formula (1)

It follows that the probability that *X* takes any value except for *u*0, *u*1, ... is zero, and thus one can write *X* as except on a set of probability zero, where 1*A* is the indicator function of *A*. This may serve as an alternative definition of discrete random variables.

9

Sampling Distributions and Confidence Intervals

Sampling Distribution

In statistics, a sampling distribution or finite-sample distribution is the probability distribution of a given statistic based on a random sample. Sampling distributions are important in statistics because they provide a major simplification on the route to statistical inference. More specifically, they allow analytical considerations to be based on the sampling distribution of a statistic, rather than on the joint probability distribution of all the individual sample values.

The sampling distribution of a statistic is the distribution of that statistic, considered as a random variable, when derived from a random sample of size n. It may be considered as the distribution of the statistic for *all possible samples from the same population* of a given size. The sampling distribution depends on the underlying distribution of the population, the statistic being considered, the sampling procedure employed, and the sample size used.

For example, consider a normal population with mean μ and variance σ^2. Assume we repeatedly take samples of a given size from this population and calculate the arithmetic mean $\bar{x}$ for each sample — this statistic is called the sample mean. Each sample has its own average value, and the distribution of these averages is called the "sampling distribution of the sample mean". This distribution is normal $\mathcal{N}(\mu, \sigma^2/n)$(n is the sample size) since the underlying population is normal, although sampling distributions may also often be close to normal even when the population distribution is not. An alternative to the sample mean is the sample median. When calculated from the same population, it has a different sampling distribution to that of the mean and is generally not normal (but it may be close for large sample sizes).

The mean of a sample from a population having a normal distribution is an example of a simple statistic taken from one of the simplest statistical populations. For other statistics and other populations the formulas are more complicated, and often they don't exist in closed-form. In such cases the sampling distributions may be approximated through Monte-Carlo simulations, bootstrap methods, or asymptotic distribution theory.

Standard error

The standard deviation of the sampling distribution of a statistic is referred to as the standard error of that quantity. For the case where the statistic is the sample mean, and samples are uncorrelated, the standard error is:

$$\sigma_{\bar{x}} = \frac{\sigma}{\sqrt{n}}$$

where σ is the standard deviation of the population distribution of that quantity and n is the size (number of items) in the sample.

An important implication of this formula is that the sample size must be quadrupled (multiplied by 4) to achieve half (1/2) the measurement error. When designing statistical studies where cost is a factor, this may have a role in understanding cost-benefit tradeoffs.

Statistical inference

In the theory of statistical inference, the idea of a sufficient statistic provides the basis of choosing a statistic (as a function of the sample data points) in such a way that no information is lost by replacing the full probabilistic description of the sample with the sampling distribution of the selected statistic.

In frequentist inference, for example in the development of a statistical hypothesis test or a confidence interval, the availability of the sampling distribution of a statistic (or an approximation to this in the form of an asymptotic distribution) can allow the ready formulation of such procedures, whereas the development of procedures starting from the joint distribution of the sample would be less straightforward.

In Bayesian inference, when the sampling distribution of a statistic is available, one can consider replacing the final outcome of such procedures, specifically the conditional distributions of any unknown quantities given the sample data, by the conditional distributions of any unknown quantities given selected sample statistics. Such a procedure would involve the sampling distribution of the statistics. The results would be identical provided the statistics chosen are jointly sufficient statistics.

Confidence interval

In statistics, a confidence interval (CI) is a type of interval estimate of a population parameter and is used to indicate the reliability of an estimate. It is an observed interval (i.e. it is calculated from the observations), in principle different from sample to sample, that frequently includes the parameter of interest if the experiment is repeated. How frequently the observed interval contains the parameter is determined by the confidence level or confidence coefficient. More specifically, the meaning of the term "confidence level" is that, if confidence intervals are constructed across many separate data analyses of repeated (and possibly different) experiments, the proportion of such intervals that contain the true value of the parameter will match the confidence level; this is guaranteed by the reasoning underlying the construction of confidence intervals. Whereas two-sided confidence limits form a confidence interval, their one-sided counterparts are referred to as lower or upper confidence bounds.

Confidence intervals consist of a range of values (interval) that act as good estimates of the unknown population parameter. However, in infrequent cases, none of these values may cover the value of the parameter. The level of confidence of the confidence interval would indicate the probability that the confidence range captures this true population parameter given a distribution of samples. It does not describe any single sample. This value is represented by a percentage, so when we say, "we are 99% confident that the true value of the parameter is in our confidence interval", we express that 99% of the observed confidence intervals will hold the true value of the parameter. After a sample is taken, the population parameter is either in the interval made or not; it is not a matter of chance. The desired level of confidence is set by the researcher (not determined by data). If a corresponding hypothesis test is performed, the confidence level is the complement of respective level of significance, i.e. a 95% confidence interval reflects a significance level of 0.05. The confidence interval contains the parameter values that, when tested, should not be rejected with the same sample. Greater levels of variance yield larger confidence intervals, and hence less precise estimates of the parameter. Confidence intervals of difference parameters not containing 0 imply that there is a statistically significant difference between the populations.

In applied practice, confidence intervals are typically stated at the 95% confidence level. However, when presented graphically, confidence intervals can be shown at several confidence levels, for example 50%, 95% and 99%.

Certain factors may affect the confidence interval size including size of sample, level of confidence, and population variability. A larger sample size normally will lead to a better estimate of the population parameter.

A confidence interval does *not* predict that the true value of the parameter has a particular probability of being in the confidence interval given the data actually obtained. Intervals with this property, called credible intervals, exist only in the paradigm of Bayesian statistics, as they require postulation of a prior distribution for the parameter of interest.

Conceptual basis

Introduction

Interval estimates can be contrasted with point estimates. A point estimate is a single value given as the estimate of a population parameter that is of interest, for example the mean of some quantity. An interval estimate specifies instead a range within which the parameter is estimated to lie. Confidence intervals are commonly reported in tables or graphs along with point estimates of the same parameters, to show the reliability of the estimates.

For example, a confidence interval can be used to describe how reliable survey results are. In a poll of election voting-intentions, the result might be that 40% of respondents intend to vote for a certain party. A 99% confidence interval for the proportion in the whole population having the same intention on the survey might be 30% to 50%. From the same data one may calculate a 90% confidence interval, which in this case might be 37% to 43%. A major factor determining the length of a confidence interval is the size of the sample used in the estimation procedure, for example the number of people taking part in a survey.

Meaning and interpretation

For users of frequentist methods, various interpretations of a confidence interval can be given.

- The confidence interval can be expressed in terms of samples (or repeated samples): "*Were this procedure to be repeated on multiple samples, the calculated confidence interval (which would differ for each sample) would encompass the true population parameter 90% of the time.*" Note that this does not refer to repeated measurement of the same sample, but repeated sampling.
- The confidence interval can be expressed in terms of a single sample: "*There is a 90% probability that the calculated confidence interval encompasses the true value of the population parameter.*" Note this is a probability statement about the confidence interval, not the population parameter. This considers the probability associated with a confidence interval from a pre-experiment point of view, in the same context in which arguments for the random allocation of treatments to study items are made. Here the experimenter sets out the way in which they intend to calculate a confidence interval and know, before they do the actual experiment, that the interval they will end up calculating has a certain chance of covering the true but unknown value. This is very similar to the "repeated sample" interpretation above, except that it avoids relying on considering hypothetical repeats of a sampling procedure that may not be repeatable in any meaningful sense. See Neyman construction.
- The explanation of a confidence interval can amount to something like: "*The confidence interval represents values for the population parameter for which the difference between the parameter and the observed estimate is not statistically significant at the 10% level*". In fact, this relates to one particular way in which a confidence interval may be constructed.

In each of the above, the following applies: If the true value of the parameter lies outside the 90% confidence interval once it has been calculated, then an event has occurred which had a probability of 10% (or less) of happening by chance.

Philosophical issues

The principle behind confidence intervals was formulated to provide an answer to the question raised in statistical inference of how to deal with the uncertainty inherent in results derived from data that are themselves only a randomly selected subset of a population. There are other answers, notably that provided by Bayesian inference in the form of credible intervals. Confidence intervals correspond to a chosen rule for determining the confidence bounds, where this rule is essentially determined before any data are obtained, or before an experiment is done. The rule is defined such that over all possible datasets that might be obtained, there is a high probability ("high" is specifically quantified) that the interval determined by the rule will include the true value of the quantity under consideration. That is a fairly straightforward and reasonable way of specifying a rule for determining uncertainty intervals. The Bayesian approach appears to offer intervals that can, subject to acceptance of an interpretation of "probability" as Bayesian probability, be interpreted as meaning that the specific interval calculated from a given dataset has a certain probability of including the true value, conditional on the data and other information available. The confidence interval approach does not allow this, since in this formulation and at this same stage, both the bounds of interval and the true values are fixed values and there is no randomness involved.

For example, in the poll example outlined in the introduction, to be 95% confident that the actual number of voters intending to vote for the party in question is between 36% and 44%, should not be interpreted in the common-sense interpretation that there is a 95% probability that the actual number of voters intending to vote for the party in question is between 36% and 44%. The actual meaning of confidence levels and confidence intervals is rather more subtle. In the above case, a correct interpretation would be as follows: If the polling were repeated a large number of times (you could produce a 95% confidence interval for your polling confidence interval), each time generating about a 95% confidence interval from the poll sample, then 95% of the generated intervals would contain the true percentage of voters who intend to vote for the given party. Each time the polling is repeated, a *different* confidence interval is produced; hence, it is not possible to make absolute statements about probabilities for any one given interval. For more information, see the section on meaning and interpretation.

The questions concerning how an interval expressing uncertainty in an estimate might be formulated, and of how such intervals might be interpreted, are not strictly mathematical problems and are philosophically problematic. Mathematics can take over once the basic principles of an approach to inference have been established, but it has only a limited role in saying why one approach should be preferred to another.

Relationship with other statistical topics

Statistical hypothesis testing

Confidence intervals are closely related to statistical significance testing. For example, if for some estimated parameter θ one wants to test the null hypothesis that $\theta = 0$ against the alternative that θ ‘“ 0, then this test can be performed by determining whether the confidence interval for θ contains 0.

More generally, given the availability of a hypothesis testing procedure that can test the null hypothesis $\theta = \theta 0$ against the alternative that θ ‘“ $\theta 0$ for any value of $\theta 0$, then a confidence interval with confidence level $\gamma = 1$ ” α can be defined as containing any number $\theta 0$ for which the corresponding null hypothesis is not rejected at significance level α.

In consequence, if the estimates of two parameters (for example, the mean values of a variable in two independent groups of objects) have confidence intervals at a given γ value that do not overlap, then the difference between the two values is significant at the corresponding value of α. However, this test is too conservative and can lead to erroneous rejection of a result that is significant at α. If two confidence intervals overlap, the two means still may be significantly different.

While the formulations of the notions of confidence intervals and of statistical hypothesis testing are distinct they are in some senses related and to some extent complementary. While not all confidence intervals are constructed in this way, one general purpose approach to constructing confidence intervals is to define a 100(1 ” α)% confidence interval to consist of all those values $\theta 0$ for which a test of the hypothesis $\theta = \theta 0$ is not rejected at a significance level of 100α%. Such an approach may not always be available since it presupposes the practical availability of an appropriate significance test. Naturally, any assumptions required for the significance test would carry over to the confidence intervals.

It may be convenient to make the general correspondence that parameter values within a confidence interval are equivalent to those values that would not be rejected by a hypothesis test, but this would be dangerous. In many instances the confidence intervals that are quoted are only approximately valid, perhaps derived from "plus or minus twice the standard error", and the implications of this for the supposedly corresponding hypothesis tests are usually unknown.

It is worth noting that the confidence interval for a parameter is not the same as the acceptance region of a test for this parameter, as is sometimes thought. The confidence interval is part of the parameter space, whereas the acceptance region is part of the sample space. For the same reason the confidence level is not the same as the complementary probability of the level of significance

Confidence region

Confidence regions generalize the confidence interval concept to deal with multiple quantities. Such regions can indicate not only the extent of likely sampling errors but can also reveal whether (for example) it is the case that if the estimate for one quantity is unreliable then the other is also likely to be unreliable.

Confidence band

Statistical theory

Definition

Let X be a random sample from a probability distribution with statistical parameters θ, which is a quantity to be estimated, and φ, representing quantities that are not of immediate interest. A *confidence interval* for the parameter θ, with confidence level or confidence coefficient γ, is an interval with random endpoints $(u(X), v(X))$, determined by the pair of random variables $u(X)$ and $v(X)$, with the property:

$$\Pr_{\theta,\varphi}(u(X) < \theta < v(X)) = \gamma \text{ for all } (\theta, \varphi).$$

The quantities φ in which there is no immediate interest are called nuisance parameters, as statistical theory still needs to find some way to deal with them. The number γ, with typical values close to but not greater than 1, is sometimes given in the form 1 " α (or as a percentage 100%·(1 " α)), where α is a small non-negative number, close to 0.

Here Prθ,φ indicates the probability distribution of X characterised by (θ, φ). An important part of this specification is that the random interval $(u(X), v(X))$ covers the unknown value θ with a high probability no matter what the true value of θ actually is.

Note that here Prθ,φ need not refer to an explicitly given parameterised family of distributions, although it often does. Just as the random variable X notionally corresponds to other possible realizations of x from the same population or from the same version of reality, the parameters (θ, φ) indicate that we need to consider other versions of reality in which the distribution of X might have different characteristics.

In a specific situation, when x is the outcome of the sample X, the interval $(u(x), v(x))$ is also referred to as a confidence interval for θ. Note that it is no longer possible to say that the (observed) interval ($u(x)$, $v(x)$) has probability γ to contain the parameter θ. This observed interval is just one realization of all possible intervals for which the probability statement holds.

Approximate confidence intervals

In many applications, confidence intervals that have exactly the required confidence level are hard to construct. But practically useful intervals can still be found: the rule for constructing the interval may be accepted as providing a confidence interval at level γ if

$$\Pr_{\theta,\phi}(u(X) < \theta < v(X)) \approx \gamma \text{ for all } (\theta, \phi)$$

to an acceptable level of approximation. Alternatively, some authors simply require that

$$\Pr_{\theta,\phi}(u(X) < \theta < v(X)) \geq \gamma \text{ for all } (\theta, \phi)$$

which is useful if the probabilities are only partially identified, or imprecise.

Desirable properties

When applying standard statistical procedures, there will often be standard ways of constructing confidence intervals. These will have been devised so as to meet certain desirable properties, which will hold given that the assumptions on which the procedure rely are true. These desirable properties may be described as: validity, optimality and invariance. Of these "validity" is most important, followed closely by "optimality". "Invariance" may be considered as a property of the method of derivation of a confidence interval rather than of the rule for constructing the interval. In non-standard applications, the same desirable properties would be sought.

Validity. This means that the nominal coverage probability (confidence level) of the confidence interval should hold, either exactly or to a good approximation.

Optimality. This means that the rule for constructing the confidence interval should make as much use of the information in the data-set as possible. Recall that one could throw away half of a dataset and still be able to derive a valid confidence interval. One way of assessing optimality is by the length of the interval, so that a rule for constructing a confidence interval is judged better than another if it leads to intervals whose lengths are typically shorter.

Invariance. In many applications the quantity being estimated might not be tightly defined as such. For example, a survey might result in an estimate of the median income in a population, but it might equally be considered as providing an estimate of the logarithm of the median income, given that this is a common scale for presenting graphical results. It would be desirable that the method used for constructing a confidence interval for the median income would give equivalent results when applied to constructing a confidence interval for the logarithm of the median income: specifically the values at the ends of the latter interval would be the logarithms of the values at the ends of former interval.

Methods of derivation

For non-standard applications, there are several routes that might be taken to derive a rule for the construction of confidence intervals. Established rules for standard procedures might be justified or explained via several of these routes. Typically a rule for constructing confidence intervals is closely tied to a particular way of finding a point estimate of the quantity being considered.

Descriptive statistics

This is closely related to the method of moments for estimation. A simple example arises where the quantity to be estimated is the mean, in which case a natural estimate is the sample mean. The usual arguments indicate that the sample variance can be used to estimate the variance of the sample mean. A naive confidence interval for the true mean can be constructed centered on the sample mean with a width which is a multiple of the square root of the sample variance.

Likelihood theory

Where estimates are constructed using the maximum likelihood principle, the theory for this provides two ways of constructing confidence intervals or confidence regions for the estimates.

Estimating equations

The estimation approach here can be considered as both a generalization of the method of moments and a generalization of the maximum likelihood approach. There are corresponding generalizations of the results of maximum likelihood theory that allow confidence intervals to be constructed based on estimates derived from estimating equations.

Via significance testing

If significance tests are available for general values of a parameter, then confidence intervals/regions can be constructed by including in the 100p% confidence region all those points for which the significance test of the null hypothesis that the true value is the given value is not rejected at a significance level of (1-p).

Bootstrapping

In situations where the distributional assumptions for that above methods are uncertain or violated, resampling methods allow construction of confidence intervals or prediction intervals. The observed data distribution and the internal correlations are used as the surrogate for the correlations in the wider population.

Examples

Practical example

A machine fills cups with a liquid, and is supposed to be adjusted so that the content of the cups is 250 g of liquid. As the machine cannot fill every cup with exactly 250 g, the content added to individual cups shows some variation, and is considered a random variable X. This variation is assumed to be normally distributed (although this assumption is not necessary for the theory to work) around the desired average of 250 g, with a standard deviation, σ, of 2.5 g. To determine if the machine is adequately calibrated, a sample of $n = 25$ cups of liquid are chosen at random and the cups are weighed. The resulting measured masses of liquid are $X1, ..., X25$, a random sample from X.

To get an impression of the expectation μ, it is sufficient to give an estimate. The appropriate estimator is the sample mean:

$$\hat{\mu} = \bar{X} = \frac{1}{n}\sum_{i=1}^{n} X_i.$$

The sample shows actual weights $x1, ..., x25$, with mean:

$$\bar{x} = \frac{1}{25}\sum_{i=1}^{25} x_i = 250.2 \text{ grams}.$$

If we take another sample of 25 cups, we could easily expect to find mass values like 250.4 or 251.1 grams. A sample mean value of 280 grams however would be extremely rare if the mean content of the cups is in fact close to 250 grams. There is a whole interval around the observed value 250.2 grams of the sample mean within which, if the whole population mean actually takes a value in this range, the observed data would not be considered particularly unusual. Such an interval is called a confidence interval for the parameter μ. How do we calculate such an interval? The endpoints of the interval have to be calculated from the sample, so they are statistics, functions of the sample $X1, ..., X25$ and hence random variables themselves.

In our case we may determine the endpoints by considering that the sample mean X from a normally distributed sample is also normally distributed, with the same expectation μ, but with a standard error of:

$$\frac{\sigma}{\sqrt{n}} = \frac{2.5 \text{ g}}{\sqrt{25}} = 0.5 \text{ grams}$$

By standardizing, we get a random variable:

$$Z = \frac{\bar{X} - \mu}{\sigma/\sqrt{n}} = \frac{\bar{X} - \mu}{0.5}$$

dependent on the parameter μ to be estimated, but with a standard normal distribution independent of the parameter μ. Hence it is possible to find numbers "z and z, independent of μ, between which Z lies with probability 1 " α, a measure of how confident we want to be.

We take 1 " α = 0.95, for example. So we have:

$$P(-z \leq Z \leq z) = 1 - \alpha = 0.95.$$

The number z follows from the cumulative distribution function, in this case the cumulative normal distribution function:

$$\Phi(z) = P(Z \leq z) = 1 - \tfrac{\alpha}{2} = 0.975,$$

$$z = \Phi^{-1}(\Phi(z)) = \Phi^{-1}(0.975) = 1.96,$$

and we get:

$$0.95 = 1 - \alpha = P(-z \leq Z \leq z) = P\left(-1.96 \leq \frac{\bar{X} - \mu}{\sigma/\sqrt{n}} \leq 1.96\right)$$

$$= P\left(\bar{X} - 1.96\frac{\sigma}{\sqrt{n}} \leq \mu \leq \bar{X} + 1.96\frac{\sigma}{\sqrt{n}}\right)$$

In other words, the lower endpoint of the 95% confidence interval is:

$$\text{Lower endpoint} = \bar{X} - 1.96\frac{\sigma}{\sqrt{n}},$$

and the upper endpoint of the 95% confidence interval is:

$$\text{Upper endpoint} = \bar{X} + 1.96\frac{\sigma}{\sqrt{n}}.$$

With the values in this example, the confidence interval is:

$$0.95 = P\left(\bar{X} - 1.96 \times 0.5 \leq \mu \leq \bar{X} + 1.96 \times 0.5\right)$$

$$= P\left(\bar{X} - 0.98 \leq \mu \leq \bar{X} + 0.98\right).$$

This might be interpreted as: with probability 0.95 we will find a confidence interval in which the value of parameter ì we will be between the stochastic endpoints

$$\bar{X} - 0.98$$

and

$$\bar{X} + 0.98.$$

This does not mean there is 0.95 probability that the value of parameter μ is in the interval obtained by using the currently computed value of the sample mean,

$$(\bar{x} - 0.98,\ \bar{x} + 0.98).$$

Instead, every time the measurements are repeated, there will be another value for the mean *X* of the sample. In 95% of the cases μ will be between the endpoints calculated from this mean, but in 5% of the cases it will not be. The actual confidence interval is calculated by entering the measured masses in the formula. Our 0.95 confidence interval becomes:

$$(\bar{x} - 0.98; \bar{x} + 0.98) = (250.2 - 0.98; 250.2 + 0.98) = (249.22; 251.18).$$

In other words, the 95% confidence interval is between the lower endpoint 249.22 g and the upper endpoint 251.18 g.

As the desired value 250 of μ is within the resulted confidence interval, there is no reason to believe the machine is wrongly calibrated.

The calculated interval has fixed endpoints, where μ might be in between (or not). Thus this event has probability either 0 or 1. One cannot say: "with probability (1 " α) the parameter μ lies in the confidence interval." One only knows that by repetition in 100(1 " α) % of the cases, μ will be in the calculated interval. In 100α% of the cases however it does not. And unfortunately one does not know in which of the cases this happens. That is (instead of using the term "probability") why one can say: "with confidence level 100(1 " α) %, μ lies in the confidence interval."

The maximum error is calculated to be 0.98 since it is the difference between value that we are confident of with upper or lower endpoint.

The figure on the right shows 50 realizations of a confidence interval for a given population mean ì. If we randomly choose one realization, the probability is 95% we end up having chosen an interval that contains the parameter; however we may be unlucky and have picked the wrong one. We will never know; we are stuck with our interval.

Alternatives and critiques

Confidence intervals are one method of interval estimation, and the most widely used in frequentist statistics. An analogous concept in Bayesian statistics is credible intervals, while an alternative frequentist method is that of prediction intervals which, rather than estimating *parameters,* estimate the outcome of *future* samples. For other approaches to expressing uncertainty using intervals, see interval estimation.

There is disagreement about which of these methods produces the most useful results: the mathematics of the computations are rarely in question–confidence intervals being based on sampling distributions, credible intervals being based on Bayes' theorem–but the application of these methods, the utility and interpretation of the produced statistics, is debated.

Users of Bayesian methods, if they produced an interval estimate, would in contrast to confidence intervals, want to say "*My degree of* belief *that the parameter is in fact in this interval is 90%,*" while users of prediction intervals would instead say "I *predict* that the *next sample* will fall in this interval 90% of the time."

Comparison to prediction intervals

A prediction interval for a random variable is defined similarly to a confidence interval for a statistical parameter. Consider an additional random variable *Y* which may or may not be statistically dependent on the random sample *X*. Then (*u*(*X*), *v*(*X*)) provides a prediction interval for the as-yet-to-be observed value *y* of *Y* if

$$\Pr_{\theta,\phi}(u(X) < Y < v(X)) = \gamma \text{ for all } (\theta, \phi).$$

Here Prθ,φ indicates the joint probability distribution of the random variables (*X*, *Y*), where this distribution depends on the statistical parameters (θ, φ).

Comparison to Bayesian interval estimates

A Bayesian interval estimate is called a credible interval. Using much of the same notation as above, the definition of a credible interval for the unknown true value of θ is, for a given γ,

$$\Pr(u(x) < \Theta < v(x) | X = x) = \gamma.$$

Here Θ is used to emphasize that the unknown value of θ is being treated as a random variable. The definitions of the two types of intervals may be compared as follows.

- The definition of a confidence interval involves probabilities calculated from the distribution of *X* for given (è, ö) (or conditional on these values) and the condition needs to hold for all values of (è, ö).

- The definition of a credible interval involves probabilities calculated from the distribution of È conditional on the observed values of $X = x$ and marginalised (or averaged) over the values of Ö, where this last quantity is the random variable corresponding to the uncertainty about the nuisance parameters in *ö*.

Note that the treatment of the nuisance parameters above is often omitted from discussions comparing confidence and credible intervals but it is markedly different between the two cases.

In some simple standard cases, the intervals produced as confidence and credible intervals from the same data set can be identical. They are very different if informative prior information is included in the Bayesian analysis; and may be very different for some parts of the space of possible data even if the Bayesian prior is relatively uninformative.

Confidence intervals for proportions and related quantities

An approximate confidence interval for a population mean can be constructed for random variables that are not normally distributed in the population, relying on the central limit theorem, if the sample sizes and counts are big enough. The formulae are identical to the case above (where the sample mean is actually normally distributed about the population mean). The approximation will be quite good with only a few dozen observations in the sample if the probability distribution of the random variable is not too different from the normal distribution (e.g. its cumulative distribution function does not have any discontinuities and its skewness is moderate).

One type of sample mean is the mean of an indicator variable, which takes on the value 1 for true and the value 0 for false. The mean of such a variable is equal to the proportion that have the variable equal to one (both in the population and in any sample). This is a useful property of indicator variables, especially for hypothesis testing. To apply the central limit theorem, one must use a large enough sample. A rough rule of thumb is that one should see at least 5 cases in which the indicator is 1 and at least 5 in which it is 0. Confidence intervals constructed using the above formulae may include negative numbers or numbers greater than 1, but proportions obviously cannot be negative or exceed 1. Additionally, sample proportions can only take on a finite number of values, so the central limit theorem and the normal distribution are not the best tools for building a confidence interval. See "Binomial proportion confidence interval" for better methods which are specific to this case.

Proportionality

In mathematics, two variables are proportional if a change in one is always accompanied by a change in the other, and if the changes are always related by use of a constant. The constant is called the coefficient of proportionality or proportionality constant.

- If one variable is always the product of the other and a constant, the two are said to be *directly proportional*. *x* and *y* are directly proportional if the ratio $\frac{y}{x}$ is constant.
- If the product of the two variables is always equal to a constant, the two are said to be *inversely proportional*. *x* and *y* are inversely proportional if the product xy is constant.

If a linear function transforms 0, *a* and *b* into 0, *c* and *d*, and if the product *a b c d* is not zero, we say *a* and *b* are proportional to *c* and *d*. An equality of two ratios such as $\frac{a}{c} = \frac{b}{d}$, where no term is zero, is called a proportio

Geometric illustration

When the duplication of a given rectangle preserves its shape, the ratio of the large dimension to the small dimension is a constant number in all the copies, and in the original rectangle. The largest rectangle of the drawing is similar to one or the other rectangle with stripes. From their width to their height, the coefficient is $\frac{d}{c} = \frac{b}{a} = \frac{d+b}{c+a}$. A ratio of their dimensions horizontally written within the image, at the top or the bottom, determines the common shape of the three similar rectangles.

The common diagonal of the similar rectangles divides each rectangle into two superposable triangles, with two different kinds of stripes. The four striped triangles and the two striped rectangles have a common vertex: the center of an homothetic transformation with a negative ratio "*k* or $\frac{-1}{k}$, that transforms one triangle and its stripes into another triangle with the same stripes, enlarged or reduced. The duplication scale of a striped triangle is the proportionality constant between the corresponding sides lengths of the triangles, equal to a positive ratio obliquely written within the image: $\frac{c}{a} = k$ or $\frac{a}{c} = \frac{1}{k}$.

In the proportion $\frac{a}{b} = \frac{c}{d}$, the terms *a* and *d* are called the extremes, while *b* and *c* are the means, because *a* and *d* are the extreme terms of the list (*a*, *b*, *c*, *d*), while *b* and *c* are in the middle of the list. From any proportion, we get another proportion by inverting the extremes or the means. And the product of the extremes equals the product of the means. Within the image, a double arrow indicates two inverted terms of the first proportion.

Consider dividing the largest rectangle in two triangles, cutting along the diagonal. If we remove two triangles from either half rectangle, we get one of the plain gray rectangles. Above and below this diagonal, the areas of the two biggest triangles of the drawing are equal, because these triangles are superposable. Above and below the subtracted areas are equal for the same reason. Therefore, the two plain gray rectangles have the same area: $a\,d = b\,c$.

Symbols

The mathematical symbol "" (U+221D in Unicode, \propto in TeX) is used to indicate that two values are proportional. For example, A "" B means the variable A is directly proportional to the variable B.

Other symbols include:

- 7" - U+2237 "PROPORTION"
- :" - U+223A "GEOMETRIC PROPORTION"

Direct proportionality

Given two variables *x* and *y*, *y is **directly proportional*** *to x* (*x and y **vary directly**,* or *x and y are in **direct variation***) if there is a non-zero constant *k* such that

$y = kx.$

The relation is often denoted, using the "" symbol, as

$y \propto x$ and the constant ratio $k = \frac{y}{x}$ is called the proportionality constant, constant of variation or constant of proportionality.

Examples

- If an object travels at a constant speed, then the distance traveled is directly proportional to the time spent traveling, with the speed being the constant of proportionality.
- The circumference of a circle is directly proportional to its diameter, with the constant of proportionality equal to ð.
- On a map drawn to scale, the distance between any two points on the map is directly proportional to the distance between the two locations that the points represent, with the constant of proportionality being the scale of the map.
- The force acting on a certain object due to gravity is directly proportional to the object's mass; the constant of proportionality between the mass and the force is known as gravitational acceleration.

Properties

Since:

$y = kx$

is equivalent to

$x = \left(\frac{1}{k}\right) y,$

it follows that if *y* is directly proportional to *x*, with (nonzero) proportionality constant *k*, then *x* is also directly proportional to *y* with proportionality constant 1/*k*.

If *y* is directly proportional to *x*, then the graph of y as a function of x will be a straight line passing through the origin with the slope of the line equal to the constant of proportionality: it corresponds to linear growth.

Inverse proportionality

The concept of *inverse proportionality* can be contrasted against *direct proportionality*. Consider two variables said to be "inversely proportional" to each other. If all other variables are held constant, the magnitude or absolute value of one inversely proportional variable will decrease if the other variable increases, while their product (the constant of proportionality *k*) is always the same.

Formally, two variables are inversely proportional (also called varying inversely, in inverse variation, in inverse proportion, in reciprocal proportion) if one of the variables is directly proportional with the multiplicative inverse (reciprocal) of the other, or equivalently if their product is a constant. It follows that the variable y is inversely proportional to the variable x if there exists a non-zero constant k such that

$$y = \frac{k}{x}$$

The constant can be found by multiplying the original x variable and the original y variable.

As an example, the time taken for a journey is inversely proportional to the speed of travel; the time needed to dig a hole is (approximately) inversely proportional to the number of people digging.

The graph of two variables varying inversely on the Cartesian coordinate plane is a hyperbola. The product of the X and Y values of each point on the curve will equal the constant of proportionality (k). Since neither x nor y can equal zero (if k is non-zero), the graph will never cross either axis.

Hyperbolic coordinates

The concepts of *direct* and *inverse* proportion lead to the location of points in the Cartesian plane by hyperbolic coordinates; the two coordinates correspond to the constant of direct proportionality that locates a point on a ray and the constant of inverse proportionality that locates a point on a hyperbola.

Exponential and logarithmic proportionality

A variable y is exponentially proportional to a variable x, if y is directly proportional to the exponential function of x, that is if there exist non-zero constants k and a

$$y = ka^x.$$

Likewise, a variable y is logarithmically proportional to a variable x, if y is directly proportional to the logarithm of x, that is if there exist non-zero constants k and a

$$y = k \log_a(x).$$

10

Hypothesis Testing

A statistical hypothesis test is a method of statistical inference using data from a scientific study. In statistics, a result is called statistically significant if it has been predicted as unlikely to have occurred by chance alone, according to a pre-determined threshold probability, the significance level. The phrase "test of significance" was coined by statistician Ronald Fisher. These tests are used in determining what outcomes of a study would lead to a rejection of the null hypothesis for a pre-specified level of significance; this can help to decide whether results contain enough information to cast doubt on conventional wisdom, given that conventional wisdom has been used to establish the null hypothesis. The *critical region* of a hypothesis test is the set of all outcomes which cause the null hypothesis to be rejected in favor of the alternative hypothesis. Statistical hypothesis testing is sometimes called confirmatory data analysis, in contrast to exploratory data analysis, which may not have pre-specified hypotheses. In the Neyman-Pearson framework, the process of distinguishing between the null & alternative hypotheses is aided by identifying two conceptual types of errors (type 1 & type 2), and by specifying parametric limits on e.g. how much type 1 error will be permitted.

Variations and sub-classes

Statistical hypothesis testing is a key technique of both Frequentist inference and Bayesian inference although they have ×notable differences. Statistical hypothesis tests define a procedure that controls (fixes) the probability of incorrectly *deciding* that a default position (null hypothesis) is incorrect based on how likely it would be for a set of observations to occur if the null hypothesis were true. Note that this probability of making an incorrect decision is not the probability that the null hypothesis is true, nor whether any specific alternative hypothesis is true. This contrasts with other possible techniques of decision theory in which the null and alternative hypothesis are treated on a more equal basis. One naive Bayesian approach to hypothesis testing is to base decisions on the posterior probability, but this fails when comparing point and continuous hypotheses. Other approaches to decision making, such as Bayesian decision theory, attempt to balance the consequences of incorrect decisions across all possibilities, rather than concentrating on a single null hypothesis. A number of other approaches to reaching a decision based on data are available via decision theory and optimal decisions, some of which have desirable properties, yet hypothesis testing is a dominant approach to data analysis in many fields of science. Extensions to the theory of hypothesis testing include the study of the power of tests, the probability of correctly rejecting the null hypothesis given that it is false. Such considerations can be used for the purpose of sample size determination prior to the collection of data.

The testing process

In the statistics literature, statistical hypothesis testing plays a fundamental role. The usual line of reasoning is as follows:

1. There is an initial research hypothesis of which the truth is unknown.
2. The first step is to state the relevant null and alternative hypotheses. This is important as mis-stating the hypotheses will muddy the rest of the process. Specifically, the null hypothesis allows to attach an attribute: it should be chosen in such a way that it allows us to conclude whether the alternative hypothesis can either be accepted or stays undecided as it was before the test.
3. The second step is to consider the statistical assumptions being made about the sample in doing the test; for example, assumptions about the statistical independence or about the form of the distributions of the observations. This is equally important as invalid assumptions will mean that the results of the test are invalid.
4. Decide which test is appropriate, and state the relevant test statistic T.
5. Derive the distribution of the test statistic under the null hypothesis from the assumptions. In standard cases this will be a well-known result. For example the test statistic might follow a Student's t distribution or a normal distribution.
6. Select a significance level (*á*), a probability threshold below which the null hypothesis will be rejected. Common values are 5% and 1%.
7. The distribution of the test statistic under the null hypothesis partitions the possible values of T into those for which the null hypothesis is rejected, the so-called critical region, and those for which it is not. The probability of the critical region is *á*.
8. Compute from the observations the observed value $t$obs of the test statistic T.
9. Decide to either reject the null hypothesis in favor of the alternative or not reject it. The decision rule is to reject the null hypothesis $H0$ if the observed value $t$obs is in the critical region, and to accept or "fail to reject" the hypothesis otherwise.

An alternative process is commonly used:

1. Compute from the observations the observed value $t$obs of the test statistic T.
2. Calculate the p-value. This is the probability, under the null hypothesis, of sampling a test statistic at least as extreme as that which was observed.
3. Reject the null hypothesis, in favor of the alternative hypothesis, if and only if the p-value is less than the significance level (the selected probability) threshold.

The two processes are equivalent. The former process was advantageous in the past when only tables of test statistics at common probability thresholds were available. It allowed a decision to be made without the calculation of a probability. It was adequate for classwork and for operational use, but it was deficient for reporting results.

The latter process relied on extensive tables or on computational support not always available. The explicit calculation of a probability is useful for reporting. The calculations are now trivially performed with appropriate software.

The difference in the two processes applied to the Radioactive suitcase example (below):

- "The Geiger-counter reading is 10. The limit is 9. Check the suitcase."
- "The Geiger-counter reading is high; 97% of safe suitcases have lower readings. The limit is 95%. Check the suitcase."

The former report is adequate, the latter gives a more detailed explanation of the data and the reason why the suitcase is being checked.

It is important to note the philosophical difference between accepting the null hypothesis and simply failing to reject it. The "fail to reject" terminology highlights the fact that the null hypothesis is assumed to be true from the start of the test; if there is a lack of evidence against it, it simply continues to be assumed true. The phrase "accept the null hypothesis" may suggest it has been proved simply because it has not been disproved, a logical fallacy known as the argument from ignorance. Unless a test with particularly high power is used, the idea of "accepting" the null hypothesis may be dangerous. Nonetheless the terminology is prevalent throughout statistics, where its meaning is well understood.

Alternatively, if the testing procedure forces us to reject the null hypothesis (H0), we can accept the alternative hypothesis (H1) and we conclude that the research hypothesis is supported by the data. This fact expresses that our procedure is based on probabilistic considerations in the sense we accept that using another set of data could lead us to a different conclusion.

The processes described here are perfectly adequate for computation. They seriously neglect the design of experiments considerations.

It is particularly critical that appropriate sample sizes be estimated before conducting the experiment.

Interpretation

If the p-value is less than the required significance level (equivalently, if the observed test statistic is in the critical region), then we say the null hypothesis is rejected at the given level of significance. Rejection of the null hypothesis is a conclusion. This is like a "guilty" verdict in a criminal trial – the evidence is sufficient to reject innocence, thus proving guilt. We might accept the alternative hypothesis (and the research hypothesis).

If the p-value is not less than the required significance level (equivalently, if the observed test statistic is outside the critical region), then the test has no result. The evidence is insufficient to support a conclusion. (This is like a jury that fails to reach a verdict.) The researcher typically gives extra consideration to those cases where the p-value is close to the significance level.

In the Lady tasting tea example (below), Fisher required the Lady to properly categorize all of the cups of tea to justify the conclusion that the result was unlikely to result from chance. He defined the critical region as that case alone. The region was defined by a probability (that the null hypothesis was correct) of less than 5%.

Whether rejection of the null hypothesis truly justifies acceptance of the research hypothesis depends on the structure of the hypotheses. Rejecting the hypothesis that a large paw print originated from a bear does not immediately prove the existence of Bigfoot. Hypothesis testing emphasizes the rejection which is based on a probability rather than the acceptance which requires extra steps of logic.

"The probability of rejecting the null hypothesis is a function of five factors: whether the test is one- or two tailed, the level of significance, the standard deviation, the amount of deviation from the null hypothesis, and the number of observations." These factors are a source of criticism.

Use and importance

Statistics are helpful in analyzing most collections of data. This is equally true of hypothesis testing which can justify conclusions even when no scientific theory exists. In the Lady tasting tea example, it was "obvious" that no difference existed between (milk poured into tea) and (tea poured into milk). The data contradicted the "obvious".

Real world applications of hypothesis testing include:

- Testing whether more men than women suffer from nightmares
- Establishing authorship of documents
- Evaluating the effect of the full moon on behavior
- Determining the range at which a bat can detect an insect by echo
- Deciding whether hospital carpeting results in more infections
- Selecting the best means to stop smoking
- Checking whether bumper stickers reflect car owner behavior
- Testing the claims of handwriting analysts

Statistical hypothesis testing plays an important role in the whole of statistics and in statistical inference. For example, Lehmann (1992) in a review of the fundamental paper by Neyman and Pearson (1933) says: "Nevertheless, despite their shortcomings, the new paradigm formulated in the 1933 paper, and the many developments carried out within its framework continue to play a central role in both the theory and practice of statistics and can be expected to do so in the foreseeable future".

Significance testing has been the favored statistical tool in some experimental social sciences (over 90% of articles in the Journal of Applied Psychology during the early 1990s). Other fields have favored the estimation of parameters (e.g., effect size). Significance testing is used as a substitute for the traditional comparison of predicted value and experimental result at the core of the scientific method. When theory is only capable of predicting the sign of a relationship, a directional (one-sided) hypothesis test can be configured so that only a statistically significant result supports theory. This form of theory appraisal is the most heavily criticized application of hypothesis testing.

Cautions

"If the government required statistical procedures to carry warning labels like those on drugs, most inference methods would have long labels indeed." This caution applies to hypothesis tests and alternatives to them.

The successful hypothesis test is associated with a probability and a type-I error rate. The conclusion *might* be wrong.

The conclusion of the test is only as solid as the sample upon which it is based. The design of the experiment is critical. A number of unexpected effects have been observed including:

- The Clever Hans effect. A horse appeared to be capable of doing simple arithmetic.
- The Hawthorne effect. Industrial workers were more productive in better illumination, and most productive in worse.
- The Placebo effect. Pills with no medically active ingredients were remarkably effective.

A statistical analysis of misleading data produces misleading conclusions. The issue of data quality can be more subtle. In forecasting for example, there is no agreement on a measure of forecast accuracy. In the absence of a consensus measurement, no decision based on measurements will be without controversy.

The book *How to Lie with Statistics* is the most popular book on statistics ever published. It does not much consider hypothesis testing, but its cautions are applicable, including: Many claims are made on the basis of samples too small to convince. If a report does not mention sample size, be doubtful. Hypothesis testing acts as a filter of statistical conclusions; only those results meeting a probability threshold are publishable. Economics also acts as a publication filter; only those results favorable to the author and funding source may be submitted for publication. The impact of filtering on publication is termed publication bias. A related problem is that of multiple testing (sometimes linked to data mining), in which a variety of tests for a variety of possible effects are applied to a single data set and only those yielding a significant result are reported. These are often dealt with by using multiplicity correction procedures that control the family wise error rate (FWER) or the false discovery rate (FDR).

Those making critical decisions based on the results of a hypothesis test are prudent to look at the details rather than the conclusion alone. In the physical sciences most results are fully accepted only when independently confirmed. The general advice concerning statistics is, "Figures never lie, but liars figure" (anonymous).

Example

Lady tasting tea

In a famous example of hypothesis testing, known as the *Lady tasting tea* example, a female colleague of Fisher claimed to be able to tell whether the tea or the milk was added first to a cup. Fisher proposed to give her eight cups, four of each variety, in random order. One could then ask what the probability was for her getting the number she got correct, but just by chance. The null hypothesis was that the Lady had no such ability. The test statistic was a simple count of the number of successes in selecting the 4 cups. The critical region was the single case of 4 successes of 4 possible based on a conventional probability criterion (< 5%; 1 of 70 H" 1.4%). Fisher asserted that no alternative hypothesis was (ever) required. The lady correctly identified every cup, which would be considered a statistically significant result.

Analogy – Courtroom trial

A statistical test procedure is comparable to a criminal trial; a defendant is considered not guilty as long as his or her guilt is not proven. The prosecutor tries to prove the guilt of the defendant. Only when there is enough charging evidence the defendant is convicted.

In the start of the procedure, there are two hypotheses H_0: "the defendant is not guilty", and H_1: "the defendant is guilty". The first one is called *null hypothesis*, and is for the time being accepted. The second one is called *alternative (hypothesis)*. It is the hypothesis one hopes to support.

The hypothesis of innocence is only rejected when an error is very unlikely, because one doesn't want to convict an innocent defendant. Such an error is called *error of the first kind* (i.e., the conviction of an innocent person), and the occurrence of this error is controlled to be rare. As a consequence of this asymmetric behaviour, the *error of the second kind* (acquitting a person who committed the crime), is often rather large.

A criminal trial can be regarded as either or both of two decision processes: guilty vs not guilty or evidence vs a threshold ("beyond a reasonable doubt"). In one view, the defendant is judged; in the other view the performance of the prosecution (which bears the burden of proof) is judged. A hypothesis test can be regarded as either a judgment of a hypothesis or as a judgment of evidence.

Example 1 – Philosopher's beans

The following example was produced by a philosopher describing scientific methods generations before hypothesis testing was formalized and popularized.

- Few beans of this handful are white.
- Most beans in this bag are white.
- Therefore: Probably, these beans were taken from another bag.
- This is an hypothetical inference.

The beans in the bag are the population. The handful are the sample. The null hypothesis is that the sample originated from the population. The criterion for rejecting the null-hypothesis is the "obvious" difference in appearance (an informal difference in the mean). The interesting result is that consideration of a real population and a real sample produced an imaginary bag. The philosopher was considering logic rather than probability. To be a real statistical hypothesis test, this example requires the formalities of a probability calculation and a comparison of that probability to a standard.

A simple generalization of the example considers a mixed bag of beans and a handful that contain either very few or very many white beans. The generalization considers both extremes. It requires more calculations and more comparisons to arrive at a formal answer, but the core philosophy is unchanged; If the composition of the handful is greatly different that of the bag, then the sample probably originated from another bag. The original example is termed a one-sided or a one-tailed test while the generalization is termed a two-sided or two-tailed test.

Example 2 – Clairvoyant card game

A person (the subject) is tested for clairvoyance. He is shown the reverse of a randomly chosen playing card 25 times and asked which of the four suits it belongs to. The number of hits, or correct answers, is called X.

As we try to find evidence of his clairvoyance, for the time being the null hypothesis is that the person is not clairvoyant. The alternative is, of course: the person is (more or less) clairvoyant.

If the null hypothesis is valid, the only thing the test person can do is guess. For every card, the probability (relative frequency) of any single suit appearing is 1/4. If the alternative is valid, the test subject will predict the suit correctly with probability greater than 1/4. We will call the probability of guessing correctly p.

When the test subject correctly predicts all 25 cards, we will consider him clairvoyant, and reject the null hypothesis. Thus also with 24 or 23 hits. With only 5 or 6 hits, on the other hand, there is no cause to consider him so. But what about 12 hits, or 17 hits? What is the critical number, c, of hits, at which point we consider the subject to be clairvoyant? How do we determine the critical value c? It is obvious that with the choice c=25 (i.e. we only accept clairvoyance when all cards are predicted correctly) we're more critical than with c=10. In the first case almost no test subjects will be recognized to be clairvoyant, in the second case, a certain number will pass the test. In practice, one decides how critical one will be. That is, one decides how often one accepts an error of the first kind – a false positive, or Type I error. With $c = 25$ the probability of such an error is:

$$P(\text{reject } H_0|H_0 \text{ is valid}) = P(X = 25|p = \tfrac{1}{4}) = (\tfrac{1}{4})^{25} \approx 10^{-15},$$

and hence, very small. The probability of a false positive is the probability of randomly guessing correctly all 25 times.

Being less critical, with c=10, gives:

$$P(\text{reject } H_0|H_0 \text{ is valid}) = P(X \geq 10|p = \tfrac{1}{4}) = \sum_{k=10}^{25} P(X = k|p = \tfrac{1}{4}) \approx 0.07.$$

Thus, $c = 10$ yields a much greater probability of false positive.

Before the test is actually performed, the maximum acceptable probability of a Type I error (α) is determined. Typically, values in the range of 1% to 5% are selected. (If the maximum acceptable error rate is zero, an infinite number of correct guesses is required.) Depending on this Type 1 error rate, the critical value c is calculated. For example, if we select an error rate of 1%, c is calculated thus:

$$P(\text{reject } H_0|H_0 \text{ is valid}) = P(X \geq c|p = \tfrac{1}{4}) \leq 0.01.$$

From all the numbers c, with this property, we choose the smallest, in order to minimize the probability of a Type II error, a false negative. For the above example, we select: $c = 13$.

Example 3 – Radioactive suitcase

As an example, consider determining whether a suitcase contains some radioactive material. Placed under a Geiger counter, it produces 10 counts per minute. The null hypothesis is that no radioactive material is in the suitcase and that all measured counts are due to ambient radioactivity typical of the surrounding air and harmless objects. We can then calculate how likely it is that we would observe 10 counts per minute if the null hypothesis were true. If the null hypothesis predicts (say) on average 9 counts per minute, then according to the Poisson distribution typical for radioactive decay there is about 41% chance of recording 10 or more counts. Thus we can say that the suitcase is compatible with the null hypothesis (this does not guarantee that there is no radioactive material, just that we don't have enough evidence to suggest there is). On the other hand, if the null hypothesis predicts 3 counts per minute (for which the Poisson distribution predicts only 0.1% chance of recording 10 or more counts) then the suitcase is not compatible with the null hypothesis, and there are likely other factors responsible to produce the measurements.

The test does not directly assert the presence of radioactive material. A *successful* test asserts that the claim of no radioactive material present is unlikely given the reading (and therefore ...). The double negative (disproving the null hypothesis) of the method is confusing, but using a counter-example to disprove is standard mathematical practice. The attraction of the method is its practicality. We know (from experience) the expected range of counts with only ambient radioactivity present, so we can say that a measurement is *unusually* large. Statistics just formalizes the intuitive by using numbers instead of adjectives. We probably do not know the characteristics of the radioactive suitcases; We just assume that they produce larger readings.

To slightly formalize intuition: Radioactivity is suspected if the Geiger-count with the suitcase is among or exceeds the greatest (5% or 1%) of the Geiger-counts made with ambient radiation alone. This makes no assumptions about the distribution of counts. Many ambient radiation observations are required to obtain good probability estimates for rare events.

The test described here is more fully the null-hypothesis statistical significance test. The null hypothesis represents what we would believe by default, before seeing any evidence. Statistical significance is a possible finding of the test, declared when the observed sample is unlikely to have occurred by chance if the null hypothesis were true. The name of the test describes its formulation and its possible outcome. One characteristic of the test is its crisp decision: to reject or not reject the null hypothesis. A calculated value is compared to a threshold, which is determined from the tolerable risk of error.

Definition of terms

The following definitions are mainly based on the exposition in the book by Lehmann and Romano:

Statistical hypothesis: A statement about the parameters describing a population (not a sample).

Statistic: A value calculated from a sample, often to summarize the sample for comparison purposes.

Simple hypothesis: Any hypothesis which specifies the population distribution completely.

Composite hypothesis : Any hypothesis which does *not* specify the population distribution completely.

Null hypothesis (H0): A simple hypothesis associated with a contradiction to a theory one would like to prove.

Alternative hypothesis (H1): A hypothesis (often composite) associated with a theory one would like to prove.

Statistical test: A procedure whose inputs are samples and whose result is a hypothesis.

Region of acceptance: The set of values of the test statistic for which we fail to reject the null hypothesis.

Region of rejection / Critical region: The set of values of the test statistic for which the null hypothesis is rejected.

Critical value: The threshold value delimiting the regions of acceptance and rejection for the test statistic.

Power of a test (1 " *â*): The test's probability of correctly rejecting the null hypothesis. The complement of the false negative rate, *â*. Power is termed **sensitivity** in biostatistics. ("This is a sensitive test. Because the result is negative, we can confidently say that the patient does not have the condition.") See sensitivity and specificity and Type I and type II errors for exhaustive definitions.

Size / Significance level of a test (*á*): For simple hypotheses, this is the test's probability of *incorrectly* rejecting the null hypothesis. The false positive rate. For composite hypotheses this is the upper bound of the probability of rejecting the null hypothesis over all cases covered by the null hypothesis. The complement of the false positive rate, (1 " *á*), is termed **specificity** in biostatistics. ("This is a specific test. Because the result is positive, we can confidently say that the patient has the condition.") See sensitivity and specificity and Type I and type II errors for exhaustive definitions.

p-value: The probability, assuming the null hypothesis is true, of observing a result at least as extreme as the test statistic.

Statistical significance test

A predecessor to the statistical hypothesis test. An experimental result was said to be statistically significant if a sample was sufficiently inconsistent with the (null) hypothesis. This was variously considered common sense, a pragmatic heuristic for identifying meaningful experimental results, a convention establishing a threshold of statistical evidence or a method for drawing conclusions from data. The statistical hypothesis test added mathematical rigor and philosophical consistency to the concept by making the alternative hypothesis explicit. The term is loosely used to describe the modern version which is now part of statistical hypothesis testing.

Conservative test

A test is conservative if, when constructed for a given nominal significance level, the true probability of *incorrectly* rejecting the null hypothesis is never greater than the nominal level.

Exact test

A test in which the significance level or critical value can be computed exactly, i.e., without any approximation. In some contexts this term is restricted to tests applied to categorical data and to permutation tests, in which computations are carried out by complete enumeration of all possible outcomes and their probabilities.

A statistical hypothesis test compares a test statistic (*z* or *t* for examples) to a threshold. The test statistic (the formula found in the table below) is based on optimality. For a fixed level of Type I error rate, use of these statistics minimizes Type II error rates (equivalent to maximizing power). The following terms describe tests in terms of such optimality:

Most powerful test

For a given *size* or *significance level*, the test with the greatest power (probability of rejection) for a given value of the parameter(s) being tested, contained in the alternative hypothesis.

Uniformly most powerful test (UMP)

A test with the greatest *power* for all values of the parameter(s) being tested, contained in the alternative hypothesis.

Common test statistics

One-sample tests are appropriate when a sample is being compared to the population from a hypothesis. The population characteristics are known from theory or are calculated from the population.

Two-sample tests are appropriate for comparing two samples, typically experimental and control samples from a scientifically controlled experiment.

Paired tests are appropriate for comparing two samples where it is impossible to control important variables. Rather than comparing two sets, members are paired between samples so the difference between the members becomes the sample. Typically the mean of the differences is then compared to zero.

Z-tests are appropriate for comparing means under stringent conditions regarding normality and a known standard deviation.

T-tests are appropriate for comparing means under relaxed conditions (less is assumed).

Tests of proportions are analogous to tests of means (the 50% proportion).

Chi-squared tests use the same calculations and the same probability distribution for different applications:

Chi-squared tests for variance are used to determine whether a normal population has a specified variance. The null hypothesis is that it does.

Chi-squared tests of independence are used for deciding whether two variables are associated or are independent. The variables are categorical rather than numeric. It can be used to decide whether left-handedness is correlated with libertarian politics (or not). The null hypothesis is that the variables are independent. The numbers used in the calculation are the observed and expected frequencies of occurrence (from contingency tables).

Chi-squared goodness of fit tests are used to determine the adequacy of curves fit to data. The null hypothesis is that the curve fit is adequate. It is common to determine curve shapes to minimize the mean square error, so it is appropriate that the goodness-of-fit calculation sums the squared errors.

F-tests (analysis of variance, ANOVA) are commonly used when deciding whether groupings of data by category are meaningful. If the variance of test scores of the left-handed in a class is much smaller than the variance of the whole class, then it may be useful to study lefties as a group. The null hypothesis is that two variances are the same – so the proposed grouping is not meaningful.

In the table below, the symbols used are defined at the bottom of the table. Many other tests can be found in other articles. Proofs exist that the test statistics are appropriate.

Origins and early controversy

Significance testing is largely the product of Karl Pearson (p-value, Pearson's chi-squared test), William Sealy Gosset (Student's t-distribution), and Ronald Fisher ("null hypothesis", analysis of variance, "significance test"), while hypothesis testing was developed by Jerzy Neyman and Egon Pearson (son of Karl). Ronald Fisher, mathematician and biologist described by Richard Dawkins as "the greatest biologist since Darwin", began his life in statistics as a Bayesian (Zabell 1992), but Fisher soon grew disenchanted with the subjectivity involved (namely use of the principle of indifference when determining prior probabilities), and sought to provide a more "objective" approach to inductive inference.

Fisher was an agricultural statistician who emphasized rigorous experimental design and methods to extract a result from few samples assuming Gaussian distributions. Neyman (who teamed with the younger Pearson) emphasized mathematical rigor and methods to obtain more results from many samples and a wider range of distributions. Modern hypothesis testing is an inconsistent hybrid of the Fisher vs Neyman/Pearson formulation, methods and terminology developed in the early 20th century. While hypothesis testing was popularized early in the 20th century, evidence of its use can be found much earlier. In the 1770s Laplace considered the statistics of almost half a million births. The statistics showed an excess of boys compared to girls. He concluded by calculation of a p-value that the excess was a real, but unexplained, effect.

Fisher popularized the "significance test". He required a null-hypothesis (corresponding to a population frequency distribution) and a sample. His (now familiar) calculations determined whether to reject the null-hypothesis or not. Significance testing did not utilize an alternative hypothesis so there was no concept of a Type II error.

The p-value was devised as an informal, but objective, index meant to help a researcher determine (based on other knowledge) whether to modify future experiments or strengthen one's faith in the null hypothesis. Hypothesis testing (and Type I/II errors) was devised by Neyman and Pearson as a more objective alternative to Fisher's p-value, also meant to determine researcher behaviour, but without requiring any inductive inference by the researcher.

Neyman & Pearson considered a different problem (which they called "hypothesis testing"). They initially considered two simple hypotheses (both with frequency distributions). They calculated two probabilities and typically selected the hypothesis associated with the higher probability (the hypothesis more likely to have generated the sample). Their method always selected a hypothesis. It also allowed the calculation of both types of error probabilities.

Fisher and Neyman/Pearson clashed bitterly. Neyman/Pearson considered their formulation to be an improved generalization of significance testing.(The defining paper was abstract. Mathematicians have generalized and refined the theory for decades.) Fisher thought that it was not applicable to scientific research because often, during the course of the experiment, it is discovered that the initial assumptions about the null hypothesis are questionable due to unexpected sources of error. He believed that the use of rigid reject/ accept decisions based on models formulated before data is collected was incompatible with this common scenario faced by scientists and attempts to apply this method to scientific research would lead to mass confusion.

The dispute between Fisher and Neyman-Pearson was waged on philosophical grounds, characterized by a philosopher as a dispute over the proper role of models in statistical inference.

Events intervened: Neyman accepted a position in the western hemisphere, breaking his partnership with Pearson and separating disputants (who had occupied the same building) by much of the planetary diameter. World War II provided an intermission in the debate. The dispute between Fisher and Neyman terminated (unresolved after 27 years) with Fisher's death in 1962. Neyman wrote a well-regarded eulogy. Some of Neyman's later publications reported p-values and significance levels.

The modern version of hypothesis testing is a hybrid of the two approaches that resulted from confusion by writers of statistical textbooks (as predicted by Fisher) beginning in the 1940s. (But signal detection, for example, still uses the Neyman/Pearson formulation.) Great conceptual differences and many caveats in addition to those mentioned above were ignored. Neyman and Pearson provided the stronger terminology, the more rigorous mathematics and the more consistent philosophy, but the subject taught today in introductory statistics has more similarities with Fisher's method than theirs. This history explains the inconsistent terminology (example: the null hypothesis is never accepted, but there is a region of acceptance).

Sometime around 1940, in an apparent effort to provide researchers with a "non-controversial" way to have their cake and eat it too, the authors of statistical text books began anonymously combining these two strategies by using the p-value in place of the test statistic (or data) to test against the Neyman-Pearson "significance level". Thus, researchers were encouraged to infer the strength of their data against some null hypothesis using p-values, while also thinking they are retaining the post-data collection objectivity provided by hypothesis testing. It then became customary for the null hypothesis, which was originally some realistic research hypothesis, to be used almost solely as a strawman "nil" hypothesis (one where a treatment has no effect, regardless of the context).

A comparison between Fisherian, frequentist (Neyman-Pearson)

Early choices of null hypothesis

Paul Meehl has argued that the epistemological importance of the choice of null hypothesis has gone largely unacknowledged. When the null hypothesis is predicted by theory, a more precise experiment will be a more severe test of the underlying theory. When the null hypothesis defaults to "no difference" or "no effect", a more precise experiment is a less severe test of the theory that motivated performing the experiment. An examination of the origins of the latter practice may therefore be useful:

1778: Pierre Laplace compares the birthrates of boys and girls in multiple European cities. He states: "it is natural to conclude that these possibilities are very nearly in the same ratio". Thus Laplace's null hypothesis that the birthrates of boys and girls should be equal given "conventional wisdom".

1900: Karl Pearson develops the chi squared test to determine "whether a given form of frequency curve will effectively describe the samples drawn from a given population." Thus the null hypothesis is that a population is described by some distribution predicted by theory. He uses as an example the numbers of five and sixes in the Weldon dice throw data.

1904: Karl Pearson develops the concept of "contingency" in order to determine whether outcomes are independent of a given categorical factor. Here the null hypothesis is by default that two things are unrelated (e.g. scar formation and death rates from small pox). The null hypothesis in this case is no longer predicted by theory or conventional wisdom, but is instead the principle of indifference that lead Fisher and others to dismiss the use of "inverse probabilities".

Null hypothesis statistical significant testing vs hypothesis testing

An example of Neyman-Pearson hypothesis testing can be made by a change to the radioactive suitcase example. If the "suitcase" is actually a shielded container for the transportation of radioactive material, then a test might be used to select among three hypotheses: no radioactive source present, one present, two (all) present. The test could be required for safety, with actions required in each case. The Neyman-Pearson lemma of hypothesis testing says that a good criterion for the selection of hypotheses is the ratio of their probabilities (a likelihood ratio). A simple method of solution is to select the hypothesis with the highest probability for the Geiger counts observed. The typical result matches intuition: few counts imply no source, many counts imply two sources and intermediate counts imply one source.

Neyman-Pearson theory can accommodate both prior probabilities and the costs of actions resulting from decisions. The former allows each test to consider the results of earlier tests (unlike Fisher's significance tests). The latter allows the consideration of economic issues (for example) as well as probabilities. A likelihood ratio remains a good criterion for selecting among hypotheses.

The two forms of hypothesis testing are based on different problem formulations. The original test is analogous to a true/false question; the Neyman-Pearson test is more like multiple choice. In the view of Tukey the former produces a conclusion on the basis of only strong evidence while the latter produces a decision on the basis of available evidence. While the two tests seem quite different both mathematically and philosophically, later developments lead to the opposite claim. Consider many tiny radioactive sources. The hypotheses become 0,1,2,3... grains of radioactive sand. There is little distinction between none or some radiation (Fisher) and 0 grains of radioactive sand versus all of the alternatives (Neyman-Pearson). The major Neyman-Pearson paper of 1933 also considered composite hypotheses (ones whose distribution includes an unknown parameter). An example proved the optimality of the (Student's) t-test, "there can be no better test for the hypothesis under consideration" (p 321). Neyman-Pearson theory was proving the optimality of Fisherian methods from its inception.

Fisher's significance testing has proven a popular flexible statistical tool in application with little mathematical growth potential. Neyman-Pearson hypothesis testing is claimed as a pillar of mathematical statistics, creating a new paradigm for the field. It also stimulated new applications in Statistical process control, detection theory, decision theory and game theory. Both formulations have been successful, but the successes have been of a different character.

The dispute over formulations is unresolved. Science primarily uses Fisher's (slightly modified) formulation as taught in introductory statistics. Statisticians study Neyman-Pearson theory in graduate school. Mathematicians are proud of uniting the formulations. Philosophers consider them separately. Learned opinions deem the formulations variously competitive (Fisher vs Neyman), incompatible or complementary. The dispute has become more complex since Bayesian inference has achieved respectability.

The terminology is inconsistent. Hypothesis testing can mean any mixture of two formulations that both changed with time. Any discussion of significance testing vs hypothesis testing is doubly vulnerable to confusion.

Fisher thought that hypothesis testing was a useful strategy for performing industrial quality control, however, he strongly disagreed that hypothesis testing could be useful for scientists. Hypothesis testing provides a means of finding test statistics used in significance testing. The concept of power is useful in explaining the consequences of adjusting the significance level and is heavily used in sample size determination. The two methods remain philosophically distinct. They usually (but *not always*) produce the same mathematical answer. The preferred answer is context dependent. While the existing merger of Fisher and Neyman-Pearson theories has been heavily criticized, modifying the merger to achieve Bayesian goals has been considered.

Criticism

Criticism of statistical hypothesis testing fills volumes citing 300–400 primary references. Much of the criticism can be summarized by the following issues:

- The interpretation of a p-value is dependent upon stopping rule and definition of multiple comparison. The former often changes during the course of a study and the latter is unavoidably ambiguous. (i.e. "p values depend on both the (data) observed and on the other possible (data) that might have been observed but weren't").
- Confusion resulting (in part) from combining the methods of Fisher and Neyman-Pearson which are conceptually distinct.
- Emphasis on statistical significance to the exclusion of estimation and confirmation by repeated experiments.
- Rigidly requiring statistical significance as a criterion for publication, resulting in publication bias. Most of the criticism is indirect. Rather than being wrong, statistical hypothesis testing is misunderstood, overused and misused.

- When used to detect whether a difference exists between groups, a paradox arises. As improvements are made to experimental design (e.g., increased precision of measurement and sample size), the test becomes more lenient. Unless one accepts the absurd assumption that all sources of noise in the data cancel out completely, the chance of finding statistical significance in either direction approaches 100%.
- Layers of philosophical concerns. The probability of statistical significance is a function of decisions made by experimenters/analysts. If the decisions are based on convention they are termed arbitrary or mindless while those not so based may be termed subjective. To minimize type II errors, large samples are recommended. In psychology practically all null hypotheses are claimed to be false for sufficiently large samples so "...it is usually nonsensical to perform an experiment with the *sole* aim of rejecting the null hypothesis.". "Statistically significant findings are often misleading" in psychology. Statistical significance does not imply practical significance and correlation does not imply causation. Casting doubt on the null hypothesis is thus far from directly supporting the research hypothesis.

"It does not tell us what we want to know". Lists of dozens of complaints are available.

Critics and supporters are largely in factual agreement regarding the characteristics of NHST: While it can provide critical information, it is *inadequate as the sole tool for statistical analysis. Successfully rejecting the null hypothesis may offer no support for the research hypothesis.* The continuing controversy concerns the selection of the best statistical practices for the near-term future given the (often poor) existing practices. Critics would prefer to ban NHST completely, forcing a complete departure from those practices, while supporters suggest a less absolute change.

Controversy over significance testing, and its effects on publication bias in particular, has produced several results. The American Psychological Association has strengthened its statistical reporting requirements after review, medical journal publishers have recognized the obligation to publish some results that are not statistically significant to combat publication bias and a journal (*Journal of Articles in Support of the Null Hypothesis*) has been created to publish such results exclusively. Textbooks have added some cautions and increased coverage of the tools necessary to estimate the size of the sample required to produce significant results. Major organizations have not abandoned use of significance tests although some have discussed doing so.

Alternatives to significance testing

The numerous criticisms of significance testing do not lead to a single alternative or even to a unified set of alternatives. A unifying position of critics is that statistics should not lead to a conclusion or a decision but to a probability or to an estimated value with a confidence interval rather than to an accept-reject decision regarding a particular hypothesis. It is unlikely that the controversy surrounding significance testing will be resolved in the near future. Its supposed flaws and unpopularity do not eliminate the need for an objective and transparent means of reaching conclusions regarding studies that produce statistical results. Critics have not unified around an alternative. Other forms of reporting confidence or uncertainty could probably grow in popularity. One strong critic of significance testing suggested a list of reporting alternatives: effect sizes for importance, prediction intervals for confidence, replications and extensions for replicability, meta-analyses for generality. None of these suggested alternatives produces a conclusion/decision. Lehmann said that hypothesis testing theory can be presented in terms of conclusions/decisions, probabilities, or confidence intervals. "The distinction between the ... approaches is largely one of reporting and interpretation."

On one "alternative" there is no disagreement: Fisher himself said, "In relation to the test of significance, we may say that a phenomenon is experimentally demonstrable when we know how to conduct an experiment which will rarely fail to give us a statistically significant result." Cohen, an influential critic of significance testing, concurred, "... don't look for a magic alternative to NHST *[null hypothesis significance testing]* ... It doesn't exist." "... given the problems of statistical induction, we must finally rely, as have the older sciences, on replication." The "alternative" to significance testing is repeated testing. The easiest way to decrease statistical uncertainty is by obtaining more data, whether by increased sample size or by repeated tests. Nickerson claimed to have never seen the publication of a literally replicated experiment in psychology. An indirect approach to replication is meta-analysis.

Bayesian inference is one alternative to significance testing. For example, Bayesian parameter estimation can provide rich information about the data from which researchers can draw inferences, while using uncertain priors that exert only minimal influence on the results when enough data is available. Psychologist Kruschke, John K. has suggested Bayesian estimation as an alternative for the t-test. Alternatively two competing models/ hypothesis can be compared using Bayes factors. Bayesian methods could be criticized for requiring information that is seldom available in the cases where significance testing is most heavily used.

Advocates of a Bayesian approach sometimes claim that the goal of a researcher is most often to objectively assess the probability that a hypothesis is true based on the data they have collected. Neither Fisher's significance testing, nor Neyman-Pearson hypothesis testing can provide this information, and do not claim to. The probability a hypothesis is true can only be derived from use of Bayes' Theorem, which was unsatisfactory to both the Fisher and Neyman-Pearson camps due to the explicit use of subjectivity in the form of the prior probability. Fisher's strategy is to sidestep this with the p-value (an objective *index* based on the data alone) followed by *inductive inference*, while Neyman-Pearson devised their approach of *inductive behaviour*.

Philosophy

Hypothesis testing and philosophy intersect. Inferential statistics, which includes hypothesis testing, is applied probability. Both probability and its application are intertwined with philosophy. Philosopher David Hume wrote, "All knowledge degenerates into probability." Competing practical definitions of probability reflect philosophical differences. The most common application of hypothesis testing is in the scientific interpretation of experimental data, which is naturally studied by the philosophy of science.

Fisher and Neyman opposed the subjectivity of probability. Their views contributed to the objective definitions. The core of their historical disagreement was philosophical.

Many of the philosophical criticisms of hypothesis testing are discussed by statisticians in other contexts, particularly correlation does not imply causation and the design of experiments. Hypothesis testing is of continuing interest to philosophers.

Education

Statistics is increasingly being taught in schools with hypothesis testing being one of the elements taught. Many conclusions reported in the popular press (political opinion polls to medical studies) are based on statistics. An informed public should understand the limitations of statistical conclusions and many college fields of study require a course in statistics for the same reason. An introductory college statistics class places much emphasis on hypothesis testing – perhaps half of the course. Such fields as literature and divinity now include findings based on statistical analysis. An introductory statistics class teaches hypothesis testing as a cookbook process. Hypothesis testing is also taught at the postgraduate level. Statisticians learn how to create good statistical test procedures (like *z*, Student's *t*, *F* and chi-squared). Statistical hypothesis testing is considered a mature area within statistics, but a limited amount of development continues.

The cookbook method of teaching introductory statistics leaves no time for history, philosophy or controversy. Hypothesis testing has been taught as received unified method. Surveys showed that graduates of the class were filled with philosophical misconceptions (on all aspects of statistical inference) that persisted among instructors. While the problem was addressed more than a decade ago, and calls for educational reform continue, students still graduate from statistics classes holding fundamental misconceptions about hypothesis testing. Ideas for improving the teaching of hypothesis testing include encouraging students to search for statistical errors in published papers, teaching the history of statistics and emphasizing the controversy in a generally dry subject

Contingency table

In statistics, a contingency table (also referred to as cross tabulation or cross tab) is a type of table in a matrix format that displays the (multivariate) frequency distribution of the variables. The term *contingency table* was first used by Karl Pearson in "On the Theory of Contingency and Its Relation to Association and Normal Correlation", part of the *Drapers' Company Research Memoirs Biometric Series I* published in 1904.

A crucial problem of multivariate statistics is finding (direct-) dependence structure underlying the variables contained in high-dimensional contingency tables. If some of the conditional independences are revealed, then even the storage of the data can be done in a smarter way). In order to do this one can use information theory concepts, which gain the information only from the distribution of probability, which can be expressed easily from the contingency table by the relative frequencies.

Example

Suppose that we have two variables, sex (male or female) and handedness (right- or left-handed). Further suppose that 100 individuals are randomly sampled from a very large population as part of a study of sex differences in handedness. A contingency table can be created to display the numbers of individuals who are male and right-handed, male and left-handed, female and right-handed, and female and left-handed. Such a contingency table is shown below.

The numbers of the males, females, and right- and left-handed individuals are called marginal totals. The grand total, i.e., the total number of individuals represented in the contingency table, is the number in the bottom right corner.

The table allows us to see at a glance that the proportion of men who are right-handed is about the same as the proportion of women who are right-handed although the proportions are not identical. The significance of the difference between the two proportions can be assessed with a variety of statistical tests including Pearson's chi-squared test, the *G*-test, Fisher's exact test, and Barnard's test, provided the entries in the table represent individuals randomly sampled from the population about which we want to draw a conclusion. If the proportions of individuals in the different columns vary significantly between rows (or vice versa), we say that there is a *contingency* between the two variables. In other words, the two variables are *not* independent. If there is no contingency, we say that the two variables are *independent*.

The example above is the simplest kind of contingency table, a table in which each variable has only two levels; this is called a 2 x 2 contingency table. In principle, any number of rows and columns may be used. There may also be more than two variables, but higher order contingency tables are difficult to represent on paper. The relation between ordinal variables, or between ordinal and categorical variables, may also be represented in contingency tables, although such a practice is rare.

Measures of association

The degree of association between the two variables can be assessed by a number of coefficients: the simplest is the phi coefficient defined by

$$\phi = \sqrt{\frac{\chi^2}{N}}$$

where χ is derived from Pearson's chi-squared test, and N is the grand total of observations. φ varies from 0 (corresponding to no association between the variables) to 1 or -1 (complete association or complete inverse association). This coefficient can only be calculated for frequency data represented in 2 x 2 tables. φ can reach a minimum value -1.00 and a maximum value of 1.00 *only* when every marginal proportion is equal to .50 (and two diagonal cells are empty). Otherwise, the phi coefficient cannot reach those minimal and maximal values.

Alternatives include the tetrachoric correlation coefficient (also only applicable to 2 × 2 tables), the contingency coefficient C, and Cramér's V.

C suffers from the disadvantage that it does not reach a maximum of 1 or the minimum of -1; the highest it can reach in a 2 x 2 table is .707; the maximum it can reach in a 4 × 4 table is 0.870. It can reach values closer to 1 in contingency tables with more categories. It should, therefore, not be used to compare associations among tables with different numbers of categories. Moreover, it does not apply to asymmetrical tables (those where the numbers of row and columns are not equal).

The formulae for the *C* and *V* coefficients are:

$$C = \sqrt{\frac{\chi^2}{N + \chi^2}}$$

and

$$V = \sqrt{\frac{\chi^2}{N(k-1)}}$$

k being the number of rows or the number of columns, whichever is less.

C can be adjusted so it reaches a maximum of 1 when there is complete association in a table of any number of rows and columns by dividing *C* by $\sqrt{\frac{k-1}{k}}$ (recall that *C* only applies to tables in which the number of rows is equal to the number of columns and therefore equal to *k*).

The tetrachoric correlation coefficient assumes that the variable underlying each dichotomous measure is normally distributed. The tetrachoric correlation coefficient provides "a convenient measure of [the Pearson product-moment] correlation when graduated measurements have been reduced to two categories." The tetrachoric correlation should not be confused with the Pearson product-moment correlation coefficient computed by assigning, say, values 0 and 1 to represent the two levels of each variable (which is mathematically equivalent to the phi coefficient). An extension of the tetrachoric correlation to tables involving variables with more than two levels is the polychoric correlation coefficient.

The Lambda coefficient is a measure of the strength of association of the cross tabulations when the variables are measured at the nominal level. Values range from 0 (no association) to 1 (the theoretical maximum possible association). Asymmetric lambda measures the percentage improvement in predicting the dependent variable. Symmetric lambda measures the percentage improvement when prediction is done in both directions.

The uncertainty coefficient is another measure for variables at the nominal level.

The values range from -1 (100% negative association, or perfect inversion) to +1 (100% positive association, or perfect agreement). A value of zero indicates the absence of association.

- Gamma test: No adjustment for either table size or ties.
- Kendall tau: Adjustment for ties.
- Tau b: For square tables.
- Tau c: For rectangular tables.

Chi-squared test

A chi-squared test, also referred to as chi-square test or χ^2 test, is any statistical hypothesis test in which the sampling distribution of the test statistic is a chi-squared distribution when the null hypothesis is true. Also considered a chi-squared test is a test in which this is asymptotically true, meaning that the sampling distribution (if the null hypothesis is true) can be made to approximate a chi-squared distribution as closely as desired by making the sample size large enough.

Some examples of chi-squared tests where the chi-squared distribution is only approximately valid:

Pearson's chi-squared test, also known as the chi-squared goodness-of-fit test or chi-squared test for independence. When the chi-squared test is mentioned without any modifiers or without other precluding context, this test is usually meant (for an exact test used in place of , see Fisher's exact test).

Yates's correction for continuity, also known as Yates' chi-squared test.

Cochran–Mantel–Haenszel chi-squared test.

McNemar's test, used in certain 2 × 2 tables with pairing

Tukey's test of additivity

The portmanteau test in time-series analysis, testing for the presence of autocorrelation

Likelihood-ratio tests in general statistical modelling, for testing whether there is evidence of the need to move from a simple model to a more complicated one (where the simple model is nested within the complicated one).

One case where the distribution of the test statistic is an exact chi-squared distribution is the test that the variance of a normally distributed population has a given value based on a sample variance. Such a test is uncommon in practice because values of variances to test against are seldom known exactly.

Chi-squared test for variance in a normal population

If a sample of size *n* is taken from a population having a normal distribution, then there is a result which allows a test to be made of whether the variance of the population has a pre-determined value. For example, a manufacturing process might have been in stable condition for a long period, allowing a value for the variance to be determined essentially without error. Suppose that a variant of the process is being tested, giving rise to a small sample of *n* product items whose variation is to be tested. The test statistic *T* in this instance could be set to be the sum of squares about the sample mean, divided by the nominal value for the variance (i.e. the value to be tested as holding). Then *T* has a chi-squared distribution with *n* Š 1 degrees of freedom. For example if the sample size is 21, the acceptance region for *T* for a significance level of 5% is the interval 9.59 to 34.17.

One-way analysis of variance

In statistics, one-way analysis of variance (abbreviated one-way ANOVA) is a technique used to compare means of two or more samples (using the F distribution). This technique can be used only for numerical data.

The ANOVA tests the null hypothesis that samples in two or more groups are drawn from populations with the same mean values. To do this, two estimates are made of the population variance. These estimates rely on various assumptions. The ANOVA produces an F-statistic, the ratio of the variance calculated among the means to the variance within the samples. If the group means are drawn from populations with the same mean values, the variance between the group means should be lower than the variance of the samples, following the central limit theorem. A higher ratio therefore implies that the samples were drawn from populations with different mean values.

Typically, however, the one-way ANOVA is used to test for differences among at least three groups, since the two-group case can be covered by a t-test (Gosset, 1908). When there are only two means to compare, the t-test and the F-test are equivalent; the relation between ANOVA and t is given by $F = t$.

Assumptions

The results of a one-way ANOVA can be considered reliable as long as the following assumptions are met:

- Response variable residuals are normally distributed (or approximately normally distributed).
- Samples are independent.
- Variances of populations are equal.
- Responses for a given group are independent and identically distributed normal random variables (not a simple random sample (SRS)).

ANOVA is a relatively robust procedure with respect to violations of the normality assumption. If data are ordinal, a non-parametric alternative to this test should be used such as Kruskal–Wallis one-way analysis of variance.

11

Regression Analysis

In statistics, regression analysis is a statistical process for estimating the relationships among variables. It includes many techniques for modeling and analyzing several variables, when the focus is on the relationship between a dependent variable and one or more independent variables. More specifically, regression analysis helps one understand how the typical value of the dependent variable (or 'criterion variable') changes when any one of the independent variables is varied, while the other independent variables are held fixed. Most commonly, regression analysis estimates the conditional expectation of the dependent variable given the independent variables – that is, the average value of the dependent variable when the independent variables are fixed. Less commonly, the focus is on a quantile, or other location parameter of the conditional distribution of the dependent variable given the independent variables. In all cases, the estimation target is a function of the independent variables called the regression function. In regression analysis, it is also of interest to characterize the variation of the dependent variable around the regression function which can be described by a probability distribution.

Regression analysis is widely used for prediction and forecasting, where its use has substantial overlap with the field of machine learning. Regression analysis is also used to understand which among the independent variables are related to the dependent variable, and to explore the forms of these relationships. In restricted circumstances, regression analysis can be used to infer causal relationships between the independent and dependent variables. However this can lead to illusions or false relationships, so caution is advisable; for example, correlation does not imply causation.

Many techniques for carrying out regression analysis have been developed. Familiar methods such as linear regression and ordinary least squares regression are parametric, in that the regression function is defined in terms of a finite number of unknown parameters that are estimated from the data. Nonparametric regression refers to techniques that allow the regression function to lie in a specified set of functions, which may be infinite-dimensional.

The performance of regression analysis methods in practice depends on the form of the data generating process, and how it relates to the regression approach being used. Since the true form of the data-generating process is generally not known, regression analysis often depends to some extent on making assumptions about this process. These assumptions are sometimes testable if a sufficient quantity of data is available. Regression models for prediction are often useful even when the assumptions are moderately violated, although they may not perform optimally. However, in many applications, especially with small effects or questions of causality based on observational data, regression methods can give misleading results.

History

The earliest form of regression was the method of least squares, which was published by Legendre in 1805, and by Gauss in 1809. Legendre and Gauss both applied the method to the problem of determining, from astronomical observations, the orbits of bodies about the Sun (mostly comets, but also later the then newly discovered minor planets). Gauss published a further development of the theory of least squares in 1821, including a version of the Gauss–Markov theorem.

The term "regression" was coined by Francis Galton in the nineteenth century to describe a biological phenomenon. The phenomenon was that the heights of descendants of tall ancestors tend to regress down towards a normal average (a phenomenon also known as regression toward the mean). For Galton, regression had only this biological meaning, but his work was later extended by Udny Yule and Karl Pearson to a more general statistical context. In the work of Yule and Pearson, the joint distribution of the response and explanatory variables is assumed to be Gaussian. This assumption was weakened by R.A. Fisher in his works of 1922 and 1925. Fisher assumed that the conditional distribution of the response variable is Gaussian, but the joint distribution need not be. In this respect, Fisher's assumption is closer to Gauss's formulation of 1821.

In the 1950s and 1960s, economists used electromechanical desk calculators to calculate regressions. Before 1970, it sometimes took up to 24 hours to receive the result from one regression.

Regression methods continue to be an area of active research. In recent decades, new methods have been developed for robust regression, regression involving correlated responses such as time series and growth curves, regression in which the predictor or response variables are curves, images, graphs, or other complex data objects, regression methods accommodating various types of missing data, nonparametric regression, Bayesian methods for regression, regression in which the predictor variables are measured with error, regression with more predictor variables than observations, and causal inference with regression.

Regression models

Regression models involve the following variables:

- The unknown parameters, denoted as â, which may represent a scalar or a vector.
- The independent variables, X.
- The dependent variable, Y.

In various fields of application, different terminologies are used in place of dependent and independent variables.

A regression model relates Y to a function of $\mathbf{X}$ and $\boldsymbol{\beta}$.

$$Y \approx f(\mathbf{X}, \beta)$$

The approximation is usually formalized as $E(Y \mid \mathbf{X}) = f(\mathbf{X}, \boldsymbol{\beta})$. To carry out regression analysis, the form of the function f must be specified. Sometimes the form of this function is based on knowledge about the relationship between Y and $\mathbf{X}$ that does not rely on the data. If no such knowledge is available, a flexible or convenient form for f is chosen.

Assume now that the vector of unknown parameters $\boldsymbol{\beta}$ is of length k. In order to perform a regression analysis the user must provide information about the dependent variable Y:

- If N data points of the form (Y, **X**) are observed, where $N < k$, most classical approaches to regression analysis cannot be performed: since the system of equations defining the regression model is underdetermined, there are not enough data to recover $\hat{\mathbf{a}}$.
- If exactly $N = k$ data points are observed, and the function f is linear, the equations $Y = f(\mathbf{X}, \hat{\mathbf{a}})$ can be solved exactly rather than approximately. This reduces to solving a set of N equations with N unknowns (the elements of $\hat{\mathbf{a}}$), which has a unique solution as long as the **X** are linearly independent. If f is nonlinear, a solution may not exist, or many solutions may exist.
- The most common situation is where $N > k$ data points are observed. In this case, there is enough information in the data to estimate a unique value for $\hat{\mathbf{a}}$ that best fits the data in some sense, and the regression model when applied to the data can be viewed as an overdetermined system in $\hat{\mathbf{a}}$.

In the last case, the regression analysis provides the tools for:

1. Finding a solution for unknown parameters $\hat{\mathbf{a}}$ that will, for example, minimize the distance between the measured and predicted values of the dependent variable Y (also known as method of least squares).
2. Under certain statistical assumptions, the regression analysis uses the surplus of information to provide statistical information about the unknown parameters $\hat{\mathbf{a}}$ and predicted values of the dependent variable Y.

Necessary number of independent measurements

Consider a regression model which has three unknown parameters, β0, β1, and β2. Suppose an experimenter performs 10 measurements all at exactly the same value of independent variable vector **X** (which contains the independent variables $X1$, $X2$, and $X3$). In this case, regression analysis fails to give a unique set of estimated values for the three unknown parameters; the experimenter did not provide enough information. The best one can do is to estimate the average value and the standard deviation of the dependent variable Y. Similarly, measuring at two different values of **X** would give enough data for a regression with two unknowns, but not for three or more unknowns.

If the experimenter had performed measurements at three different values of the independent variable vector **X**, then regression analysis would provide a unique set of estimates for the three unknown parameters in $\boldsymbol{\beta}$.

In the case of general linear regression, the above statement is equivalent to the requirement that the matrix **XX** is invertible.

Statistical assumptions

When the number of measurements, N, is larger than the number of unknown parameters, k, and the measurement errors εi are normally distributed then *the excess of information* contained in (N“ k) measurements is used to make statistical predictions about the unknown parameters. This excess of information is referred to as the degrees of freedom of the regression.

Underlying assumptions

Classical assumptions for regression analysis include:

- The sample is representative of the population for the inference prediction.
- The error is a random variable with a mean of zero conditional on the explanatory variables.
- The independent variables are measured with no error. (Note: If this is not so, modeling may be done instead using errors-in-variables model techniques).
- The predictors are linearly independent, i.e. it is not possible to express any predictor as a linear combination of the others.
- The errors are uncorrelated, that is, the variance–covariance matrix of the errors is diagonal and each non-zero element is the variance of the error.
- The variance of the error is constant across observations (homoscedasticity). If not, weighted least squares or other methods might instead be used.

These are sufficient conditions for the least-squares estimator to possess desirable properties; in particular, these assumptions imply that the parameter estimates will be unbiased, consistent, and efficient in the class of linear unbiased estimators. It is important to note that actual data rarely satisfies the assumptions. That is, the method is used even though the assumptions are not true. Variation from the assumptions can sometimes be used as a measure of how far the model is from being useful. Many of these assumptions may be relaxed in more advanced treatments. Reports of statistical analyses usually include analyses of tests on the sample data and methodology for the fit and usefulness of the model.

Assumptions include the geometrical support of the variables. Independent and dependent variables often refer to values measured at point locations. There may be spatial trends and spatial autocorrelation in the variables that violate statistical assumptions of regression. Geographic weighted regression is one technique to deal with such data. Also, variables may include values aggregated by areas. With aggregated data the modifiable areal unit problem can cause extreme variation in regression parameters. When analyzing data aggregated by political boundaries, postal codes or census areas results may be very distinct with a different choice of units.

Linear regression

In linear regression, the model specification is that the dependent variable, $y_i$is a linear combination of the *parameters* (but need not be linear in the *independent variables*). For example, in simple linear regression for modeling $n$data points there is one independent variable: x_i, and two parameters, $\beta_0$and β_1:

straight line: $y_i = \beta_0 + \beta_1 x_i + \varepsilon_i, \quad i = 1, \dots, n.$

In multiple linear regression, there are several independent variables or functions of independent variables.

Adding a term in *xi* to the preceding regression gives:

parabola: $y_i = \beta_0 + \beta_1 x_i + \beta_2 x_i^2 + \varepsilon_i,\ i = 1, \ldots, n.$

This is still linear regression; although the expression on the right hand side is quadratic in the independent variable x_i, it is linear in the parameters β_0, $\beta_1$and β_2.

In both cases, $\varepsilon_i$is an error term and the subscript $i$indexes a particular observation.

Given a random sample from the population, we estimate the population parameters and obtain the sample linear regression model:

$$\widehat{y}_i = \widehat{\beta}_0 + \widehat{\beta}_1 x_i.$$

The residual, $e_i = y_i - \widehat{y}_i$, is the difference between the value of the dependent variable predicted by the model, $\widehat{y}_i$, and the true value of the dependent variable, y_i. One method of estimation is ordinary least squares. This method obtains parameter estimates that minimize the sum of squared residuals, SSE, also sometimes denoted RSS:

$$SSE = \sum_{i=1}^{n} e_i^2.$$

Minimization of this function results in a set of normal equations, a set of simultaneous linear equations in the parameters, which are solved to yield the parameter estimators, $\widehat{\beta}_0, \widehat{\beta}_1$

In the case of simple regression, the formulas for the least squares estimates are

$$\widehat{\beta}_1 = \frac{\sum(x_i - \bar{x})(y_i - \bar{y})}{\sum(x_i - \bar{x})^2} \text{ and } \widehat{\beta}_0 = \bar{y} - \widehat{\beta}_1 \bar{x}$$

where $\bar{x}$is the mean (average) of the $x$values and $\bar{y}$is the mean of the $y$values.

Under the assumption that the population error term has a constant variance, the estimate of that variance is given by:

$$\hat{\sigma}_\varepsilon^2 = \frac{SSE}{n-2}.$$

This is called the mean square error (MSE) of the regression. The denominator is the sample size reduced by the number of model parameters estimated from the same data, (*n-p*) for *p* regressors or (*n-p*-1) if an intercept is used. In this case, *p*=1 so the denominator is *n*-2.

Thc standard errors of the parameter estimates are given by

$$\hat{\sigma}_{\beta_0} = \hat{\sigma}_\varepsilon \sqrt{\frac{1}{n} + \frac{\bar{x}^2}{\sum(x_i - \bar{x})^2}}$$

$$\hat{\sigma}_{\beta_1} = \hat{\sigma}_\varepsilon \sqrt{\frac{1}{\sum(x_i - \bar{x})^2}}.$$

Under the further assumption that the population error term is normally distributed, the researcher can use these estimated standard errors to create confidence intervals and conduct hypothesis tests about the population parameters.

General linear model

For a derivation, see linear least squares

For a numerical example, see linear regression

In the more general multiple regression model, there are p independent variables:

$$y_i = \beta_1 x_{i1} + \beta_2 x_{i2} + \cdots + \beta_p x_{ip} + \varepsilon_i,$$

where xij is the i observation on the j independent variable, and where the first independent variable takes the value 1 for all i (so $\beta_1$is the regression intercept).

The least squares parameter estimates are obtained from p normal equations. The residual can be written as

$$\varepsilon_i = y_i - \hat{\beta}_1 x_{i1} - \cdots - \hat{\beta}_p x_{ip}.$$

The **normal equations** are

$$\sum_{i=1}^{n} \sum_{k=1}^{p} X_{ij} X_{ik} \hat{\beta}_k = \sum_{i=1}^{n} X_{ij} y_i, \ j = 1, \ldots, p.$$

In matrix notation, the normal equations are written as

$$(\mathbf{X}^\top \mathbf{X}) \hat{\boldsymbol{\beta}} = \mathbf{X}^\top \mathbf{Y},$$

where the ij element of X is xij, the i element of the column vector Y is yi, and the j element of $\hat{\beta}$is $\hat{\beta}_j$. Thus X is $n \times p$, Y is $n \times 1$, and is $p \times 1$. The solution is

$$\hat{\boldsymbol{\beta}} = (\mathbf{X}^\top \mathbf{X})^{-1} \mathbf{X}^\top \mathbf{Y}.$$

Diagnostics

Once a regression model has been constructed, it may be important to confirm the goodness of fit of the model and the statistical significance of the estimated parameters. Commonly used checks of goodness of fit include the R-squared, analyses of the pattern of residuals and hypothesis testing. Statistical significance can be checked by an F-test of the overall fit, followed by t-tests of individual parameters.

Interpretations of these diagnostic tests rest heavily on the model assumptions. Although examination of the residuals can be used to invalidate a model, the results of a t-test or F-test are sometimes more difficult to interpret if the model's assumptions are violated. For example, if the error term does not have a normal distribution, in small samples the estimated parameters will not follow normal distributions and complicate inference. With relatively large samples, however, a central limit theorem can be invoked such that hypothesis testing may proceed using asymptotic approximations.

"Limited dependent" variables

The phrase "limited dependent" is used in econometric statistics for categorical and constrained variables.

The response variable may be non-continuous ("limited" to lie on some subset of the real line). For binary (zero or one) variables, if analysis proceeds with least-squares linear regression, the model is called the linear probability model. Nonlinear models for binary dependent variables include the probit and logit model. The multivariate probit model is a standard method of estimating a joint relationship between several binary dependent variables and some independent variables. For categorical variables with more than two values there is the multinomial logit. For ordinal variables with more than two values, there are the ordered logit and ordered probit models. Censored regression models may be used when the dependent variable is only sometimes observed, and Heckman correction type models may be used when the sample is not randomly selected from the population of interest. An alternative to such procedures is linear regression based on polychoric correlation (or polyserial correlations) between the categorical variables. Such procedures differ in the assumptions made about the distribution of the variables in the population. If the variable is positive with low values and represents the repetition of the occurrence of an event, then count models like the Poisson regression or the negative binomial model may be used instead.

Interpolation and extrapolation

Regression models predict a value of the *Y* variable given known values of the *X* variables. Prediction *within* the range of values in the dataset used for model-fitting is known informally as interpolation. Prediction *outside* this range of the data is known as extrapolation. Performing extrapolation relies strongly on the regression assumptions. The further the extrapolation goes outside the data, the more room there is for the model to fail due to differences between the assumptions and the sample data or the true values.

It is generally advised that when performing extrapolation, one should accompany the estimated value of the dependent variable with a prediction interval that represents the uncertainty. Such intervals tend to expand rapidly as the values of the independent variable(s) moved outside the range covered by the observed data.

For such reasons and others, some tend to say that it might be unwise to undertake extrapolation.

However, this does not cover the full set of modelling errors that may be being made: in particular, the assumption of a particular form for the relation between *Y* and *X*. A properly conducted regression analysis will include an assessment of how well the assumed form is matched by the observed data, but it can only do so within the range of values of the independent variables actually available. This means that any extrapolation is particularly reliant on the assumptions being made about the structural form of the regression relationship. Best-practice advice here is that a linear-in-variables and linear-in-parameters relationship should not be chosen simply for computational convenience, but that all available knowledge should be deployed in constructing a regression model. If this knowledge includes the fact that the dependent variable cannot go outside a certain range of values, this can be made use of in selecting the model – even if the observed dataset has no values particularly near such bounds. The implications of this step of choosing an appropriate functional form for the regression can be great when extrapolation is considered. At a minimum, it can ensure that any extrapolation arising from a fitted model is "realistic" (or in accord with what is known).

Nonlinear regression

When the model function is not linear in the parameters, the sum of squares must be minimized by an iterative procedure. This introduces many complications which are summarized in Differences between linear and non-linear least squares

Power and sample size calculations

There are no generally agreed methods for relating the number of observations versus the number of independent variables in the model. One rule of thumb suggested by Good and Hardin is $N = m^n$, where N is the sample size, n is the number of independent variables and m is the number of observations needed to reach the desired precision if the model had only one independent variable. For example, a researcher is building a linear regression model using a dataset that contains 1000 patients (). If he decides that five observations are needed to precisely define a straight line (), then the maximum number of independent variables his model can support is 4, because

$$\frac{\log 1000}{\log 5} = 4.29$$

Other methods

Although the parameters of a regression model are usually estimated using the method of least squares, other methods which have been used include:

- Bayesian methods, e.g. Bayesian linear regression
- Percentage regression, for situations where reducing *percentage* errors is deemed more appropriate.
- Least absolute deviations, which is more robust in the presence of outliers, leading to quantile regression
- Nonparametric regression, requires a large number of observations and is computationally intensive
- Distance metric learning, which is learned by the search of a meaningful distance metric in a given input space.

Software

All major statistical software packages perform least squares regression analysis and inference. Simple linear regression and multiple regression using least squares can be done in some spreadsheet applications and on some calculators. While many statistical software packages can perform various types of nonparametric and robust regression, these methods are less standardized; different software packages implement different methods, and a method with a given name may be implemented differently in different packages. Specialized regression software has been developed for use in fields such as survey analysis and neuroimaging.

12

Quality and Six Sigma Management Application of Statistic

Six Sigma is a set of techniques and tools for process improvement. It was developed by Motorola in 1986, coinciding with the Japanese asset price bubble which is reflected in its terminology. Jack Welch made it central to his business strategy at General Electric in 1995. Today, it is used in many industrial sectors.

Six Sigma seeks to improve the quality of process outputs by identifying and removing the causes of defects (errors) and minimizing variability in manufacturing and business processes. It uses a set of quality management methods, including statistical methods, and creates a special infrastructure of people within the organization ("Champions", "Black Belts", "Green Belts", "Yellow Belts", etc.) who are experts in these methods. Each Six Sigma project carried out within an organization follows a defined sequence of steps and has quantified value targets, for example: reduce process cycle time, reduce pollution, reduce costs, increase customer satisfaction, and increase profits. These are also core to principles of Total Quality Management (TQM) as described by Peter Drucker and Tom Peters (particularly in his book "In Search of Excellence" in which he refers to the Motorola six sigma principles).

The term Six Sigma originated from terminology associated with manufacturing, specifically terms associated with statistical modeling of manufacturing processes. The maturity of a manufacturing process can be described by a *sigma* rating indicating its yield or the percentage of defect-free products it creates. A six sigma process is one in which 99.99966% of the products manufactured are statistically expected to be free of defects (3.4 defective parts/million), although, as discussed below, this defect level corresponds to only a 4.5 sigma level. Motorola set a goal of "six sigma" for all of its manufacturing operations, and this goal became a by-word for the management and engineering practices used to achieve it.

Doctrine

Six Sigma doctrine asserts that:

- Continuous efforts to achieve stable and predictable process results (i.e., reduce process variation) are of vital importance to business success.
- Manufacturing and business processes have characteristics that can be measured, analyzed, controlled and improved.
- Achieving sustained quality improvement requires commitment from the entire organization, particularly from top-level management.

Features that set Six Sigma apart from previous quality improvement initiatives include:

- A clear focus on achieving measurable and quantifiable financial returns from any Six Sigma project.
- An increased emphasis on strong and passionate management leadership and support.
- A clear commitment to making decisions on the basis of verifiable data and statistical methods, rather than assumptions and guesswork.

The term "six sigma" comes from statistics and is used in statistical quality control, which evaluates process capability. Originally, it referred to the ability of manufacturing processes to produce a very high proportion of output within specification. Processes that operate with "six sigma quality" over the short term are assumed to produce long-term defect levels below 3.4 defects per million opportunities (DPMO). Six Sigma's implicit goal is to improve all processes, but not to the 3.4 DPMO level necessarily. Organizations need to determine an appropriate sigma level for each of their most important processes and strive to achieve these. As a result of this goal, it is incumbent on management of the organization to prioritize areas of improvement.

"Six Sigma" was registered June 11, 1991 as U.S. Service Mark 74,026,418. In 2005 Motorola attributed over US$17 billion in savings to Six Sigma. Other early adopters of Six Sigma include Honeywell (previously known as AlliedSignal) and General Electric, where Jack Welch introduced the method. By the late 1990s, about two-thirds of the Fortune 500 organizations had begun Six Sigma initiatives with the aim of reducing costs and improving quality.

In recent years, some practitioners have combined Six Sigma ideas with lean manufacturing to create a methodology named Lean Six Sigma. The Lean Six Sigma methodology views lean manufacturing, which addresses process flow and waste issues, and Six Sigma, with its focus on variation and design, as complementary disciplines aimed at promoting "business and operational excellence". Companies such as GE, Verizon, GENPACT, and IBM use Lean Six Sigma to focus transformation efforts not just on efficiency but also on growth. It serves as a foundation for innovation throughout the organization, from manufacturing and software development to sales and service delivery functions.

The International Organisation for Standardisation (ISO) has published ISO 13053:2011 defining the six sigma process.

Methodologies

Six Sigma projects follow two project methodologies inspired by Deming's Plan-Do-Check-Act Cycle. These methodologies, composed of five phases each, bear the acronyms DMAIC and DMADV.

- DMAIC is used for projects aimed at improving an existing business process. DMAIC is pronounced as "duh-may-ick" (<ÌdŒ Èmej jk>).
- DMADV is used for projects aimed at creating new product or process designs. DMADV is pronounced as "duh-mad-vee" (<ÌdŒ Èmæd vi>).

DMAIC

The DMAIC project methodology has five phases:

- *Define* the system, the voice of the customer and their requirements, and the project goals, specifically.
- *Measure* key aspects of the current process and collect relevant data.
- *Analyze* the data to investigate and verify cause-and-effect relationships. Determine what the relationships are, and attempt to ensure that all factors have been considered. Seek out root cause of the defect under investigation.
- *Improve* or optimize the current process based upon data analysis using techniques such as design of experiments, poka yoke or mistake proofing, and standard work to create a new, future state process. Set up pilot runs to establish process capability.
- *Control* the future state process to ensure that any deviations from the target are corrected before they result in defects. Implement control systems such as statistical process control, production boards, visual workplaces, and continuously monitor the process.

Some organizations add a ***Recognize*** step at the beginning, which is to recognize the right problem to work on, thus yielding an RDMAIC methodology.

DMADV or DFSS

The DMADV project methodology, known as DFSS ("**D**esign **F**or **S**ix **S**igma"), features five phases:

- *Define* design goals that are consistent with customer demands and the enterprise strategy.
- *Measure* and identify CTQs (characteristics that are **C**ritical **T**o **Q**uality), product capabilities, production process capability, and risks.
- *Analyze* to develop and design alternatives
- *Design* an improved alternative, best suited per analysis in the previous step
- *Verify* the design, set up pilot runs, implement the production process and hand it over to the process owner(s).

Quality management tools and methods

Within the individual phases of a DMAIC or DMADV project, Six Sigma utilizes many established quality-management tools that are also used outside Six Sigma. The following table shows an overview of the main methods used.

- 5 Whys
- Statistical and fitting tools
    - Analysis of variance
    - General linear model
    - ANOVA Gauge R&R
    - Regression analysis
    - Correlation
    - Scatter diagram
    - Chi-squared test

- Axiomatic design
- Business Process Mapping/Check sheet
- Cause & effects diagram (also known as fishbone or Ishikawa diagram)
- Control chart/Control plan (also known as a swimlane map)/Run charts
- Cost-benefit analysis
- CTQ tree
- Design of experiments/Stratification
- Histograms/Pareto analysis/Pareto chart
- Pick chart/Process capability/Rolled throughput yield
- Quality Function Deployment (QFD)
- Quantitative marketing research through use of Enterprise Feedback Management (EFM) systems
- Root cause analysis
- SIPOC analysis (**S**uppliers, **I**nputs, **P**rocess, **O**utputs, **C**ustomers)
- COPIS analysis (Customer centric version/perspective of SIPOC)
- Taguchi methods/Taguchi Loss Function
- Value stream mapping

Implementation roles

One key innovation of Six Sigma involves the absolute "professionalizing" of quality management functions. Prior to Six Sigma, quality management in practice was largely relegated to the production floor and to statisticians in a separate quality department. Formal Six Sigma programs adopt a kind of elite ranking terminology (similar to some martial arts systems, like Kung-Fu and Judo) to define a hierarchy (and special career path) that kicks across all business functions and levels.

Six Sigma identifies several key roles for its successful implementation.

Executive Leadership includes the CEO and other members of top management. They are responsible for setting up a vision for Six Sigma implementation. They also empower the other role holders with the freedom and resources to explore new ideas for breakthrough improvements.

Champions take responsibility for Six Sigma implementation across the organization in an integrated manner. The Executive Leadership draws them from upper management. Champions also act as mentors to Black Belts.

Master Black Belts, identified by champions, act as in-house coaches on Six Sigma. They devote 100% of their time to Six Sigma. They assist champions and guide Black Belts and Green Belts. Apart from statistical tasks, they spend their time on ensuring consistent application of Six Sigma across various functions and departments.

Black Belts operate under Master Black Belts to apply Six Sigma methodology to specific projects. They devote 100% of their valued time to Six Sigma. They primarily focus on Six

Sigma project execution and special leadership with special tasks, whereas Champions and Master Black Belts focus on identifying projects/functions for Six Sigma.

Green Belts are the employees who take up Six Sigma implementation along with their other job responsibilities, operating under the guidance of Black Belts. Some organizations use additional belt colours, such as *Yellow Belts*, for employees that have basic training in Six Sigma tools and generally participate in projects and "White belts" for those locally trained in the concepts but do not participate in the project team. "Orange belts" are also mentioned to be used for special cases.

Certification

General Electric and Motorola developed certification programs as part of their Six Sigma implementation, verifying individuals' command of the Six Sigma methods at the relevant skill level (Green Belt, Black Belt etc.). Following this approach, many organizations in the 1990s started offering Six Sigma certifications to their employees. Criteria for Green Belt and Black Belt certification vary; some companies simply require participation in a course and a Six Sigma project. There is no standard certification body, and different certification services are offered by various quality associations and other providers against a fee. The American Society for Quality for example requires Black Belt applicants to pass a written exam and to provide a signed affidavit stating that they have completed two projects, or one project combined with three years' practical experience in the body of knowledge.

Etymology of "six sigma process"

The term "six sigma process" comes from the notion that if one has six standard deviations between the process mean and the nearest specification limit, as shown in the graph, practically no items will fail to meet specifications. This is based on the calculation method employed in process capability studies.

Capability studies measure the number of standard deviations between the process mean and the nearest specification limit in sigma units, represented by the Greek letter σ (sigma). As process standard deviation goes up, or the mean of the process moves away from the center of the tolerance, fewer standard deviations will fit between the mean and the nearest specification limit, decreasing the sigma number and increasing the likelihood of items outside specification.

Role of the 1.5 sigma shift

Experience has shown that processes usually do not perform as well in the long term as they do in the short term. As a result, the number of sigmas that will fit between the process mean and the nearest specification limit may well drop over time, compared to an initial short-term study. To account for this real-life increase in process variation over time, an empirically-based 1.5 sigma shift is introduced into the calculation. According to this idea, a process that fits 6 sigma between the process mean and the nearest specification limit in a short-term study will in the long term fit only 4.5 sigma – either because the process mean will move over time, or because the long-term standard deviation of the process will be greater than that observed in the short term, or both.

Hence the widely accepted definition of a six sigma process is a process that produces 3.4 defective parts per million opportunities (DPMO). This is based on the fact that a process that is normally distributed will have 3.4 parts per million beyond a point that is 4.5 standard deviations above or below the mean (one-sided capability study). So the 3.4 DPMO of a six sigma process in fact corresponds to 4.5 sigma, namely 6 sigma minus the 1.5-sigma shift introduced to account for long-term variation. This allows for the fact that special causes may result in a deterioration in process performance over time, and is designed to prevent underestimation of the defect levels likely to be encountered in real-life operation.

The role of the sigma shift is mainly academic. The purpose of six sigma is to generate organizational performance improvement. It is up to the organization to determine, based on customer expectations, what the appropriate sigma level of a process is. The purpose of the sigma value is as a comparative figure to determine whether a process is improving, deteriorating, stagnant or non-competitive with others in the same business. Six sigma (3.4 DPMO) is not the goal of all processes.

Sigma levels

The table below gives long-term DPMO values corresponding to various short-term sigma levels. It must be understood that these figures assume that the process mean will shift by 1.5 sigma toward the side with the critical specification limit. In other words, they assume that after the initial study determining the short-term sigma level, the long-term Cpk value will turn out to be 0.5 less than the short-term Cpk value. So, for example, the DPMO figure given for 1 sigma assumes that the long-term process mean will be 0.5 sigma *beyond* the specification limit (Cpk = –0.17), rather than 1 sigma *within* it, as it was in the short-term study (Cpk = 0.33). Note that the defect percentages indicate only defects exceeding the specification limit to which the process mean is nearest. Defects beyond the far specification limit are not included in the percentages.

Application

Six Sigma mostly finds application in large organizations. An important factor in the spread of Six Sigma was GE's 1998 announcement of $350 million in savings thanks to Six Sigma, a figure that later grew to more than $1 billion. According to industry consultants like Thomas Pyzdek and John Kullmann, companies with fewer than 500 employees are less suited to Six Sigma implementation, or need to adapt the standard approach to make it work for them. Six Sigma however contains a large number of tools and techniques that work well in small to mid-size organizations. The fact that an organization is not big enough to be able to afford Black Belts does not diminish its abilities to make improvements using this set of tools and techniques. The infrastructure described as necessary to support Six Sigma is a result of the size of the organization rather than a requirement of Six Sigma itself.

Criticism

Lack of originality

Noted quality expert Joseph M. Juran has described Six Sigma as "a basic version of quality improvement", stating that "there is nothing new there. It includes what we used to call facilitators. They've adopted more flamboyant terms, like belts with different colors. I think that concept has merit to set apart, to create specialists who can be very helpful. Again, that's not a new idea. The American Society for Quality long ago established certificates, such as for reliability engineers."

Role of consultants

The use of "Black Belts" as itinerant change agents has (controversially) fostered an industry of training and certification. Critics argue there is overselling of Six Sigma by too great a number of consulting firms, many of which claim expertise in Six Sigma when they have only a rudimentary understanding of the tools and techniques involved, or the markets or industries in which they are acting.

Potential negative effects

A *Fortune* article stated that "of 58 large companies that have announced Six Sigma programs, 91 percent have trailed the S&P 500 since". The statement was attributed to "an analysis by Charles Holland of consulting firm Qualpro (which espouses a competing quality-improvement process)". The summary of the article is that Six Sigma is effective at what it is intended to do, but that it is "narrowly designed to fix an existing process" and does not help in "coming up with new products or disruptive technologies." Advocates of Six Sigma have argued that many of these claims are in error or ill-informed.

Over-reliance on statistical tools

A more direct criticism is the "rigid" nature of Six Sigma with its over-reliance on methods and tools. In most cases, more attention is paid to reducing variation and searching for any significant factors and less attention is paid to developing robustness in the first place (which can altogether eliminate the need for reducing variation). The extensive reliance on significance testing and use of multiple regression techniques increases the risk of making commonly-unknown types of statistical errors or mistakes. A possible consequence of Six Sigma's array of P-value misconceptions is the false belief that the probability of a conclusion being in error can be calculated from the data in a single experiment without reference to external evidence or the plausibility of the underlying mechanism. One of the most serious but all-too-common misuses of inferential statistics is to take a model that was developed through exploratory model building and subject it to the same sorts of statistical tests that are used to validate a model that was specified in advance. Another comment refers to the often mentioned Transfer Function, which seems to be a flawed theory if looked at in detail. Since significance tests were first popularized many objections have been voiced by prominent and respected statisticians. The volume of criticism and rebuttal has filled books with language seldom used in the scholarly debate of a dry subject. Much of the first criticism was already published more than 40 years ago. Refer to: Statistical hypothesis testing#Criticism for details. Articles featuring critics have appeared in the November–December 2006 issue of USA Army Logistician regarding Six-Sigma: "The dangers of a single paradigmatic orientation (in this case, that of technical rationality) can blind us to values associated with double-loop learning and the learning organization, organization adaptability, workforce creativity and development, humanizing the workplace, cultural awareness, and strategy making." Nassim Nicholas Taleb consider risk managers little more than "blind users" of statistical tools and methods. He states that statistics is fundamentally incomplete as a field as it cannot predict the risk of rare events - something Six Sigma is specially concerned with. Furthermore, errors in prediction are likely to occur as a result of ignorance for or distinction between epistemic and other uncertainties. These errors are the biggest in time variant (reliability) related failures.

Stifling creativity in research environments

A *BusinessWeek* article says that James McNerney's introduction of Six Sigma at 3M had the effect of stifling creativity and reports its removal from the research function. It cites two Wharton School professors who say that Six Sigma leads to incremental innovation at the expense of blue skies research. This phenomenon is further explored in the book *Going Lean*, which describes a related approach known as lean dynamics and provides data to show that Ford's "6 Sigma" program did little to change its fortunes.

According to an article by John Dodge, editor in chief of *Design News*, use of Six Sigma is inappropriate in a research environment. Dodge states "excessive metrics, steps, measurements and Six Sigma's intense focus on reducing variability water down the discovery process. Under Six Sigma, the free-wheeling nature of brainstorming and the serendipitous side of discovery is stifled." He concludes "there's general agreement that freedom in basic or pure research is preferable while Six Sigma works best in incremental innovation when there's an expressed commercial goal."

Lack of systematic documentation

One criticism voiced by Yasar Jarrar and Andy Neely from the Cranfield School of Management's Centre for Business Performance is that while Six Sigma is a powerful approach, it can also unduly dominate an organization's culture; and they add that much of the Six Sigma literature lacks academic rigor:

Probably more to the Six Sigma literature than concepts, relates to the evidence for Six Sigma's success. So far, documented case studies using the Six Sigma methods are presented as the strongest evidence for its success. However, looking at these documented cases, and apart from a few that are detailed from the experience of leading organizations like GE and Motorola, most cases are not documented in a systemic or academic manner. In fact, the majority are case studies illustrated on websites, and are, at best, sketchy. They provide no mention of any specific Six Sigma methods that were used to resolve the problems. It has been argued that by relying on the Six Sigma criteria, management is lulled into the idea that something is being done about quality, whereas any resulting improvement is accidental (Latzko 1995). Thus, when looking at the evidence put forward for Six Sigma success, mostly by consultants and people with vested interests, the question that begs to be asked is: are we making a true improvement with Six Sigma methods or just getting skilled at telling stories? Everyone seems to believe that we are making true improvements, but there is some way to go to document these empirically and clarify the causal relations.

1.5 sigma shift

The statistician Donald J. Wheeler has dismissed the 1.5 sigma shift as "goofy" because of its arbitrary nature. Its universal applicability is seen as doubtful.

The 1.5 sigma shift has also become contentious because it results in stated "sigma levels" that reflect short-term rather than long-term performance: a process that has long-term defect levels corresponding to 4.5 sigma performance is, by Six Sigma convention, described as a "six sigma process." The accepted Six Sigma scoring system thus cannot be equated to actual normal distribution probabilities for the stated number of standard deviations, and this has been a key bone of contention over how Six Sigma measures are defined. The fact that it is rarely explained that a "6 sigma" process will have long-term defect rates corresponding to 4.5 sigma performance rather than actual 6 sigma performance has led several commentators to express the opinion that Six Sigma is a confidence trick.

Total quality management

Total quality management (TQM) consists of organization-wide efforts to install and make permanent a climate in which an organization continuously improves its ability to deliver high-quality products and services to customers. While there is no widely agreed-upon approach, TQM efforts typically draw heavily on the previously developed tools and techniques of quality control. TQM enjoyed widespread attention during the late 1980s and early 1990s before being overshadowed by ISO 9000, Lean manufacturing, and Six Sigma.

History

In the late 1970s and early 1980s, the developed countries of North America and Western Europe suffered economically in the face of stiff competition from Japan's ability to produce high-quality goods at competitive cost. For the first time since the start of the Industrial Revolution, the United Kingdom became a net importer of finished goods. The United States undertook its own soul-searching, expressed most pointedly in the television broadcast of *If Japan Can... Why Can't We?* Firms began reexamining the techniques of quality control invented over the past 50 years and how those techniques had been so successfully employed by the Japanese. It was in the midst of this economic turmoil that TQM took root.

The exact origin of the term "total quality management" is uncertain. It is almost certainly inspired by Armand V. Feigenbaum's multi-edition book *Total Quality Control* (OCLC 299383303) and Kaoru Ishikawa's *What Is Total Quality Control? The Japanese Way* (OCLC 11467749). It may have been first coined in the United Kingdom by the Department of Trade and Industry during its 1983 "National Quality Campaign". Or it may have been first coined in the United States by the Naval Air Systems Command to describe its quality-improvement efforts in 1985.

Development in the United States

In the spring of 1984, an arm of the United States Navy asked some of its civilian researchers to assess statistical process control and the work of several prominent quality consultants and to make recommendations as to how to apply their approaches to improve the Navy's operational effectiveness. The recommendation was to adopt the teachings of W. Edwards Deming. The Navy branded the effort "Total Quality Management" in 1985.

From the Navy, TQM spread throughout the US Federal Government, resulting in the following:

- The creation of the Malcolm Baldrige National Quality Award in August 1987

- The creation of the Federal Quality Institute in June 1988
- The adoption of TQM by many elements of government and the armed forces, including the United States Department of Defense, United States Army, and United States Coast Guard

The private sector began using TQM principles not only as a means to recapture market share from the Japanese, but also to remain competitive when bidding for contracts from the Federal Government since "total quality" requires involving suppliers, not just employees, in process improvement efforts.

Features

There is no widespread agreement as to what TQM is and what actions it requires of organizations, however a review of the original United States Navy effort gives a rough understanding of what is involved in TQM. The key concepts in the TQM effort undertaken by the Navy in the 1980s include:

- "Quality is defined by customers' requirements."
- "Top management has direct responsibility for quality improvement."
- "Increased quality comes from systematic analysis and improvement of work processes."
- "Quality improvement is a continuous effort and conducted throughout the organization."

The Navy used the following tools and techniques:

- The PDCA cycle to drive issues to resolution
- *Ad hoc* cross-functional teams (similar to quality circles) responsible for addressing immediate process issues
- Standing cross-functional teams responsible for the improvement of processes over the long term
- Active management participation through steering committees
- Use of the Seven Basic Tools of Quality to analyze quality-related issues

Notable definitions

While there is no generally accepted definition of TQM, several notable organizations have attempted to define it. These include:

United States Department of Defense (1988)

"Total Quality Management (TQM) in the Department of Defense is a strategy for continuously improving performance at every level, and in all areas of responsibility. It combines fundamental management techniques, existing improvement efforts, and specialized technical tools under a disciplined structure focused on continuously improving all processes. Improved performance is directed at satisfying such broad goals as cost, quality, schedule, and mission need and suitability. Increasing user satisfaction is the overriding objective. The TQM effort builds on the pioneering work of Dr. W. E. Deming, Dr. J. H. Juran, and others, and benefits from both private and public sector experience with continuous process improvement."

British Standards Institution standard BS 7850-1:1992

"A management philosophy and company practices that aim to harness the human and material resources of an organization in the most effective way to achieve the objectives of the organization."

International Organization for Standardization standard ISO 8402:1994

"A management approach of an organisation centred on quality, based on the participation of all its members and aiming at long term success through customer satisfaction and benefits to all members of the organisation and society."

The American Society for Quality

"A term first used to describe a management approach to quality improvement. Since then, TQM has taken on many meanings. Simply put, it is a management approach to long-term success through customer satisfaction. TQM is based on all members of an organization participating in improving processes, products, services and the culture in which they work. The methods for implementing this approach are found in the teachings of such quality leaders as Philip B. Crosby, W. Edwards Deming, Armand V. Feigenbaum, Kaoru Ishikawa and Joseph M. Juran."

The Chartered Quality Institute

"TQM is a philosophy for managing an organisation in a way which enables it to meet stakeholder needs and expectations efficiently and effectively, without compromising ethical values."

Malcolm Baldrige National Quality Award criteria

In the United States, the Baldridge Award, created by Public Law 100-107, annually recognizes American businesses, educational institutions, and healthcare organizations that run high-quality operations. Organizations are judged on criteria from seven categories:

1. Leadership
2. Strategic planning
3. Customer focus
4. Measurement, analysis, and knowledge management
5. Workforce focus
6. Operations focus
7. Results

Example criteria are:

- How do you obtain information on your customers' satisfaction relative to their satisfaction with your competitors?
- How do you select, collect, align, and integrate data and information for tracking daily operations?

- How do you manage your workforce, its needs, and your needs to ensure continuity, prevent workforce reductions, and minimize the impact of workforce reductions, if they do become necessary?

Joseph M. Juran believed the Baldrige Award judging criteria to be the most widely accepted description of what TQM entails.

Standards

During the 1990s, standards bodies in Belgium, France, Germany, Turkey, and the United Kingdom attempted to standardize TQM. While many of these standards have since been explicitly withdrawn, they all are effectively superseded by ISO 9000:

Total Quality Management: Guide to Management Principles, London, England: British Standards Institution, 1992, ISBN 9780580211560, OCLC 655881602, BS 7850

Electronic Components Committee (1994), *Guide to Total Quality Management (TQM) for CECC-Approved Organizations*, Brussels, Belgium: European Committee for Electrotechnical Standardization, CECC 00 806 Issue 1

System zur Zukunftssicherung: Total Quality Management (TQM), Düsseldorf, Germany: Verein Deutscher Ingenieure, 1996, OCLC 632959402, VDI 5500

Total Quality and Marketing/Management Tools, Paris, France: AFNOR, 1998, FD X50-680

Total Quality Management: Guide to Management Principles, Turkish Standards Institution (TSE), 2006, TS 13133

Legacy

Interest in TQM as an academic subject peaked around 1993.

The Federal Quality Institute was shuttered in September 1995 as part of the Clinton administration's efforts to streamline government. The European Centre for Total Quality Management closed in August 2009, a casualty of the Great Recession.

TQM as a vaguely defined quality management approach was largely supplanted by the ISO 9000 collection of standards and their formal certification processes in the 1990s. Business interest in quality improvement under the TQM name also faded as Jack Welch's success attracted attention to Six Sigma and Toyota's success attracted attention to Lean manufacturing, though the three share many of the same tools, techniques, and significant portions of the same philosophy.

13

Understanding Advanced Statistical Methods

Anyone who listens to the radio, watches television, and reads books, newspapers, and magazines cannot help but be aware of statistics, which is the science of collecting, analyzing, presenting, and interpreting data. Statistics appear in the claims of advertisers, in predictions of election results and opinion polls, in cost-of-living indexes, and in reports of business trends and cycles. Every science depends to some extent upon the gathering of data and the interpreting of the data by statistical methods. On the basis of statistics, important decisions are made in the fields of government, industry, and education. Even the average person bases many personal decisions on information that has been supplied by statisticians.

The term statistics is used in two different ways. When used in the plural, it refers to numerical data. For example, one would say, "Statistics show highway accidents to be caused by..." When used in the singular, it means statistical methods, as in "Statistics is the body of principles and methods that has been developed for collecting, analyzing, presenting, and interpreting large masses of numerical data." Without statistical treatment of data, there would be no way to put the "facts" together to see what they mean. The results of statistical investigations may sometimes be stated in a single sentence, as in weather forecasting. Often, however, they are presented in the form of numerical tables, as in census reports, or are shown pictorially in the form of graphs or charts.

The word "Statistic" derived from Italian word-'Statista' or Latin word 'Status'; both meaning political state i.e. it denotes status of political accounts of facts. The word Statistics generally connotes:

- It refers to numerical facts.
- It also signifies the method or methods of dealing with numerical facts.
- It refers to summarised figures of numerical facts.

DEFINITIONS

"Statistics is the science and art that gathers and corodinates numerous fact within a determined fied, treats these mathemetically so that the numerical relation between these facts may be displaced by clearly and freed from anomalies and chance factors." – English and English

"Statistics comprise the collection, tabulation, presentation and analysis of an aggregate of facts, collected in a methodical , without bias and related to a predetermined purpose."- WG Sutcliffe

"Statistic is a branch of cientific methodology. It deal with collection, classification, description, and interpretation of data obtained by the conduct of urvey and experiments. Its esential purpose is to describe and draw infernces about the numerical properties of the populations." – George Ferguson.

Meaning

In the firstly place, the word statistics refers to "numerical facts systematically arranged". In this sense, the word statistics is always used in the plural. We have, for instance, statistics of prices, statistics of road, accidents, statistics of crimes, statistics of births, statistics of educational institutions, etc. In all these examples, the word statistics denotes a set of numerical data in the respected fields. This is the meaning the man in the street gives to the word statistics and the most people usually use the word data instead.

In the second places, the word statistics is defined as a descipline that includes procedures and techniques used to collect, process and analyse numerical data to make inferences and to reach decisions in the face of uncertainty. In this sense, the word statistics is used in the singular. As it embodies more or less all stages of the general process of learning, sometimes called scientific method, statistics is characterized as a science. Thus the word statistics used in the plural refers to a set of numerical information and in the singular, denotes the science of basing decision on numerical data. It should be noted that statistics as a subject is mathematical in character.

Thirdly, the word statistics are numerical quantities calculated from sample observations; a single quantity has been a calculated is called a statistic. The mean of a sample for instance is a statistic. The word statistics is plural when used in this sense.

The word statistics has three different meanings (sense) which are discussed below:

(1) Plural Sense (2) Singular Sense (3) Plural of the word "Statistic"

(1) Plural Sense: In plural sense, the word statistics refer to numerical facts and figures collected in a systematic manner with a definite purpose in any field of study. In this sense, statistics are also aggregates of facts which are expressed in numerical form. For example, Statistics on industrial production, statistics or population growth of a country in different years etc.

(2) Singular Sense: In singular sense, it refers to the science comprising methods which are used in collection, analysis, interpretation and presentation of numerical data. These methods are used to draw conclusion about the population parameter.

For Example: If we want to have a study about the distribution of weights of students in a certain college.

First of all, we will collect the information on the weights which may be obtained from the records of the college or we may collect from the students directly. The large number of weight figures will confuse the mind. In this situation we may arrange the weights in groups such as: "50 Kg to 60 Kg" "60 Kg to 70 Kg" and so on and find the number of students fall in each group. This step is called a presentation of data. We may still go further and compute the averages and some other measures which may give us complete description of the original data.

(3) Plural of Word "Statistic":The word statistics is used as the plural of the word "Statistic" which refers to a numerical quantity like mean, median, variance etc..., calculated from sample value.

For Example: If we select 15 student from a class of 80 students, measure their heights and find the average height. This average would be a statistic.

Use of Statistical Methods

Statistical methods are powerful and important tools with which to interpret the complex world of today. Statistics provides techniques for discovering knowledge and for simplifying large masses of data of ordinary numbers and also provides a means for presenting information in meaningful and understandable form and is a vehicle for transmitting and storing information and for stating the results of measurement and enumeration. It also is a way for solving certain kinds of problems and it provides methods by which data may be collected and analysed. Statistics serves as the informational segment of decision-making process. Management at all levels is guided by facts obtained through analysis of records rather than upon knowledge obtained merely through personal observation and experience. Through application of appropriate statistical methods, current performance may be measured, significant relationships may be studied, past experience may be analysed and probable future trends appraised. To acquire knowledge and to express it precisely, statistical methods and statistics, have a vital role to play.Statistics has a long and venerable history. In all the countries of ancient culture, where history has been written, proofs are available that they had a system of collection of statistics.

Nature of Statistics

Statistics can be described as all of the following:

- Academic discipline: one with academic departments, curricula and degrees; national and international societies; and specialized journals.
- Scientific field (a branch of science) – widely-recognized category of specialized expertise within science, and typically embodies its own terminology and nomenclature. Such a field will usually be represented by one or more scientific journals, where peer reviewed research is published.
- Formal science – branch of knowledge concerned with formal systems.
- Mathematical science – field of science that is primarily mathematical in nature but may not be universally considered subfields of mathematics proper. Statistics, for example, is mathematical in its methods but grew out of political arithmetic which merged with inverse probability and grew through applications in the social sciences and some areas of physics and biometrics to become its own separate, though closely allied, field.

Statistics is primarily a problem solving field of study and knowledge. Statisticians should have a drive and desire to solve mathematical and data problems, and should get satisfaction from working towards a solution. A good statistician should not feel beaten or defeated by a problem, even if it appears difficult - instead, they should rise to the challenge of coming up with the solution.

Statistics is also all about understanding and interpreting data. A good knowledge of mathematics is obviously essential, but statistics also requires strong communication skills in order to discuss data and any problems surrounding it. Statisticians usually work within a team, for example, with other statisticians, or as advisers to businesses, so they need to be able to communicate effectively with others within a professional environment. In addition, difficult problems require a team effort, and in order to fully understand the data at hand, communication may be essential.

Furthermore, statistics is about being knowledgeable in general. Statistics is not usually an isolated field - as I said above, statisticians usually work within businesses or companies. Therefore, they need a good knowledge base about the field in which they work, whether it be fashion, food, medicine or automobiles. Strong knowledge about your specific field allows a statistician to interpret data more accurately, and draw more reliable and applicable conclusions from the data in order to benefit the company or business.

Statisticians also work closely with computing technology, so should be well-versed an experienced in the latest data programming and organizing technology. Today, statisticians work with such vast amounts of data on such a regular basis that the role of computer technology cannot be ignored in the field of statistics. Statisticians should therefore be not only proficient, but confident, in using technology and software and applying it to particular sets of data.

Divisions of Statistics

There are two divisions in statistics:

Descriptive and Inferential statistics.

Descriptive statistical procedures are used to describe a group of numbers. These tools reduce raw data to a more meaningful form. You've used descriptive statistics when averaging test grades during the semester to determine what grade you'll get. The single average, say, a 94, represents all the grades you've earned in the course throughout the entire semester. (Whether this 94 translates to an "A" or a "C" depends on factors outside of statistics!). Descriptive statistics are covered in chapters 15 (mean and standard deviation) and 22 (correlation).Inferential infers some information about a population (e.g. hypothesis testing, confidence intervals, ANOVA).

Inferential statistics are used to infer findings from a smaller group to a larger one. When the group we want to study is too large to study as a whole, we can draw a sample of subjects from the group and study them. Descriptive statistics about the sample is not our interest. We want to develop conclusions about the large group as a whole. Procedures that allow us to make inferences from samples to populations are called inferential statistics.

For example, there are over 36,000 pastors in the Southern Baptist Convention. It is impossible to interview or survey or test all 36,000 subjects. Round-trip postage alone would cost over $21,000. But we could randomly select, say, one percent (1%) or 360 pastors for the study, analyze the data of the 360, and infer the characteristics of the 36,000.

Modern Statistics

The history of statistics can be said to start around 1749 although, over time, there have been changes to the interpretation of what the word statistics means. In early times, the meaning was restricted to information about states. This was later extended to include all collections of information of all types, and later still it was extended to include the analysis and interpretation of such data. In modern terms, "statistics" means both sets of collected information, as in national accounts and temperature records, and analytical work which requires statistical inference.

Statistical activities are often associated with models expressed using probabilities, and requireprobability theory for them to be put on a firm theoretical basis: see History of probability.

A number of statistical concepts have had an important impact on a wide range of sciences. These include the design of experiments and approaches to statistical inference such as Bayesian inference, each of which can be considered to have their own sequence in the development of the ideas underlying modern statistics.

During the 20th century, the creation of precise instruments for agricultural research, public health concerns (epidemiology, biostatistics, etc.), industrial quality control, and economic and social purposes (unemployment rate, econometry, etc.) necessitated substantial advances in statistical practices.

Today the use of statistics has broadened far beyond its origins. Individuals and organizations use statistics to understand data and make informed decisions throughout the natural and social sciences, medicine, business, and other areas.

Statistics is generally regarded not as a subfield of mathematics but rather as a distinct, albeit allied, field. Many universities maintain separate mathematics and statistics departments. Statistics is also taught in departments as diverse as psychology, education, and public health.

The foundation of statistics

There are many different deûnitions of statistics. Depending on the precise nature of the work that a statistician does, they tend to put different degrees of emphasis on terms such as data, uncertainty, information, analysis, understanding, prediction, inference, summarization, and so on. The range of deûnitions arises from the diversity of kinds of statistical exercises, something which was also noted by David Bartholomew in his Presidential address (Bartholomew, 1995). In that address, he identiûed four different types of statistics, ranging from concern with collecting and presenting data to reveal their main features, through the formal inferential procedures which tend to be taught on statistics courses, via attempts to understand horrendously complex stochastic systems, to issues of interacting in higher level discussions about domains with large amounts of intrinsic uncertainty.

I think, however, that the diversity is also a consequence of how the discipline of statistics developed. Statistics as we now know it is the conûuence of several strands of thought and has evolved through several phases. Each of these strands, and each of these phases, has left its mark, and each continues to be of interest.

The important strands include the following.

(a) The theory of probability: the beginnings of the development of a formal calculus of probability is often dated from around 1650, when mathematicians focused their attention on some issues arising in games of chance. Kolmogorov's axioms, which were formulated around 1930, are now the basis of modern statistical treatments of probability, whichever interpretation one puts on that word.

(b) Surveys of people for governmental and economic purposes, as well as the collection of administrative data: indeed, the word 'statistics' derives from the Italian stato, meaning state, and with this meaning dates back at least as far as the 16th century. This work is related to the construction of life tables for insurance purposes.

(c) The third strand is the development of arithmetic tools for coping with observational and measurement error, especially in disciplines such as astronomy and mechanics

Development of Modern Statistics

The development of statistics

The notion of statistics as a primarily mathematical discipline really developed during the 20th century, perhaps up to around 1970, during which period the foundations of modern statistical inference were laid. However, during more recent decades the effect of the computer has been felt, so there is nowadays as much justiûcation for regarding the discipline as a computational one as a mathematical one. Certainly, the computer has revolutionized statistics and its practice.

The computer and the particular requirements of the different domains to which statistics has been applied have been the two primary factors in inûuencing the direction in which it has developed in the past few decades.

One of the consquences of the ubiquity of statistics is that it has a tendency to diversify and specialize into different application areas. In some sense, this is a good thing. Such growth and change characterize a dynamic discipline, evolving to ûll new data analytic niches. A discipline which failed to change and adjust to new challenges would rapidly die. However, it also has consequences which may not be beneûcial. Just as evolution produces new species, which cannot interbreed with their cousins, so data analytic evolution has generated subdisciplines such as econometrics, chemometrics and environmetrics. Not all practitioners of these disciplines willdeûne themselves as statisticians, perhaps arguing that they have particular expertise that is not possessed by statisticians. To some extent that argument is always valid—the very breadth of statistics ensures that different practitioners, in different application areas, are likely to have rather different skills. It is a well-known fact that statisticians working within any particular application area do develop an understanding of and expertise within that area, which enables them to make signiûcant, sometimes fundamental, contributions to it. But I think that this has also served to fracture the idea that they have a common statistical core. I think that the discipline as a whole suffers when this common core is not acknowledged.

If, in some cases, subdisciplines have spun off from statistics, and also adopted ideas from other sources, in other cases statistical ideas have been rediscovered. Typically, of course, it then takes some time before it is recognized that the ideas are the same, merely with different names. Such duplication of research effort is unfortunate. It does not seem to be restricted to any particular application domain but occurs in both the natural and the social sciences, and in engineering and commercial applications. At the least it can lead to cases of reinvention of the wheel and failure to take advantage of advances. I believe that this is a consequence of lack of awareness of the common foundation, and that it arises from too narrow a view of what statistics is. The problem is illustrated by an examination of US patents and patent applications. Unlike in the UK and the European Union, in the USA it is possible to patent 'business processes', and statistical techniques often fall into this category. Such an examination shows many instances of apparent rediscovery of well-known and well-understood statistical techniques which have been around for years.

It gained its momentum after industrial revolution in Europe. A.J. Wickens, while delivering Presidential address of the American Statistical Association in 1952 said, "Statistics of a sort can, of course, be traced back to ancient times, but they have flowered since the industrial revolution. Beginning in the 19th century, statistical records were developed to describe the society of that era, and to throw light on its economic and social problems. No doubt, they influenced the course of men's thinking then, and even in some instances, may have led to new policies and new laws, but primarily their uses were descriptive. In the beginning of 20th century, and especially since World War I(1914-1918), statistics have been in practice to settle problems, and to determine course of action." There were duo main reasons which were responsible for the growth and development of statistics. They were :

(i) The concerned machinery of different countries used to collect statistics for evaluating their military strength and taxable capacity of their subject. This was the reason for giving the tag of statistics as the 'science of king's, or 'science of statecraft' or 'political arithmetic'.

(ii) It is interesting to know that gamblers of the seventeenth century were also responsible for the early development of statistics. In fact, it was blessings in disguise. Many of the gamblers were mathematicians of their times and some had cordial relations with mathematicians.

R.A. Fisher is notable figure in the history of statistics. His book, Statistical Methods for Research Workers, published in 1925 starts the theory of modern statistics.Pearson was pioneer in developing many of the correlation and regression formulas that are in use today. His researches inspired many statisticians. William S. Gosset (1876-1937), a student of Karl Pearson, propounded a number of statistical formulas under the name of 'Student'. His contribution is also worth praising. To draw solid conclusions from statistical data, fisher propounded many concepts and tests. Alexander McFarlane Movo in his book, An Introduction to the Theory of Statistics, appreciating the contribution of Fisher to the Science of statistics observes, "Fisher is the real giant in the development of the theory of statistics. His first paper was published in 1912 and his work continues unabated today. Although hundreds of scholars have contributed to the science of statistics, this one man must be credited with at least half of the essential and important developments as the theory now stands."

Limitations of Statistics

Statistics is indispensable to almost all sciences - social, physical and natural. It is very often used in most of the spheres of human activity. In spite of the wide scope of the subject it has certain limitations. Some important limitations of statistics are the following:

1. Statistics does not study qualitative phenomena: Statistics deals with facts and figures. So the quality aspect of a variable or the subjective phenomenon falls out of the scope of statistics. For example, qualities like beauty, honesty, intelligence etc. cannot be numerically expressed. So these characteristics cannot be examined statistically. This limits the scope of the subject.
2. Statistical laws are not exact: Statistical laws are not exact as incase of natural sciences. These laws are true only on average. They hold good under certain conditions. They cannot be universally applied. So statistics has less practical utility.
3. Statistics does not study individuals: Statistics deals with aggregate of facts. Single or isolated figures are not statistics. This is considered to be a major handicap of statistics.

4. Statistics can be misused:

Statistics is mostly a tool of analysis. Statistical techniques are used to analyze and interpret the collected information in an enquiry. As it is, statistics does not prove or disprove anything. It is just a means to an end. Statements supported by statistics are more appealing and are commonly believed. For this, statistics is often misused. Statistical methods rightly used are beneficial but if misused these become harmful. Statistical methods used by less expert hands will lead to inaccurate results. Here the fault does not lie with the subject of statistics but with the person who makes wrong use of it.

Overiding limitations of statistics

There is little in life that can compare with the sheer excitement of data analysis, especially if done early on a Sunday morning after a good party. However wonderful statistics are, they are not flawless and have some very important limitations.

How representative is your sample?

Most of us use samples to represent a population, with the number of data points collected in the sample depending on the resources available. If we were to catch the nearest beetle and measure its length, would we be able to say that length is typical (average) of that species? Not with any degree of confidence! It may have just emerged as an adult, or it may have just escaped from a growth-hormone development laboratory and is 20 times the biggest size ever recorded before. For reasons such as these we must collect as many measurements as we can to get an idea of the variability within a population. Then we can find out how representative the sample is by calculating standard error. The lower the standard error is relative to the mean the closer the sample is to representing the population.

Samples used in statistical tests that do not represent the population adequately can give reliable results but with little relevance to the population that it came from.

How well does your data fit the requirements of the tests?

All statistical tests are limited to particular types of data they can be applied to. For instance, some tests are based on the data having a normal distribution. By using this "normal" pattern in the data they provide us with the results.

NOTE: Many books and web sites refer to these "limitations" as "assumptions". The author feels that this word is too obscure and plays down their importance. Therefore, in order to give them the right emphasis they will be referred to as "REQUIREMENTS" throughout this web site. Where applicable, requirements that are not as rigid in application as others will be highlighted.

Results based on data with strong departures from the requirements of the test used will be less reliable than results from data that meet the requirements of the test.

What the P-value says about your hypotheses

It would be nice if the P-value or "probability value" informed us of the probability of the null hypothesis (HO) occurring. If only life was so simple! The P-value is the probability that the observed differences (e.g. between the means in a t-test, or slope of the line and zero in a correlation) occur only by chance. We then use the reverse logic that if the differences occur by chance so seldom (typically when P<5%), real differences must exist. This has serious implications on what you say about the hypothesis you accept:

By accepting an alternative hypothesis at the 5% confidence level you can say that 95% of the time a difference or a relationship would be found in consecutive samples from the same area (that there is a 5% chance that the differences occur only by chance).

Accepting a null hypothesis does not mean that the samples are the same or that there is no relationship, just that the evidence in the samples is not strong enough to support the opposite. However, most would accept that the two samples were from the same population (comparison) or that the slope of the line is equal to zero (correlation).

Distrust of Statistics

It is a general belief that "statistics can prove anything." This statement is partly true and false. It is false because mere statistics should not be taken for granted without proper verification. It is true because statistics is often used by unscrupulous people to achieve their personal ends. This results in loss of faith or confidence on statistics or in causing distrust of statistics.

Distrust of statistics literally means lack of trust in statistical data, statistical analysis and the conclusions derived from it. We often hear statements like.

(i). Statistics is an unreliable science

(ii). Statistics are lies of the first order.

(iii). There are three type of lies-lies, damned lies and statistics.

(iv). Figures do not lie, liars figure.

These are expressions of distrust in statistics. These views of statistics stem from the misuse of statistics by the interested parties.Publicity, advertisers of various products, Governments and other organizations are trying to promote their sectional interest using statistics and statistical methods. This causes distrust of statistics.

Some of the important reasons of distrust in statistics are the following:

(a) Facts based on figures are more convincing. But these figures can be manipulated according to one's wishes. This misguides public causing distrust in statistics.

(b) Sometimes statistical analyses are misinterpreted causing distrust in statistics. Supposing the mortality rates of patients are more in Indian hospitals. From this one may wrongly conclude that it is safer to treat the patients at home. This type of misinterpretation also causes distrust in statistics.

Statistics are useful tools. One uses them according to his knowledge and experience. Use of statistics makes a statement more convincing. But its misuse causes distrust. So it is necessary that people should be adequately prepared to know the reality or to shift the truth from untruth, good statistics from bad statistics. WI. King has rightly observed "statistics are like clay of which you can make a 'God' or a 'Devil' as you please."

The causes of Distrust of Statistics

The distrust of statistics refers to the lack of confidence in statistical datum. Undoubtedly, statistical tools have yielded important results in almost every field knowledge.

But still science of statistics is looked upon with a suspicious eye by so people. On the other hand, some people looked upon it with the eyes of respect.

In the words of Stephen Leacock, "In the earlier times people had no statistics a they have to fall back on lies. Hence the huge exaggerations of primitive literature-giants or miracles or wonders! They did it with lies and we do with statistics, but it is all the same."

Yet, there are another quarter of people who look upon it with suspicion. They belie that figures are tissues of falsehood or figures can prove anything. Disraeli once quoted "there are three degrees of lies-lies, damned lies and statistics". In realization statistics should not be blamed for this distrust.

Statistics are like clay of which can make God or Devil as you please. We should examine whether the figures unbiased and properly collected and scientifically collected. Statistics does not prove disprove a thing. It is merely a tool.

Causes of Distrust

The distrust of statistics occurs due to the following reasons:

1 .Incomplete knowledge of statistical methods.
2. Unrealistic assumptions.
3. Deliberate misuse of statistics.
4. Ignoring limitations of statistics.
5. Misuse of statistics
6. Wrong application of statistical methods like inappropriate comparisons, statistical errors, false percentages etc.

Removal of Distrust

To overcome the problems of distrust following precautions should be taken into consideration:

(i) Limitations of statistics should be kept in mind,

(ii) Only experts should make use of the statistics,

(iii) Data should be used after a careful enquiry,

(iv) Great care and caution should be exercised while using statistics,

(v) Experts of statistics must exercise self-restrain or statistics must exercise self-restrain,

(vi) Free and frank discussion can go a long way to overcome the problem of distrust. Thus, from the above observations it becomes very much clear that statistics are nothing but only a pack of lies. Therefore, fault does not lie with statistics. These techniques are innocent techniques which may be used for the betterment of the society.

A knife may be used in cutting one's throat instead of cutting fruits and vegetables. Fault is not with knife but with a person who handles it.

Similarly, if the statistician misuses data then the fault purely lies on the statistician and not on the data. It is pertinently observed, "Figures would not lie, but liars figure".

In reality, statistics should not be relied upon blindly nor distrusted out rightly. Statistics should not be used as blind man uses a lamp post for support rather than for illumination, whereas it's real purpose is to serve as illumination and not as a support.

According to W.I. King "The science of statistics is a most useful servant but only of great value to those who understand its proper use."

Thus, from the above, we can conclude that statistics is not bad though innocent. Sir. F. Galton has aptly remarked, "Some people hate the very name of statistics, but I find them full of beauty and interest. Whenever, they are not brutalized but delicately handled by the higher methods and are properly interpreted, their power in dealing with complicated phenomenon is extra-ordinary."

Why laymen have a distrust of statistics?

It's not just laymen. Many experts express doubts in the manner in which certain statistics are developed or presented.

The most likely cause for biased statistics is the person or organization has a self interest in obtaining certain results. The manner in which subjective statistics are developed may include:

a) Excluding some information. For example, a survey of 1,000 people shows a slight preference to brand A over brand B, but if we just take the first two days of the survey, Brand B is better, so if our company produces brand B, we take the first two days.

b) Unfair comparisons. For example, I want to show that my new fertilizer is better than all others. I fertilize my corn plant with brand A which is specially prepared for vegetables, and in the comparison plot, I use brand B, which is for lawns. I can claim that my product beat out the most commonly used fertilizer.

c) Unrealistic Assumptions. See attached link. Scientists conducted a study of Florida panthers and concluded that the restricted area was not a problem. However, they only considered day time activity, while it is a well known fact, that panthers are more active at night.

d) Surveys with loaded questions: For example, the question, Given that 40% of all accidents are alcohol related and laws are not being enforced for lack of manpower, do you think we need more policemen? Question is put in a fashion to steer respondent in one direction.

e) Biased presentations= Many examples are available. In fact there's a book on how to lie with graphs.

Statistics and its Importance

Statistics is simply the most important tool of the sciences, particularly biology. Because scientists often must use large amounts of data to gain a representative sample of a population, it is not possible to simply look at the numbers and understand what is happening. Statistics allows a trained person to see the significance of data, the relationship between seemingly unrelated phenomena, and predict what may happen in the future or determine what may have happened in the past.

Statistics, however, is not only useful in science. Insurance agencies use actuary tables to determine the likelihood that you will have a car accident and will adjust your premiums accordingly. Doctors can determine the likelihood that you will develop cancer or a have a heart attack. And, political scientists use statistics to determine how citizens feel about current issues and their likelihood to vote for a particular candidate.

Like most people, you probably feel that it is important to "take control of your life." But what does this mean? Parly it means being able to properly evaluate the data and claims that bombard you every day. If you cannot distinguish good from faulty reasoning, then you are vulnerable to manipulation and to decisions that are not in your best interest. Statistics provides tools that you need in order to react intelligently to information you hear or read. In this sense, statistics is one of the most important subject matter that you ever study.

To be more specific, here are some claims that we have heard on several occassions. (We are not saying that each one of these claims is true!)

- 4 out of 5 dentists recommend Dentyne
- Almost 85% of lung cancers in men and 45% in women are tobacco-related.
- Condoms are effective 94% of the time.
- Native Americans are significantly more likely to be hit crossing the streets than are people of other ethnicities.
- People tend to be more persuasive when they look others directly in the eye and speak loudly and quickly.
- Women make 75 cents to every dollar a man makes when they work the same job.
- A surprising new study shows that eating egg whites can increase one's lifespan.
- People predict that it is very unlikely there will ever be another baseball player with a batting average over 400.
- There is an 80% chance that in a room full of 30 people that at least two people will share the same birthday.
- 79.48% of all statistics are made up on the spot.

All of these claims are statistical in character. We suspect that some of them sound familiar; if not, we bet that you have heard other claims like them. Notice how diverse the examples are. They come from psychology, health, law, sports, business, etc. Indeed, data and data-interpretation show up in discourse from virtually every facet of contemporary life.

Statistics are often presented in an effort to add credibility to an argument or advice. You can see this by paying attention to television advertisements. Many of the numbers thrown about in this way do not represent careful statistical analysis. They can be misleading, and push you into decisions that you might find cause to regret. For these reasons, learning about statistics is a long step towards taking control of your life. (It is not, of course, the only step needed for this purpose.) The present on-line textbook is designed to help you learn statistical essentials. It will make you into an intelligent consumer of statistical claims.

You can take the first step right away. To be an intelligent consumer of statistics, your first reflex must be to question the statistics that you encounter. The British Prime Minister

Benjamin Disraeli famously said, "There are three kinds of lies — lies, damned lies, and statistics." This quote reminds us why it is so important to understand statistics. So let us invite you to reform your statistical habits from now on. No longer will you blindly accept numbers or findings. Instead, you will begin to think about the numbers, their sources, and most importantly, the procedures used to generate them.

We have put the emphasis on defending ourselves against fraudulent claims wrapped up as statistics. We close this section on a more positive note. Just as important as detecting the deceptive use of statistics is the appreciation of the proper use of statistics. You must also learn to recognize statistical evidence that supports a stated conclusion. Statistics are all around you, sometimes used well, sometimes not. We must learn how to distinguish the two cases.

Importance of Basic Statistics

Basic Statistics is a form of mathematics that allows you to properly collect, analyze, interpret and present data in an easy to understand format. It is a basic skill needed to ensure proper understanding of many of the more centralized statistic fields.

Importance of Statistics

We are bombarded with data in everyday life. These days, we encounter the use of statistics in everything ranging from news reports, sports averages, weather, elections, business reports, stocks to advertisements, economic conditions etc.

Importance of basic statistics in everyday life cannot be stressed enough. Inclusion of basic statistics in high school curriculumis uncommon but proves highly beneficial to supplement certain careers in future. This field may be the most widely used of all and most people don't even know they are using it.

Many of today's brightest business minds use this study to create charts and graph that allow them to stress a certain aspect of the business they are dealing with. Market research agencies, News rooms, marketing divisions of large corporations, NGOs, accounting firms etc. are full of people who specialize in basic statistics.

Who should take it?

Basically, anyone who is planning on entering the business, accounting, psychology or research based fields would benefit from the study of basic statistics. This also applies to anyone entering college to obtain an MBA or a specialized degree like social sciences, requiring higher study of statistical methods. Such students would be advised to complete this course at the high school level itself to be able to complete the requirements with ease.

Statistical Awareness with Triola Textbooks

Just turning on the television exposes us to surveys and percent this and percent that. How many dinners have been ruined with a survey taker calling? For some particular reason humans are fascinated with how many of us want to do this or that. We need to know not just about ourselves but also, in exact (+-) numbers, how many or what percent. Curiosity dictates it.

But is it really?

These statistics are supposed to mean something. Statistical textbooks like the Triola textbook series show how the numbers are arrived at, but what do they really mean? You have a mean and a statistical deviation derived through the Triola textbookequation but what does it mean to us?

The people need to know.

Enter the experts

These people supposedly understand what the Triola textbook equations and numbers mean. They can apply the numbers to show how people are behaving and give it weight in the decision making process. But wait, there is a problem. This expert says it means this and this one says it means that. How can this be? These are statistics! They govern everything and must be correct and accurate in the calculus.

Maybe yes and maybe no

Never mind the experts. Enter the data. Depending upon the data that is used the end result can mean just about anything you want it to mean. The data may seem to be the correct data to enter into the equations, and most likely is, but to what end? Ultimately, the numbers never lie. It is just a question of which numbers you care to use. The experts have to eat to after all.

Today we learn the main difference in philosophy in practice between objective, predictive Bayesian and classical analyses. To illustrate, I'm going to ask you some questions that will seem like tricks: but they are not. The answers are all obvious.

Here's the situation: you are an emergency room physician checking people for suspicion of appendicitis. Suppose you are interested in whether temperature helps predict appendicitis. Another way to state this: suppose temperature is correlated with appendicitis. Yet another way: does temperature have any relationship with appendicitis? Get it? We want to check whether temperature and appendicitis have any relationship. This is what you want to know.

Now, let's imagination that temperature is in no way associated with appendicitis. That is, knowing whether a person has a fever, is normal, or is hypothermic means nothing to appendicitis. It is the same as the number of green lollipops your corner grocery store has and that number's association with appendicitis. That is, knowing the temperature or the number of lollipops tells you nothing about appendicitis.

Got it? Good, then answer this: Given this evidence, what is the probability that more people with high temperatures have appendicitis than do people with low temperatures? The answer is the same as this: what is the probability that more people whose corner stores have many lollipops have appendicitis than do people whose corner stores have few lollipops?

If these variables are in no way related to appendicitis, then the answer is obvious: any changes in the number of people with appendicitis is due to other factors (which we may or may not have measured). If we did see more people with appendicitis in the high lollipop (temperature) group, then this is just a coincidence. The probability is 50%

OK so far? Now let's imagine we ran a standard (logistic) regression of temperature to predict appendicitis. The software would spit out a p-value for the classical hypothesis test with the "null" hypothesis that the parameter associated with temperature is 0. Which is to say, that temperature has no effect. Let's imagine the p-value associated with this test is 0.003. What would a classical statistician do?

Yes, "reject" the hypothesis that the parameter associated with temperature is 0 and say, therefore, that it is non-zero. That is, he would conclude that temperature is associated with appendicitis. Very well. But our statistician at least wants to check the (subjective) Bayesian way and so computes the posterior probability distribution for the parameter.

He discovers that, given the model is correct and the data he saw, that the probability the parameter associated with temperature is greater than 0 is, say, 99.9%. Which is to say, he is pretty darn sure that temperature is positively associated with appendicitis: higher temperatures predict more appendicitis cases.

The statistician now rests. He should not. Here's why.

Suppose we know with certainty a parameter in a logistic regression model has the value 0.000001. What is the probability that this parameter is greater than 0? Think carefully now. The answer should be obvious.

In all cases I have ever heard of, 0.000001 > 0. Therefore, the parameter is greater than zero. If this were so, the p-value we would get in any hypothesis test would show a value of 0. Now that's significant! The posterior probability would also show that the probability the parameter is greater than 0 is 100%. Thus, we could publish our paper that the variable associated with this parameter is "highly" statistical significant, even to Bayesians.

But none of these facts answer our main question: how does temperature affect appendicitis. That's what we started wanting to know, and with the classical analysis we stop short of learning the complete answer. Sure, the temperature parameter's value of 0.000001 is greater than 0, but it is so small as to be useless.

What we should be doing is calculating the probability that we see more (new) people with appendicitis and high temperatures than (new) people with appendicitis and low temperatures. We already agreed that if temperature had no effect, then this probability would be 50%.

If, then, after we fit our model (with the low p-values and the high posterior probabilities), we push ahead and compute the uncertainty in new observations and so discover that the probability we see more people with high temperatures and appendicitis is only 52%, what have we learned?

Well, that while temperature may formally be related to appendicitis, its predictive value is very low, and probably negligible. Knowing the value of a person's temperature barely- -cver so barely—changed our uncertainty in the values of new observables. It changed it so little that even though all classical measures say we should consider it, we really probably shouldn't.

And that is the difference between the old and the new.

Main Functions of Statistics

(1) Statistics helps in providing a better understanding and exact description of a phenomenon of nature.

(2) Statistical helps in proper and efficient planning of a statistical inquiry in any field of study.

(3) Statistical helps in collecting an appropriate quantitativedata.

(4) Statistics helps in presenting complex data in a suitable tabular, diagrammatic and graphic form for an easy and clearcomprehension of the data.

(5) Statistics helps in understanding the nature and pattern of variability of a phenomenon through quantitative obersevations.

(6) Statistics helps in drawing valid inference, along with a measure of their reliability about the population parameters from the sample data.

Basic Statistical Functions

Octave supports various helpful statistical functions. Many are useful as initial steps to prepare a data set for further analysis. Others provide different measures from those of the basic descriptive statistics.

— Function File: center (x)

— Function File: center (x, dim)

If x is a vector, subtract its mean. If x is a matrix, do the above for each column. If the optional argument dim is given, operate along this dimension.

— Function File: zscore (x)

— Function File: zscore (x, dim)

If x is a vector, subtract its mean and divide by its standard deviation.

If x is a matrix, do the above along the first non-singleton dimension. If the optional argument dim is given, operate along this dimension.

— Function File: n = histc (x, edges)

— Function File: n = histc (x, edges, dim)

— Function File: [n, idx] = histc (...)

Produce histogram counts.

When x is a vector, the function counts the number of elements of x that fall in the histogram bins defined by edges. This must be a vector of monotonically increasing values that define the edges of the histogram bins. n(k) contains the number of elements in x for which edges(k) <= x <edges(k+1). The final element of n contains the number of elements of x exactly equal to the last element of edges.

When x is an N-dimensional array, the computation is carried out along dimension dim. If not specified dim defaults to the first non-singleton dimension.

When a second output argument is requested an index matrix is also returned. The idx matrix has the same size as x. Each element of idx contains the index of the histogram bin in which the corresponding element of x was counted.

— Function File: c = nchoosek (n, k)

— Function File: c = nchoosek (set, k)

Compute the binomial coefficient or all combinations of a set of items.

If n is a scalar then calculate the binomial coefficient of n and k which is defined as

/ \

| n | n (n-1) (n-2) ... (n-k+1) n!

| | = ———————————— = ————

| k | k! k! (n-k)!

\ /

This is the number of combinations of n items taken in groups of size k.

If the first argument is a vector, set, then generate all combinations of the elements of set, taken k at a time, with one row per combination. The result c has k columns andnchoosek (length (set), k) rows.

For example:

How many ways can three items be grouped into pairs?

nchoosek (3, 2)

⇒! 3

What are the possible pairs?

nchoosek (1:3, 2)

⇒! 1 2

1 3

2 3

nchoosek works only for non-negative, integer arguments. Use bincoeff for non-integer and negative scalar arguments, or for computing many binomial coefficients at once with vector inputs for n or k.

— Function File: perms (v)

Generate all permutations of v, one row per permutation. The result has size factorial (n) * n, where n is the length of v.

As an example, perms([1, 2, 3]) returns the matrix

1 2 3

2 1 3

1 3 2

2 3 1

3 1 2

3 2 1

— Function File: ranks (x, dim)

Return the ranks of x along the first non-singleton dimension adjusted for ties. If the optional argument dim is given, operate along this dimension.

— Function File: run_count (x, n)

— Function File: run_count (x, n, dim)

Count the upward runs along the first non-singleton dimension of x of length 1, 2, ..., n-1 and greater than or equal to n.

If the optional argument dim is given then operate along this dimension.

— Function File: [count, value] = runlength (x)

Find the lengths of all sequences of common values. Return the vector of lengths and the value that was repeated.

runlength ([2, 2, 0, 4, 4, 4, 0, 1, 1, 1, 1])

⇒! [2, 1, 3, 1, 4]

— Function File: probit (p)

For each component of p, return the probit (the quantile of the standard normal distribution) of p.

— Function File: logit (p)

For each component of p, return the logit of p defined as

logit (p) = log (p / (1-p))

— Function File: cloglog (x)

Return the complementary log-log function of x, defined as

cloglog (x) = - log (- log (x))

— Function File: mahalanobis (x, y)

Return the Mahalanobis' D-square distance between the multivariate samples x and y, which must have the same number of components (columns), but may have a different number of observations (rows).

— Function File: [t, l_x] = table (x)

— Function File: [t, l_x, l_y] = table (x, y)

Create a contingency table t from data vectors. The l_x and l_y vectors are the corresponding levels.

Currently, only 1- and 2-dimensional tables are supported.

Whether Statistics is a science or an Art

Is statistics a science?

There are many philosophical theories of science. I will outline a particular view of science to provide a context for an explanation of why I am unhappy with the division of statistics into frequency and Bayesian branches.

I consider a direction in intellectual activity a hard-core science if scientists active in this area either achieved consensus on all essential issues or have a reasonable hope of achieving consensus on all essential issues in the future. Physics is an example of such a science. I realize that, in reality, achieving consensus is far from straightforward. For example, Ernst Mach opposed the atomic theory of matter even after substantial empirical evidence had been collected in favor of this theory. The current status of the string theory provides another example of difficulties on the way to consensus. It is not clear when and how physicists will achieve consensus on the string theory in view of the formidable difficulties in designing experiments that could verify this theory. Nevertheless, it is fair to say that physicists achieved consensus on relativity theory and quantum physics, two fundamental theories with highly counterintuitive claims.

It is a good idea to compare physics to historical research. Some historical facts are controversial - there is no consensus whether they occurred. But the main reason why historians do not have a consensus similar to that found in physics is that one of the most interesting and significant activities of historians is to select historical facts and interpret them. The price, probably unavoidable, that historians have to pay is that historical research cannot generate predictions of future political and economic events that come even close in reliability to predictions generated by physics.

Why do I care about consensus? The universe is incredibly complex. I have direct access to a tiny portion of all facts and similarly I am aware of and can understand only a handful of laws governing the universe. Consensus among scientists is the closest thing to objective truth that exists in practice. I believe that most scientists are smart and honest. I believe in their theories because my only other choice is to be irrational or paranoid.

The further we go from natural science towards humanities, art and religion, the less consensus we find; the more we have to rely on our own judgment. I do appreciate historical research and art but for qualities much different from intellectual certainty.

I believe that statistics can be a science in the same sense as physics. The fact that it is split into two branches, frequency and Bayesian, is unsettling. There is no consensus among statisticians on some fundamental issues. This means that users of statistics must apply their own judgment - they cannot fully rely on results of research performed by statisticians in the same way that they can do it in an idealized science that I described above. Statistics does not generate intellectual material of the same kind as in historical research or art so it should try to evolve in the direction of natural sciences such as physics, in terms of consensus.

In order to know whether statistics is a science or an art or both, it is necessary to understand the meaning of science and art. Webster's dictionary defines science as 'accumulated and accepted knowledge that has been systematised and formulated with reference to the discovery of general truths or the operation of general law." In brief, Science is a body of systematized knowledge. It studies cause and effect and tries to find out generalisations which are called laws of that science. It does not tell whether the results are good or bad. It only describes what are the facts. It is like a lighthouse that gives light to the ships to find out their own ways but does not indicate in which direction they should go. The ships have to find their own direction with the help of the light. Thus any branch of systematised knowledge that states true facts after analysis of cause and effect, will be classed as a science.

According to Karl Pearson that knowledge which (a) gives mental education to the citizens, (b) throws light on important social problems,(c) gives happiness in practical life, and (d) gives satisfaction to out artistic faculties, may be called science. All these qualities are found in statistics, hence it can be regarded as science.

Science has two characteristics: one, skeptical attitude of the scientist and second, methodology, A scientist has a skeptical attitude for every phenomenon and therefore is keen to uncover the truth. Care is taken in evaluating the facts scientifically and reasons are examined and accepted on solid grounds. Tolerance limit is decided for probable error. Scientific methodology is kept on a very high standard. The science of statistics possesses both the characteristics, hence it should be called a science.

However, statistics is not a science like physics, chemistry, economics and sociology. It may be called a science of scientific methods. Statistics help other sciences to derive their own laws. Statistical knowledge is not for its own sake but for the sake of other knowledge. This is a difference between science of statistics and other sciences. But it is very useful in the advancement of knowledge. That is why it is said that "science without statistics bears no fruit, statistics without science has no root."

This statement indicates the usefulness of statistics in the development of other sciences. According to Tippett," As a science, the statistical method is a part of the general scientific method and is based on the same fundamental ideas and processes."

Bibliography

- A Theory of Probable Inference", *Studies in Logic*, pp. 126-181, Little, Brown, and Company. (Reprinted 1983, John Benjamins Publishing Company, ISBN 90-272-3271-7)
- Agresti, Alan; David B. Hichcock (2005). "Bayesian Inference for Categorical Data Analysis". *Statistical Methods & Applications* 14 (14): 298. doi:10.1007/s10260-005-0121-y.
- Anderson, D.R.; Sweeney, D.J.; Williams, T.A.. (1994) *Introduction to Statistics: Concepts and Applications*, pp. 5–9. West Group. ISBN 978-0-314-03309-3
- Babbie, Earl R. (2009). *The Practice of Social Research* (12th ed.). Wadsworth. pp. 436–440. ISBN 0-495-59841-0.
- Bickel, Peter J.; Doksum, Kjell A. (2001). *Mathematical statistics: Basic and selected topics* 1 (Second (updated printing 2007) ed.). Pearson Prentice-Hall. ISBN 0-13-850363-X. MR 443141.
- Chance, Beth L.; Rossman, Allan J. (2005). *Investigating Statistical Concepts, Applications, and Methods*. Duxbury Press. ISBN 978-0-495-05064-3.
- Cox, D. R. (2006). *Principles of Statistical Inference*, CUP. ISBN 0-521-68567-2.
- Deduction, Induction, and Hypothesis", *Popular Science Monthly*, v. 13, pp. 470–482. *Internet Archive* Eprint.
- Dodge, Y. (2003) *The Oxford Dictionary of Statistical Terms*, OUP for International Statistical Institute. ISBN 0-19-920613-9 (entry for "central tendency")
- Fisher, Ronald (1955) "Statistical methods and scientific induction" *Journal of the Royal Statistical Society, Series B*, 17, 69—78. (criticism of statistical theories of Jerzy Neyman and Abraham Wald)
- Freedman, David A. (2009). *Statistical models: Theory and practice* (revised ed.). Cambridge University Press. pp. xiv+442 pp. ISBN 978-0-521-74385-3. MR 2489600.
- Freund, John. (1973) *Introduction to Probability*. Dickenson ISBN 978-0822100782 (p. 1)
- Galton F (1877) Typical laws of heredity. Nature 15: 492-553
- Garver (1932) Concerning the limits of a mesuare of skewness. Ann Math Stats 3(4) 141–142

- Hacking, I. (2006) *The Emergence of Probability: A Philosophical Study of Early Ideas about Probability, Induction and Statistical Inference*, Cambridge University Press, ISBN 978-0-521-68557-3
- Hájek, Alan. "Interpretations of Probability". *The Stanford Encyclopedia of Philosophy (Winter 2012 Edition), Edward N. Zalta (ed.)*. Retrieved 22 April 2013.
- Hansen, Mark H.; Yu, Bin (June 2001). "Model Selection and the Principle of Minimum Description Length: Review paper". *Journal of the American Statistical Association* 96 (454): 746–774. doi:10.1198/016214501753168398.
- Hays, William Lee, (1973) *Statistics for the Social Sciences*, Holt, Rinehart and Winston, p.xii, ISBN 978-0-03-077945-9
- Helen Mary Walker (1975). *Studies in the history of statistical method.* Arno Press.
- Hinkelmann, Klaus; Kempthorne, Oscar (2008). *Introduction to Experimental Design* (Second ed.). Wiley. ISBN 978-0-471-72756-9.
- Hogg, Robert V.; Craig, Allen; McKean, Joseph W. (2004). *Introduction to Mathematical Statistics* (6th ed.). Upper Saddle River: Pearson. ISBN 0-13-008507-3.
- Hotelling H, Solomons LM (1932) The limits of a measure of skewness. Annals Math Stat 3, 141–114
- Investopedia, Descriptive Statistics Terms
- J. Franklin, The Science of Conjecture: Evidence and Probability before Pascal,Johns Hopkins Univ Pr 2002
- Jeffrey, R.C., *Probability and the Art of Judgment,* Cambridge University Press. (1992). pp. 54-55 . ISBN 0-521-39459-7
- Johnson NL, Rogers CA (1951) "The moment problem for unimodal distributions". *Annals of Mathematical Statistics*, 22 (3) 433–439
- Kolmogorov, Andrei N. (1963a). "On Tables of Random Numbers". *Sankhyâ Ser. A.* 25: 369–375. MR 178484.
- Kolmogorov, Andrei N. (1963b). "On Tables of Random Numbers". Theoretical Computer Science 207 (2): 387–395. doi:10.1016/S0304-3975(98)00075-9. MR 1643414.
- Le Cam, Lucian. (1986) Asymptotic Methods of Statistical Decision Theory, Springer. ISBN 0-387-96307-3
- Lund Research Ltd. "Descriptive and Inferential Statistics". statistics.laerd.com. Retrieved 2014-03-23.

Index

A

Algorithm 175

Ambient 202

Analysis 1-2, 4-5, 11-12, 24, 26-27, 29, 58-59, 126-127, 170, 194, 214, 216, 218, 227-228

Argument 252

Azimuth 69

B

Behavior 15

Binary 222

Bivariate 37, 42, 58-59, 127

Bootstrap 41

Business 225, 249

C

Capacity 18

Comparison 25

Complex 167

Components 39, 152

Conformity 56

Convex 130

Covariance 155

Customer 235

D

Density 66-67, 109, 146, 149, 166

Dimension 252, 254

Dispersion 87-88, 90, 92, 95-96, 101, 130-132

E

Elements 252

Endpoints 188

Extensions 167

F

Family 109

Football 74

H

Hawthorne 7

Histogram 252

Hypothesis 9-10, 29, 77, 168, 183, 194-197, 199-211, 213, 245, 251

I

Investment 49

Investors 49

J

Journal 209

K

Kurtosis 107-111

L

Lambda 213

Laplace 61, 135, 176

Linear 30, 56, 131, 219, 221, 223-224

M

Management 22, 225, 228, 233-236

Matrix 40, 167, 252

Mechanics 138

Median 58, 63-65, 93-95, 102-103, 129-130, 155, 185

Metabolic 44-45

Models 12, 223

Moments 162-163

Monotone 79

N

Normality 173

Numbers 81-82, 116, 141, 150, 175, 250

O

Operations 235

Orthogonal 123

P

Parents 118

Philosophy 210

Physics 24, 255

Placebo 18

Planners 26

Plural 1, 238

Poisson 152, 156-157

Population 1-3, 5-6, 10, 19-20, 22, 26, 29, 31, 34, 36, 43-47, 55, 65, 70-72, 97, 116-118, 120, 132, 179-182, 190, 200, 202, 204, 214, 221, 244

Prediction 189, 223

Predictor 217

Protocol 7

Psychology 23

P-value 196, 205, 244, 251

Q

Quantum 138

R

Radius 68

Random 8, 10, 29, 40, 46-47, 55, 66, 97, 115-116, 119, 122, 145-147, 149-150, 159, 164-167, 174-175, 178-179, 184, 187, 189-190

Regression 10, 35, 59, 83, 121, 216-219, 221-224

Residuals 83-85

Robust 37

Runners 77

S

Samples 4, 87, 159, 169, 179, 204, 214, 245

Scientists 255

Scores 56, 87, 174

Scurvy 121

Signals 152

Singular 1, 149, 238

Skewness 102-103, 105, 107

Software 224

Standards 236

Statistics 1-6, 8, 11-14, 20-23, 25-29, 55, 59, 74, 82, 106, 124, 126-127, 171, 179-180, 189, 197, 199, 205, 208, 211, 237-249, 252, 255-256, 258

Symptoms 113

System 6

T

Tribune 120

Triola 250

Truncate 118

V

Validation 83

Variables 2, 6, 8, 16, 30-31, 34, 40, 53, 59, 66, 68, 77-78, 83, 123-124, 127, 145-146, 159-160, 163-165, 173, 190, 192, 204, 211-213, 216-217, 219, 222-224

Variation 86-88, 96, 101, 130-131

Vectors 35

Voters 22